The Secret History of Gold

The Secret History of Gold

Myth, Money, Politics and Power

DOMINIC FRISBY

PENGUIN LIFE

AN IMPRINT OF

PENGUIN BOOKS

PENGUIN LIFE

UK | USA | Canada | Ireland | Australia
India | New Zealand | South Africa

Penguin Life is part of the Penguin Random House group of companies
whose addresses can be found at global.penguinrandomhouse.com.

Penguin Random House UK,
One Embassy Gardens, 8 Viaduct Gardens, London SW11 7BW

penguin.co.uk

Penguin
Random House
UK

First published 2025

001

Set in 12/14.75pt Dante MT Std
Typeset by Six Red Marbles UK, Thetford, Norfolk
Printed at Thomson Press India Ltd, New Delhi

The authorized representative in the EEA is Penguin Random House Ireland,
Morrison Chambers, 32 Nassau Street, Dublin D02 YH68

A CIP catalogue record for this book is available from the British Library

ISBN: 978–0–241–72834–5

Penguin Random House is committed to a sustainable future
for our business, our readers and our planet. This book is made from
Forest Stewardship Council® certified paper.

MIX
Paper | Supporting
responsible forestry
FSC® C018179

Contents

For my beautiful mother, the first person
I ever saw wearing gold, and for my father, who paid for it.

Glossary of Terms

Fiat money is a term you will hear a lot in this book. It means national currencies – the dollar, pound, euro or yen, for example – that are not backed by anything tangible, just law. Under a gold standard the pound and dollar were backed by and exchangeable for gold. Now they have no backing, except the law, so they are fiat – meaning 'by decree'.

Weights and Measures:

In general terms, I have tried to use the measure that is the most digestible. This has resulted in an inconsistent but workable mix of metric and traditional. For large measures I use metric tonnes, but for smaller amounts I tend to use ounces, as they are the more universal measure for gold. Sometimes, for the sake of clarity, I use both. For example, I might say: 1 kg/32 oz.

To help you visualise these numbers: an ounce of gold would be about the same size as a typical large chocolate coin, or a USB flash drive. A tonne of gold, meanwhile, would be about the size of a beachball, albeit one you couldn't lift, or a medium-sized suitcase – 1.8 cubic feet/52 litres. If it were a cube, it would have sides just under 15 inches/37.5 centimetres.

By the way, when I say an ounce or oz, I am referring to a troy ounce, which is the measure used for metal. A troy ounce is actually slightly heavier than a normal ounce. Don't ask. Long story.

Also, except where precise figures are required, I use round numbers. There are 32,151 troy ounces in a tonne, but 32,000 makes easier reading.

I.

The Eternal Metal

'Gold will be slave or master'

Horace

In 2021, a metal detectorist with the eyebrow-raising name of Ole Ginnerup Schytz dug up a hoard of Viking gold in a field in Denmark. The gold was just as it was when it was buried 1,500 years before, if a little dirtier. The same goes for the jewellery unearthed at the Varna Necropolis in Bulgaria in 1972. The beads, bracelets, rings and necklaces are as good as when they were buried 6,700 years ago.

In the Egyptian Museum in Cairo, there is a golden tooth bridge – a gold wire used to bind teeth and dental implants – made over 4,000 years ago. It could go in your mouth today.

No other substance is as long-lasting as gold – not diamonds, not tungsten carbide, not boron nitride. Gold does not corrode; it does not tarnish or decay; it does not break down over time. This sets it apart from every other substance. Iron rusts, wood rots, silver tarnishes. Gold never changes. Left alone, it stays itself. And it never loses its shine – how about that?

Despite its permanence, you can shape this enormously ductile metal into pretty much anything. An ounce of gold can be stretched into a wire 50 miles long or plate a copper wire 1,000 miles long. It can be beaten into a leaf just one atom thick.[1] Yet there is one thing you cannot do and that is destroy it. Life may be temporary, but gold is permanent. It really is forever.

This means that all the gold that has ever been mined, estimated to be 216,000 tonnes, still exists somewhere. Put together it would fit into a cube with 22-metre sides. Visualise a square building seven storeys high - and that would be all the gold ever.

With some effort, you can dissolve gold in certain chemical solutions, alloy it with other metals, or even vaporise it. But the gold will always be there.[2] It is theoretically possible to destroy gold through nuclear reactions and other such extreme methods, but in practical terms, gold is, as Spandau Ballet famously sang, indestructible. It is the closest thing we have on earth to immortality.

Perhaps that is why almost every ancient culture we know of associated gold with the eternal. The Egyptians believed the flesh of gods was made of gold, and that it gave you safe passage into the afterlife. In Greek myth, the Golden Apples of the Hesperides, which Hercules was sent to retrieve, conferred immortality on whoever ate them. The South Americans saw gold as the link between humanity and the cosmos. They were not far wrong.

Gold was present in the dust that formed the solar system. It sits in the earth's crust today, just as it did when our planet was formed some 4.6 billion years ago. That little bit of gold you may be wearing on your finger or around your neck is actually older than the earth itself. In fact, it is older than the solar system. To touch gold is as close as you will ever come to touching eternity.

And yet the world's most famous investor is not impressed.

'It gets dug out of the ground in Africa, or some place,' said Warren Buffett. 'Then we melt it down, dig another hole, bury it again and pay people to stand around guarding it. It has no utility. Anyone watching from Mars would be scratching their head.'[3]

He's right. Gold does nothing. It does not even pay a yield. It just sits there inert. We use other metals to construct things, cut things or conduct things, but gold's industrial uses are minimal. It is a good conductor of electricity, but copper and silver are better and cheaper. It has some use in dentistry, medical applications and nanotechnology. It is finding more and more use in outer space – back whence it came – where it is used to coat spacecraft, astronauts' visors and heat shields. But, in the grand scheme of things, these uses are paltry.

Gold's only purpose is to store and display prosperity. It is dense and tangible wealth: pure money.

Though you may not realise it, we still use gold as money today. Not so much as a medium to exchange value but store it.

In 1850, about 27 per cent of all the gold in the world was in the form of gold coinage and central bank or government reserves. Today, even with the gold standard long since dead, 'the percentage is about the same'.[4]

The most powerful nation on earth, the United States, keeps 70 per cent of its foreign exchange holdings in gold.[5] Its great rival, China, is both the world's largest producer and the world's largest importer. It has built up reserves that, as we shall discover, are likely as great as the USA's. Ordinary people and institutions the world over use gold to store wealth. Across myriad cultures gold is gifted at landmark life events – births and weddings – because of its intrinsic value.

In fact, gold's purchasing power has increased over the millennia, as human beings have grown more productive. The same ounce of gold said by economic historians to have bought King Nebuchadnezzar of Babylon 350 loaves of bread could buy you more than 1,000 loaves today. The same gold dinar (roughly ⅛ oz) that, in the time of the Koran in the seventh century, bought you a lamb would buy you three lambs today. Those same four or five aurei (¾ oz) which bought you a fine linen tunic in ancient Rome would buy you considerably more clothing today.[6]

In 1972, 0.06 ounces of gold would buy you a barrel of oil. Here we are in 2024 and a barrel of oil costs 0.02 ounces of gold – it's significantly cheaper than it was fifty years ago.

House prices, too, if you measure them in gold, have stayed constant. It is only when they are measured in fiat currency that they have appreciated so relentlessly (and destructively).

In other words, an ounce of gold buys you as much, and sometimes more, food, clothing, energy and shelter as it did ten years ago, a hundred years ago or even thousands of years ago. As gold lasts, so does its purchasing power. You cannot say the same about modern national currencies.

Rare and expensive to mine, the supply of gold is constrained. This is in stark contrast to modern money – electronic, debt-based fiat money to give it its full name – the supply of which multiplies every year as governments spend and borrowing balloons.

As if by Natural Law, gold supply has increased at the same rate as the global population – roughly 3 per cent per annum. The population of the world has slightly more than doubled since 1971. So has gold supply. The correlation has held for centuries, except for one fifty-year period during the gold rushes of the late nineteenth century, when gold supply per capita increased.[7]

Gold has the added attraction of being beautiful. It shines and glistens and sparkles. It captivates and allures. The word 'gold' derives from the Sanskrit 'jval', meaning 'to shine'. That's why we use it as jewellery – to show off our wealth and success, as well as to store it. Indeed, in nomadic prehistory, and still in parts of the world today, carrying your wealth on your person as jewellery was the safest way to keep it.

The universe has given us this captivatingly beautiful, dense, inert, malleable, scarce, useless and permanent substance whose only use is to be money. To quote historian Peter Bernstein, 'nothing is as useless and useful all at the same time'.[8]

But after thousands of years of gold being official money, in the early twentieth century there was a seismic shift. Neither the British, German nor French government had enough gold to pay for the First World War. They abandoned gold backing to print the money they needed. In the inter-war years, nations briefly attempted a return to gold standards, but they failed. The two prevailing monetary theories clashed: gold-backed versus state-issued currency. Gold standard advocates, such as Montagu Norman, Governor of the Bank of England, considered gold to be one of the key pillars of a free society along with property rights and habeas corpus. 'We have gold because we cannot trust governments,' said President Herbert Hoover in 1933.[9] This was a sentiment echoed by one of the founders of the London School of Economics, George Bernard Shaw – to whom I am grateful for demonstrating that it is possible to have a career as both a comedian and a financial writer. 'You have to choose (as a voter)' he said, 'between trusting to the natural stability of gold and the natural stability of the honesty and intelligence of the members of the Government . . . I advise you, as long as the Capitalist system lasts, to vote for gold.'[10]

On the other hand, many, such as economist John Maynard Keynes, advocated the idea of fiat currency to give government greater control over the economy and the ability to manipulate the money supply. Keynes put fixation with gold in the Freudian realms of sex and religion. The gold standard, he famously said after the First World War – and rightly, as it turned out – was 'already a barbarous relic'.[11] Freud himself related fascination with gold to the erotic fantasies and interests of early childhood.

Needless to say, Keynes and fiat money prevailed. By the end of the 1930s, most of Europe had left the gold standard. The US followed, but not completely until 1971, in order to meet the ballooning costs of its welfare system and its war in Vietnam.

But compare both gold's universality (everyone everywhere knows gold has value) and its purchasing power to national currencies and you have to wonder why we don't use it officially today. There is a very good reason: power.

Sticking to the discipline of the gold standard means governments can't just create money or run deficits to the same extent. Instead, they have to rein in their spending, which they are not prepared to do, especially in the twenty-first century, when they make so many promises to win elections. Balanced books, let alone independent money, have become an impossibility. If you seek an answer as to why the state has grown so large in the west, look no further than our system of money. When one body in a society has the power to create money at no cost to itself, it is inevitable that that body will grow disproportionately large. So it is in the twenty-first century, where state spending in many social democracies is now not far off 50 per cent of GDP, sometimes higher.

Many arguments about gold will quickly slide into a political argument about the role of government. It is a deeply political metal. Those who favour gold tend to favour small government, free markets and individual responsibility. I count myself in that camp. Those who dismiss it tend to favour large government and state planning.

I have argued many times that money is the blood of a society. It must be healthy. So much starts with money. Values, morals, behaviour, ambitions, manners, even family size. Money must be sound and true. At the moment it is neither. Gold, however, is both. 'Because gold is honest money it is disliked by dishonest men,' said former Republican Congressman Ron Paul.[12] As Dorothy is advised in *The Wizard of Oz* (which was, as we shall discover, part allegory), maybe the time has come to once again 'follow the yellow brick road'.

On the other hand, maybe the twilight of gold has arrived, as Niall Ferguson argued in his history of debt and money, *The Cash Nexus*. Gold's future, he said, is 'mainly as jewellery' or 'in parts of the world with primitive or unstable monetary and financial systems'.[13] Gold may have been money for 5,000 years, or even 50,000 years, but so was the horse a means of transport, and then along came the motor car.

A history of gold is inevitably a history of money, but it is also a history of greed, obsession and ambition. Gold is beautiful. Gold is compelling. It is wealth in its purest, most distilled form. 'Gold is a child of Zeus,' runs the ancient Greek lyric. 'Neither moth nor rust devoureth it; but the mind of man is devoured by this supreme possession.'[14] Perhaps that's why Thomas Edison said gold was 'an invention of Satan'.[15] Wealth, and all the emotions that come with it, can do strange things to people.

Gold has led people to do the most brilliant, the most brave, the most inventive, the most innovative and the most terrible things. 'More men have been knocked off balance by gold than by love,' runs the saying, usually attributed to Benjamin Disraeli. Where gold is concerned, emotion, not logic, prevails. Even in today's markets it is a speculative asset whose price is driven by greed and fear, not by fundamental production numbers.

Its gleam has drawn man across oceans, across continents and into the unknown. It lured Jason and the Argonauts, Alexander the Great, numerous Caesars, da Gama, Cortés, Pizarro and Raleigh. Brilliant new civilisations have emerged as a result of the quest for gold, yet so have slavery, war, deceit, death and devastation. Describing the gold mines of ancient Egypt, the historian Diodorus Siculus wrote, 'there is absolutely no consideration nor relaxation for sick or maimed, for aged man or weak woman. All are forced to labour at their tasks until they die, worn out by misery amid their toil.'[16] His description could apply to many an illegal mine in Africa today.

The English critic John Ruskin told a story of a man who boarded a ship with all his money: a bag of gold coins. Several days into the voyage a terrible storm blew up. 'Abandon ship!' came the cry. The man strapped his bag around his waist and jumped overboard, only to sink to the bottom of the sea. 'Now,' asked Ruskin, 'as he was sinking – had he the gold? Or had the gold him?'[17]

As the Chinese proverb goes, 'The miser does not own the gold; the gold owns the miser.'

Gold may be a dead metal. Inert, unchanging and lifeless. But its hold over humanity never relents. It has adorned us since before the dawn of civilisation and, as money, underpinned economies ever since. Desire for it has driven mankind forwards, the prime impulse for quest and conquest, for exploration and discovery. From its origins in the hearts of dying stars to its quiet presence today beneath the machinery of modern finance, gold has seen it all. How many secrets does this silent witness keep? This book tells the story of gold. It unveils the schemes, intrigues and forces that have shaped our world in the relentless pursuit of this ancient asset, which, even in this digital age, still wields immense power.

2.

The Ancient Genesis of Gold

'Gold makes the ugly beautiful'

Molière

Plato and Aristotle both thought you could make gold by mixing sunlight with water. Alchemists thought you could get it from lead.

Scientists think they actually witnessed gold being created in 2017.

Two neutron stars, 130 million light years away, each the size of a city yet heavier than the sun, collided in a colossal explosion known as a kilonova.[1] Enormous amounts of energy were released in the form of gravitational waves and electromagnetic radiation, including visible light, all observed by telescopes around the world as it rippled through space-time to earth.

By the metals' reflective properties, astronomers estimated the amount of heavy elements produced by the collision. Something like 16,000 earth masses of material hurtled into space, creating '10 times the Earth's mass in gold and platinum alone'.[2] (Gold, by the way, makes up about one-billionth of the earth's mass, and most of that is still in the planet's core.)

'A significant fraction, maybe half, maybe more, of the heavy elements in the Universe are actually produced by this kind of collision,' says physicist Patrick Sutton.[3] Scientists argue that in the extreme heat and pressure inside neutron stars, atomic nuclei grab on to free neutrons in a process called 'neutron capture'. The resulting nuclear reactions then lead to the formation of gold. When these neutron stars eventually die, they explode as supernovae and disperse the gold and other elements into space.

Perhaps the ancient South Americans were not so wrong to see gold as the tears of the sun.

Our solar system (the sun and everything that orbits it) is believed to have formed from the cloud of gas and dust – a so-called solar nebula – produced by one such stellar collision. Small, solid objects – planetesimals – then formed in a process known as accretion, as gravitational attraction pulled the small particles together. These planetesimals grew through continued accretion and collision to eventually form the planets. Thus did gold make its way into the earth's crust.

Though rare, gold can be found in high concentrations in certain meteorites, known as 'carbonaceous chondrites', which formed in the early solar nebula. As such, additional gold has been brought here via asteroids and meteorites over the aeons.

So, gold is in fact older than the solar system; it is as old as stardust.

A Primal Instinct

'The desire for gold is the most universal and deeply rooted commercial instinct of the human race'

Gerald Loeb, trader[4]

As prehistoric man hunted and gathered his way through the Stone Age, thousands of years before the dawn of civilisation, he would have come across native metals – the metals that occur in nature in a relatively pure state: silver, tin, lead, iron, copper and gold. Gold was, says geochemist R. W. Boyle, the very first metal he used, 'the first metal known to the early hominids and humankind'.[5] Is that so?

The earliest known gold artefacts date back about 6,700 years to the Neolithic period – jewellery discovered by accident in 1972 in graves near Varna, Bulgaria: beads, rings, brooches, crowns, necklaces, amulets, even a gold phallus cover, with holes for threads to tie it on, presumably to emphasise the owner's status as a leading pro-creator. All show considerable craft, demonstrating that humans had been working with gold for many years already. The gold is heavy too, weighing over 1.5 kg/48 oz, and pure. This treasure predates smelting, the Bronze Age and the use of lead, tin and iron, which all began around 5,000 years ago. The Varna discovery is not just evidence of early gold use, it shows us that wealth accumulation, social structure, specialisation and trade networks already existed.

There are examples of copper tools, beads and awls that are older – in Iraqi caves dating back perhaps 11,000 years – but that does not necessarily mean man was using copper first. It is sadly a recurring theme throughout history, from tomb robbers in Egypt to conquistadors in South America, that wherever people have found gold, they have tended to melt it down and resmelt it, placing greater value on the raw material than on the craft, so most evidence of early gold use has been erased. (This also means that little bit of gold wrapped around your finger might once have adorned the head of a pharaoh or the neck of a hominid hunter-gatherer. You never know.)

Small bits of native gold have been found in ancient Spanish caves that were inhabited 40,000 years ago in the late Palaeolithic period.[6] Were they used as jewellery or tokens perhaps? If so, this would be the earliest known use of any metal. There is no such evidence of copper, though it's unlikely the copper would have survived so long without disintegrating.

Which metal did we actually use first – copper, gold or perhaps even silver? I want to say gold. Of course, I do. But we'll call it a dead heat. Either way the earliest use of metal was as jewellery.

Stone Age man found gold in river beds – glistening nuggets in the sediment, relatively easy to spot. Alluvial gold was more plentiful then than it is now – centuries of human scavenging have depleted the supply – and it will have compelled Stone Age man just as it compels us today. It was easy to shape into beads and other basic jewellery. There was no need for heat, just a rock to pound it with. As well as for decoration, gold would have been used as reward: as an expression of gratitude, as a gift, as a prize, even as a tool of barter. In other words, we were using it just as we use it today: to display, store and exchange value. Even in prehistory, gold was performing the monetary role it has always performed – and always will.

Stone Age man had the same basic emotions as we do today – fear, desire, love, hate, greed – which derive from our most basic instinct: survival. First, you must find water, food, clothing and shelter, for yourself and for those close to you. Then there is the urge to ensure the survival of your species: to reproduce. What frequently goes unmentioned, though, is our instinct for beauty and the emotions it inspires. What we find beautiful is often good for us in some way – the sound of running water, an open landscape with varied animal and plant life, a fit and healthy potential mate. The experience of beauty correlates with activity in the emotional brain – in the medial orbito-frontal cortex. This region of the brain lights up when we see beauty, whether in art, music or even mathematics. We find gold beautiful. As a symbol of accomplishment, it indicates, among other things, reproductive fitness: 'Look at me, I can get this rare and shiny substance.' It also denotes status. In the words of the ancient Greek sophist Hippias, 'The beautiful, is nothing else but gold . . . even what before appears ugly will appear beautiful when adorned with gold.'[7] Molière said something similar.

Beauty has long been associated by philosophers with truth and goodness. 'Beauty is truth, truth beauty,—that is all / Ye know on earth,' said John Keats.[8] Beauty is not just aesthetic but an indicator of deeper truth and moral goodness. This is why we find symmetry, proportion and harmony – all mathematical concepts – beautiful: they reflect an underlying order or 'truth' in nature. Indeed, the Egyptians used the most perfect of geometric figures, the circle, as a symbol for this most perfect and noblest of the metals.

Gold's association with goodness is one of the most common metaphors in literature, no matter what language. In English we talk of golden ages, golden boys, golden rules and hearts of gold. The 'golden thread', given to Theseus by his lover Ariadne to help him escape the Minotaur's labyrinth, symbolises wisdom and guidance.

In Arthurian legend, the Holy Grail was a golden symbol of God's grace. In Hercules' quest for Zeus's golden apples, gold is a symbol of incorruptible purity and purpose. Frodo's mission to destroy the Ring of Power is a twist on this convention (the ring is evil even if Frodo's quest is pure). Today, the young student gets a gold star, the athlete a gold medal. It is a symbol of achievement. 'The finest compliment you can pay a man', said daredevil Evel Knievel, 'is that his word was as good as gold.'

Almost every early civilisation, whether Sumerian, Akkadian, Assyrian, Babylonian, Indus Valley, Chinese or Egyptian, prized and utilised gold extensively. The same applies to pretty much every civilisation since. You could take a time machine to any society at any point in history, and they would instinctively understand that gold has value. It is a truly universal money which transcends culture and time. Our instinct for gold is more than just learned behaviour. It is primal. So, too, are the emotions gold inspires.

Now regarded as one of the cradles of civilisation, the first cities evolved around 4000 BC in Sumer, southern Mesopotamia. There, 'Sumerian jewellery fulfilled practically all the ornamental functions which were to occur during the course of history,' says jewellery historian Guido Gregorietti.[9] 'In fact, there were more different types of jewellery than there are today.' High levels of skill in engraving, relief, filigree, lost-wax casting and granulation are all evident. The archaeologist Sir Leonard Woolley, who spent at least twelve years at excavations in Ur in Sumer, said, 'Its craftsmen possessed a knowledge and technical skill which few have ever rivalled.'[10]

Where did the gold come from? Much is thought to have come from placer deposits in the upper Tigris and Euphrates, and some from the Zagros Mountains to the east in Persia. Much came via trade. One tablet mentions Dilmun, an ancient kingdom surrounding modern-day Bahrain, another Pakistan. Gold also came from Egypt, where it could be found in the rich alluvial deposits along the upper reaches of the Nile in Nubia and in the many mines between the river and Red Sea. These were probably the source of King Solomon's gold, too.

References to the geological setting of gold at this time are sparse, but the most ancient of geological maps known shows gold in Egypt,[11] and the first mention of gold in the Bible (Genesis 2:10–12) points to alluvial gold:

10 And a river went out of Eden to water the garden;
   and from thence it was parted, and became into four heads.
11 The name of the first is Pison: that is it which compasseth
   the whole land of Havilah, where there is gold;
12 And the gold of that land is good.

In this case, 'good' means 'pure'.

Gold's Link to the Divine

'No other object has commanded so much
veneration over such a long period of time'

Peter Bernstein, historian[12]

Today, we know of around ninety metals. Until the thirteenth century, we knew of just seven: gold, silver, copper, tin, lead, iron and mercury. (Actually, we also knew about zinc, antimony and arsenic, but they were not considered metals.) There were seven known celestial bodies, and each became associated with a metal: the 'mysterious' moon with silver; Mars, rusty and blood-red, with iron; Mercury with its fluid namesake; Jupiter with tin; Venus with copper; Saturn with lead. Alchemists would even refer to metals by their planetary names – a nod to each metal's essence So lead, for example, was Saturn. Gold was, inevitably, associated with the sun. Alchemists would call it 'Sol'.

Each of the seven metals claimed a day of the week, too. Silver Monday, iron Tuesday, mercury Wednesday. Gold's day, of course, was Sunday.

The number seven was pre-eminent in the ancient mind: planets, metals, days.

To the ancient Greeks, the sun was a golden chariot driven across the sky each day by the god Apollo. The Egyptian sun god, Ra, was depicted as a yellow blaze of gold. The Latin word for gold, 'aurum', means glowing dawn, and derives from Aurora, the goddess of dawn, who rose each morning to announce the sun's arrival. The root of the words by which the Celts and Greeks referred to gold is the Sanskrit 'harat', which means 'colour of the sun'.

Early alchemists thought the centre of the earth was an inferno produced by the rays of the seven known planets upon the earth. Thus, Apollo (the sun) gave rise to gold, Diana (the moon) to silver, Mars to iron and so on.

There are even whispers of an ancient and superior culture which preceded us, and of aliens landing on earth thousands of years ago in great spaceships, which the ancients took to be chariots of the gods. They came for gold, and they bred humans to mine it for them. Among the things they left behind them on earth were the pyramids. There is some evidence that the capstones on top of the pyramids – the pyramidia – were gilded with a thin layer of gold or electrum (gold-silver alloy),[13] which would have had all sorts of celestial and religious connotations. It would be remiss of me not to mention that this version of events is disputed.

While silver, like the moon, was perceived as feminine – intuitive, enigmatic, reflective – gold was a masculine metal, bold and dominant, strong and powerful, connected not just with the sun but with the lion. This association lives on today, from the lion rampant (standing on its hind legs) found on so many family crests to the three gold lions on the English coat of arms. Gold represented wealth, prosperity, authority and charisma. It was a symbol of knowledge and enlightenment, its radiant qualities mirroring the illumination provided by the sun. Scholars and sages adorned themselves with it to reflect their intellectual and spiritual pursuits.

When you touch gold, 'you're in touch with sunshine', as Bernstein put it.[14] The sun's energy was thought to have infused gold with special healing properties. Ancient healers and priests often used gold in their remedies and elixirs, attributing its regenerative powers to the sun's life-giving energy. Wearing gold could help physical well-being and aid in recovery from ailments. The ancient Greek sun god Apollo was the god of healing and diseases, while his son, Asclepius, was the god of medicine. Apollo delivered people from epidemics, but could bring ill-health and deadly plague. Modern science confirms these instincts, with Vitamin D, which we get from sunlight, now seen as so important for our general well-being. As the sun was a guardian against darkness and evil, so could gold ward off negative energies and offer spiritual protection. Thus talismans and amulets were often made of gold.

Many swear by gold's healing powers. Ayurvedic medicine recommends gold powder or pills for many ailments. Gold salts, in the form of specific compounds, have been used for decades to alleviate inflammation and slow the progression of rheumatoid arthritis. Gold nanoparticles show promising potential in targeting cancer cells.

Monarchs draped themselves in gold to show their power: to dazzle, to command and to demonstrate godlike status. They still do. Just recently, the new British king, Charles III, rode to his coronation in a golden carriage. In early ancient Egypt, gold was a royal prerogative, thereby reinforcing the pharaohs' godlike status. Pharaohs were buried with their gold to aid their travel into the next world. Tutankhamun, son of Ra, was buried in a golden shrine. Gold was a gift both from the gods and to the gods.

According to the Bible, too, which mentions gold over 400 times, gold and silver belong to God: 'The silver is mine, and the gold is mine, saith the Lord of hosts.'[15] However, given that in those days the distinctions between God, church, king and ruler were not always that clear, that might have been a ploy to control capital.

3.

Myths and Dragons, Coins and Kings

'Some things that should not have been forgotten were lost.
History became legend. Legend became myth'

Peter Jackson, director, *The Fellowship of the Ring*[1]

The golden fleece, so the story goes, came from a magical ram with golden wool, sent by the gods to rescue two children, Phrixus and Helle. Helle fell into the sea and died (creating the Hellespont), but Phrixus survived and rode the ram to the kingdom of Colchis. He then sacrificed the ram to Zeus to thank him for his safety, and he gave the fleece to Aietes, the king, who hung it from a tree in a sacred grove. There, it was guarded by bulls with hooves of brass and breath of fire, and a dragon that never slept, whose teeth became soldiers when planted in the ground.

Not an easy thing to steal. Yet Jason, the rightful king of far-away Iolcos, was challenged to retrieve it and bring it back to his homeland in order to reclaim his own lost throne.

You might think that this well-known Greek myth is just that – a myth. But myths and legends are born from real-life events. The stories are told and retold, each time with a little embellishment here, a little restructuring there, and so do today's current affairs become tomorrow's history and, eventually, the myth and legend of the future. The protagonists of those stories will be the heroes and gods of tomorrow. The tale of Jason and the Argonauts, and their quest for the golden fleece, went through just such a transformation. In reality, Jason, like the prospectors of any gold rush, was a young explorer seeking his fortune. The 'golden fleece' was, actually, an ancient method of panning gold. Let me explain.

Colchis – in modern-day Georgia – lies to the east of the Black Sea, and the streams coming down from the Caucasus Mountains made it a prolific source of alluvial gold. Those same streams of the Caucasus may have supplied Mesopotamia centuries before. In Colchis, the locals used sheepskin to pan them for gold. They stretched the fleeces over wooden frames and lodged them in the water. The tight curls of the wool would catch the specks of gold being carried down from the placer deposits upstream. They then hung the fleece up to dry and combed out the gold. If you have a fleece full of gold hanging out to dry in a tree, you are going to make sure it is well guarded – by bulls and dragons, if necessary. It's quite easy to see how this practice evolved into the myth of the golden fleece, as the story spread west to Greece and then down through time.

Pelias, king of Iolcos, had promised Jason the throne if he brought back the golden fleece. Jason built a ship and assembled the Argonauts – a crew which included such heroes as Hercules, the twins Castor and Pollux, and Orpheus – then set off on what is seen by some as the first long-distance voyage ever undertaken: the first time a Greek successfully navigated the hostile currents of the Bosphorus. Along the way, the Argonauts fought giants, killed harpies and fathered a new race, before arriving in Colchis where the king's daughter, Medea, fell for Jason. She showed him how to overcome the formidable guards and steal the fleece, which he did, before fleeing back to Iolcos with Medea to reclaim his throne.

As is so often the way with rags-to-riches stories involving gold, it soon started to go wrong when they got home. Pelias went back on his promise to hand over the throne. So Medea tricked his daughters into murdering him. Jason and Medea were exiled, and they fled to the city of Corinth, where Jason dumped Medea and married the King of Corinth's daughter instead. Medea would have her revenge – who wouldn't? – a revenge which has become the subject of many a drama since. She murdered Jason's newly betrothed and then her own two sons, fathered by Jason, and fled. Jason returned home to Iolcos, where he died alone and unhappy, asleep on the rotting *Argo*.

It's a buccaneering adventure story with a typically tragic end. The formula of hero, dark power and female helper has become the backbone of numerous plots since, not least in Hollywood. But it is also the classic story of a gold prospector who takes incredible risks, furthers general knowledge in doing so, and gets rich, only to be struck by hubris and misfortune for it all to go wrong. As we shall see, in the history of prospecting this plot is by no means unique.

A Golden Apple Triggers History's First Great War

'It's very simple when you analyze it . . .
the cause of all wars is gold'

Henry Ford[2]

Gold and war have always been bedfellows.

Zeus was holding a banquet on Mount Olympus to celebrate the wedding of Pelias (him again) and Thetis, and all the gods were invited, all except one – Eris, goddess of chaos. Eris, ego bruised by the snub, threw a golden apple into the party with the word 'Kallisti' inscribed on it: 'For the most beautiful'.

Immediately, the goddesses Hera, Athena and Aphrodite began to quarrel. Each felt they should have the apple, for they were the most beautiful. It fell to Zeus to pass judgement. Who should he choose? Hera, his wife, or one of his two daughters? Tricky. Whoever he chose, he would incur the fury of the other two. So, instead, he nominated the Trojan prince Paris, who was sitting on a nearby mountainside, to decide.

The goddesses then undressed, bathed and came in turn before Paris, in a kind of divine lap dance, to make their case. But Paris could not decide, so the goddesses tried to bribe him. Hera offered Paris power: control of all Europe and Asia. Athena offered him wisdom and victory in battle. Aphrodite offered him the love of the most beautiful woman on earth.

Paris, being a bloke, went for option three.

The most beautiful woman on earth was, of course, Helen of Sparta. What Aphrodite had not mentioned, however, was that Helen was married – to Menelaus, King of Sparta. When Paris ran away with Helen, the greatest war the world had ever known was precipitated: the Trojan War.

All because of a golden apple.

How King Midas Was Not a Myth: The Alluvial Deposits of the River Pactolus

'Gold . . . what can it not do and undo?'

William Shakespeare, *Cymbeline*

The most famous golden myth of all is one of the later Greek myths: the story of Midas, and how his touch turned everything to gold.

What isn't widely known is how the Midas Touch led to one of the most successful, long-lasting and underrated technologies in history.

The story, as told by Ovid in *Metamorphoses*, is that Dionysus, god of wine, parties and pleasure, and his entourage had been on something of a binge through Phrygia (now part of Turkey), where Midas was king. Midas found Dionysus' tutor Silenus passed out in his rose garden and nursed him back to health. After eleven days – that must have been some hangover – Midas took Silenus back to Dionysus, who was so delighted to see his old mentor safe and well that he offered Midas whatever reward he wished for. Midas thought hard and then asked that everything he touched should turn to gold. Dionysus urged the king to reconsider, but Midas was sure and so his wish was granted.

At first, Midas was thrilled. He turned a twig, then a stone to gold.

He turned the roses in his garden to gold. Delighted, he ordered his servants to make him a feast, but, when he turned his food and drink to gold, he realised he might have a problem. Then his daughter came to him, crying that their roses had lost their smell. Midas hugged her and she too turned to gold. What had been his beloved daughter was now a statue, albeit a golden one. Despairing, he prayed to Dionysus to deliver him from his curse. 'Go and wash your hands in the River Pactolus,' Dionysus told him.

Midas did so, and the cure worked. Midas' power flowed into the water and the sands of the river turned to gold. Whatever he put in the water, his daughter included, was turned back into what it had been before Midas touched it.

So does that more famous part of Midas' story end with its obvious moral: greed can overpower good sense.

But the sands of the River Pactolus now held treasure: alluvial gold. Lots of it.

King Alyattes I and the Western World's First Coins

'Although gold and silver are not by nature money,
money is by nature gold and silver'

Karl Marx[3]

The Pactolus flowed right through the middle of the Lydian Empire, which, at its height, stretched across all western Asia Minor. The Lydians were, in the sixth century BC, says Greek historian Herodotus, 'the first to strike and use coins of gold and silver'.[4]

Given that we still use coins today, some 2,600 years later, coinage has proved a remarkably successful technology, perhaps the most successful fintech of all time. But here we have another case of history becoming legend and legend myth, to paraphrase Peter Jackson.

Midas did actually exist – most Greek mythological figures did. He was likely Mita of Mushki, who ruled in the late eighth century BC. His golden touch, though, is no doubt an embellishment. One of his descendants, some 200 years or so later, was the Lydian King Alyattes I, the first western king to issue coins. He minted them from the alluvial gold-silver alloy, electrum, found in the bed of the Pactolus. This was the gold supposedly left there by Midas. It was a 'huge alluvial deposit too', said mining analyst Robert Weinberg after a visit there in 2004. 'All the gold scoured out of the oxidised ore in the mountains would have precipitated into the river century after century.'[5]

Really, Alyattes' coins were little more than blobs of metal. The innovation of his son, Croesus, around 550 BC, was to have the electrum coins of his father melted down and the gold separated from the silver, before reminting them.[6] On one side of his new coins was the image of a lion and a bull; on the other were punch marks to show their value. (Faces did not appear on coins till later.) Effectively, Croesus launched not only the first imperial currency in the history of the world, but also the bimetallic standard (gold and silver) – the backbone of money for over 2,000 years. This, as we shall discover, would become a huge political issue in both eighteenth-century Britain and nineteenth-century America.

Croesus' coins, mined from that huge alluvial deposit, were not only accepted but demanded. Lydia was prosperous as a result, and, as his coins began circulating so widely and effectively, Croesus' reputation as an extremely rich man was secured for all time. Within a century, the new technology was being used in Persia in the east, across Asia Minor and Greece and at least as far as Sicily in the west. Coins provided both geographical and social mobility: people could move around and carry certifiable value with them, thus trade and exchange spread with newfound ease. As any Matt Ridley acolyte will tell you, it is through trade and exchange that mankind progresses. From Persia and the Phoenician city states to Greece, Macedonia, Sicily and Carthage, there was economic expansion; credit and investment; cultural exchange; improved shipping; the development of record-keeping and writing, not to mention governance. Civilisation was able to accelerate.

Croesus' basic denomination was divided into smaller denominations of thirds, sixths and twelfths. These evolved into the twenty-four carats we use today. Not only was he 'as rich as Croesus', but he had, it seems, the Midas Touch.

One unintended consequence of Croesus' coins was to advertise to all the world that gold could be found in the bed of the Pactolus. Another was to fire his bellicose ambition, and he used his coins to pay mercenaries for an invasion of Persia. Gold, not for the first or last time, was both instigator and propagator of war: people start wars to get gold, and they pay for wars with gold. This is a pattern that, unfortunately, never stops repeating.

Despite the forecasts of the Oracle at Delphi that 'a great kingdom would be destroyed', Croesus' invasion failed. Seeking revenge – and, no doubt, Pactolus gold – Persian King Cyrus the Great marched on the Lydian capital, Sardis, in 546 BC, and took the city after a fourteen-day siege. So did the Lydian Empire come to an end. As Herodotus put it, 'the oracle was fulfilled; Croesus did destroy a great kingdom – his own.'

Lands as far as the Aegean fall under Persian control, and the Pactolus gold and silver were now the mint supply for Persian coins, most notably the daric, named after Cyrus' son Darius. The daric circulated throughout the Persian Empire and beyond for some 200 years, the most important international coin, minted from Midas' gold.

Gold facilitates many things. One of them, as we already have seen, is war. Two hundred years of conflict between Persian and Greek ensued. Along with the daric, this came to an end with the conquests of Alexander the Great, another warmonger. There is no shortage of violence in the history of this extraordinary substance.

How Gold Is Measured

I expect you know that an inch is the width of a thumb, and a foot is, well, a foot (with a boot on). In the past, when people didn't have modern measuring equipment, they made do with the most immediate thing they had, which was their body, and so most traditional weights and measures derive from the human anatomy in some way. A cubit is the distance from the elbow to the tip of the outstretched fingers – a foot and a half. A yard is a pace – three feet.

The mina is one of the oldest measures we know of, used in ancient Sumer and then through Semitic, Greek and Latin civilisations. It was roughly a pound, which is roughly a handful. Because they are based around the body, you will find that most traditional measures (Americans call them English measures; the British call them Imperial) correspond to the weights and measures used by the ancients.

However, when it came to very small items, body parts did not work, so we used grains and seeds. The grain was a foundational measure of weight – seeds of wheat, barley or carob. All are remarkably consistent in size and weight. 'An English Penny, which is called the Sterling, round without clipping, shall weigh Thirty-two Grains of Wheat dry in the midst of the Ear,' proclaimed the thirteenth-century law, the Assize of Bread and Ale. Even today, gold is measured in grains, though not actual grains, as the measure has been standardised.

Barley seeds – or barleycorns to give them their proper name – are also how we measure shoe sizes. A size-nine shoe is one barleycorn longer than a size eight. Even metric continental shoe sizes increase in barleycorn increments.

In ancient Rome, the siliqua, which is Latin for 'carob tree', was a unit of weight which equalled three barleycorns or four wheat grains.[7] Hundreds of years later, Johnson's *Dictionary* (1755) defined a carat as four grains – the word 'carat' deriving from the

Greek 'keration', meaning 'fruit of the carob tree'. The Roman solidus coin weighed twenty-four siliquas, as did the Arabic dinar.

This is why the modern measurement of gold purity is based on twenty-four parts. Pure gold is twenty-four-carat, while an alloy containing 50 per cent gold is twelve-carat.

This table shows gold purity.

Carat	Gold Purity	% of Other Metals
24	100%	0%
22	91.6%	8.4%
18	75%	25%
14	58.5%	41.5%
10	41.7%	58.3%
8	33.3%	66.7%

But what would gold be mixed with?

It depends what the purpose is. People have always mixed other metals with gold: some trying to make gold harder, some to make it more beautiful, some to defraud buyers.

Pink or rose gold is made by mixing gold with copper. The amount of copper used can vary, resulting in different shades of pink.

White gold is made by mixing gold with white metals such as nickel, palladium or zinc, and sometimes coated with rhodium to enhance its whiteness. 'High-end' or 'premium' white gold sees gold mixed with platinum. Gold and platinum have similar chemical properties, so they can be easily alloyed. The result is usually harder and more resistant to scratching than pure gold.

Green gold is made by mixing gold with silver, which can give it a greenish hue. It can be found naturally, as electrum, or created artificially for use in jewellery.

Blue gold is a rare alloy made by mixing gold with indium, which gives it a bluish hue. It is usually used for specialised applications in electronics and nanotechnology.

There are other types of gold alloys, such as black gold (made by adding cobalt or other dark metals), purple gold (made by adding aluminium) and grey gold (made by adding iron). They are not common.

4.

Gold in the Classical World

'Whoever has the gold makes the rules'

Johnny Hart, cartoonist[1]

The Royal Tombs at Vergina, where Philip II of Macedon, father of Alexander the Great, is buried, are one of the most dramatic displays of gold you will ever see.

Luckily, they were only discovered in 1977. Much before that and chances are the gold would have been taken and resmelted. The opulence is quite something: golden crowns, intricate jewellery and stunning weaponry. The golden larnax (chest), which held the cremated remains of the king, is made with over 11 kg/350 oz of pure gold. The golden wreath, fashioned to look like an oak wreath, complete with delicate leaves and acorns, shows just how skilful the ancient goldsmiths were. Philip II was a rich and powerful man.

But Macedonia was an unusual kingdom in the ancient world for having so much gold. In ancient Greece, if anything, there was a shortage. Silver paid for much of the Peloponnesian War, although many a fine gold statue (including at least seven of the goddess Nike) was stripped of its gold casing to help fund the effort. Exhausting conflict between Athens and Sparta, and then Sparta and Thebes, paved the way for the rise of Macedonia, in whose mountains there was plenty of gold and plenty of silver to be mined.

Early in his reign, and quite deliberately, the young Philip captured the plentiful mines of eastern Macedonia and reorganised them on a grand scale to provide him with a substantial income for decades, equivalent to some two tonnes per year,[2] and enabling him to start issuing coins.

After his father's assassination, Alexander, who had been tutored as a child by Aristotle – not many of us can say that – became king at the age of twenty. Alexander the Great, King of Macedonia, became one of the most successful military commanders in history. He was just thirty-three when he died, having reigned from 336 to 323 BC, and having spent most of his adult life, it seems, on military campaigns. By the time he was thirty, he controlled one of the largest empires ever known, stretching from Greece in the west and Egypt in the south all the way through Persia and Pakistan to north-western India. Despite often being outnumbered, he never lost a battle. His thirteen years of rule really did change the face of the world.

Though he was better known for his military exploits, his contribution to the evolution of money and coinage was also significant.

At first, he stuck with the coins of his father, but before long he began minting small coins of his own from the mines of Macedonia and Thrace. His money followed his armies – he had soldiers to pay. As he conquered, he plundered, and then minted coins from the mines and the huge bullion stocks he took, especially in Persia.

'It is hardly coincidence,' says the British Museum's Dyfri Williams, 'that the route of Alexander's conquests passed through all the main gold-supplying regions of the former Persian Empire.'[3] As well as the mines, Alexander occupied key trade routes, and he found huge caches: an abandoned royal baggage train after the Battle of Issus, another half tonne at Damascus and, best of all, the main treasure of the empire at Susa and Persepolis – perhaps as much as 47 tonnes of gold and 4,200 tonnes of silver in total.[4] By the time he died, not even a third of that was left. Armies need paying. Loyalty needs rewarding. Easy come, easy go, as they say.

Alexander established twenty-six mints across his vast empire, often close to mines – seven in Europe, eighteen in Asia and one in

Africa – and the instruction to all of them was that his coins should all be struck to be the same. He was standardising money and creating an internationally recognised currency.

Nor did he skimp on the job. Alexander's money was sound. His stater, one of the highest-denomination coins, had a gold purity of around 98 per cent, among the purest of ancient coins. His silver tetradrachms were similarly pure. At just over ½ oz, these became the most widely used coins of all: international, imperial money used in state transactions, to pay his armies, to pay off Celtic invaders from the north and, of course, in the marketplace. The stature and value of his coins were such that his successors continued to mint similar coins for the next 250 years.

His coins served not just as a means to pay his army and as a tool of commerce, but as propaganda. He melted down pillaged coins and then struck new ones with images of Greek gods. Gone were the previously widespread darics. It must have been somewhat demoralising for the conquered Persians, ancient rivals of the Greeks, to see their own culture and history quite literally struck off. But for Alexander, here was a means of embedding his leadership in the minds of the conquered. Money was becoming an important tool of government, as it remains today, beyond its function as a medium of exchange.

His gold stater was just over ¼ oz (about 8.67 g) – a fraction heavier than a US quarter or a UK 2p piece. On the front was the helmeted head of Athena, goddess of wisdom and war, and on the reverse the standing figure of Nike, goddess of victory, who holds a wreath in one hand and, in the other, a naval standard. Behind her we read the word 'Alexandrou' ('of Alexander').

The tetradrachm became the most widespread coin in the eastern Mediterranean. A drachma (which meant 'handful' – referring to a measure of metal rods that were used before coins) would amount to about a day's wages for a common labourer – a tetradrachm would thus be about four days' wages. They comprised a little over ½ oz (17 g) of silver. The Athenian owl tetradrachm was common, but, with Alexander's innovation to strike coins everywhere he went, his tetradrachms can be seen as the world's first global currency. Judas, for example, was almost certainly paid in tetradrachms to betray Jesus. Thirty of them – around sixteen ounces – so about 120 days' wages.

More were minted than any other ancient coin – and they were minted for over 300 years. Thousands still exist today, many in excellent condition. Have a look on eBay: they don't always trade at as high a premium to the metal content as you might expect. On the front they carry the head of Hercules, god of strength, and founder of Macedonia, wearing a lion skin. On the back is Zeus, god of power, seated on a throne, holding a sceptre in one hand and an eagle in the other. As with the stater, behind Zeus we read that word again, 'Alexandrou'. The depiction of Hercules – usually beardless and young – showed a remarkable likeness to the young Alexander. Thereby did he open the door to the practice of stamping coins with the heads of rulers, rather than gods.

Alexander died in 323 BC, and one of his successors, Ptolemy I, went one step further and inscribed coins with portraits of Alexander himself. One example shows the Hercules-resembling Alexander with an elephant scalp with tusks and a trunk on his head, symbolising his conquest of India, where Alexander brought coinage for the first time. Within a few decades, with Demetrius I probably being the first, rulers were blatantly putting their own heads on coins. The portrait became an important tool of propaganda.

Alexander's empire, in terms of land mass, was one of the greatest in history. Only the Mongol, British and Soviet Empires were larger. He might have conquered with his armies, but he consolidated with money: by taking control of gold and silver supply and using it to impose his currency, the most international money the world had ever seen. Gold may enable war; it also enables rule. In all the years since, there has never been a global reserve currency that did not start out based on gold and, sometimes, silver. This is a lesson we shall see time and time again: whoever has the gold makes the rules.

How the Romans Destroyed Their Money

'Aurum potestas est' ('Gold is power')

Roman proverb

The Roman silver coin, the denarius, started out at 95–98 per cent pure silver. By 275 AD, the silver content was not even 1 per cent. The amount of gold in a gold coin was almost halved.

How could a coin of the world's most powerful empire go from pure silver to practically none?

The Romans are probably more famous for debasing their money than for their money itself, but for that debasement to have been so prolonged (it went on for hundreds of years) and, some might say, effective, it needed an established, widely recognised and credible money as a starting point.

At its mightiest, as many as 50 million people lived in the Roman Empire. The peace was kept by the formidable Roman army amounting to more than 100,000 troops, all paid in hard cash, gold and silver.

The quantity of gold in circulation was on a scale never before witnessed, and never equalled until the gold rushes of the nineteenth century. One calculation puts it at 880 tonnes at the height of the empire, around 160 AD.[5] To get to that point took some 400 years, at least.

The geology of central Italy is not particularly abundant in gold and silver. Bronze (copper and tin) was the early currency of choice. But as the republic expanded, it gained access to more gold and silver, either from loot, tribute or mine supply. Rome's forays against Carthage in the Second Punic War secured huge gold stocks, as well as control of Spain's silver mines. 'Then Macedon, Greece, Asia, Numidia, the East, Gaul and finally Egypt fed the Roman coffer,' says historian Fernand Braudel. 'The sums involved were massive and the immediate impact of these accretions of wealth would be dramatic.'[6]

The first gold staters were minted at around the same time as the first silver denarius in 211 BC, but the denarius was the more successful of the two, largely because silver supply was more abundant.

For the next 500 years, the denarius, containing just over ⅛ oz (4 g) of silver – a little bit more than the weight of a 1c or 1p coin – would be the main circulating currency of Rome. One denarius was exchangeable for ten bronze weights ('asses'), hence its name denarius – 'of ten'. The purchasing power of a denarius would be more than the underlying metal value – ranging between 1.5 and 3 times the value. That's seigniorage for you.

The denarius lives on today, especially in many Latin languages. One Italian word for money is 'denaro', 'dinero' is Spanish, 'dinheiro' is Portuguese, 'denar' is Slovenian. In many Arab nations, the currency is the dinar. It became the symbol for the old English penny: 'd', as in 1d.

Gold emerged as a major element under Julius and then Augustus Caesar about 200 years later. The aureus, weighing 8 g / ¼ oz, was at the heart of the system. One aureus was worth 25 silver denarii, meaning an effective gold-to-silver ratio of 1:12.

The Romans Were Not Flat-Earthers

Consider this Trajan aureus (98–117 AD). On the reverse we see Providentia, Roman goddess of foresight, overlooking a globe (the world, the empire).

And here is a Roman aureus of Hadrian from 117 AD – the year he became emperor, and when the Roman Empire was at its greatest extent. On the reverse it shows Trajan, the previous emperor (on the right), passing a globe to Hadrian, who accepts it.

This surely kills the notion that people thought the earth was flat. The Romans clearly knew it was round. (And indeed the Greeks before them: Aristotle said 'the Earth is spherical'.)

We can tell a great deal about a civilisation from their coins.

The Mighty Spanish Mines of Rome and Their Eventual Exhaustion

'It rivals the achievements of the Giants. By the light of lamps, long galleries are cut into the mountain. Men work in long shifts measured by lamps, and may not see daylight for months'

Pliny the Elder[7]

The aqueducts in León and along the western flank of Puerto del Palo in Asturias, along with the Montefurado tunnel in Galicia, are regarded as some of the finest examples of hydrological engineering in the Roman world. We tend to think the aqueducts were there to bring water to Roman cities, so citizens could all enjoy their hot baths. In fact, their purpose was often to bring water to the mines.

Gunpowder and explosives had not yet been discovered. The Romans used a method called 'fire-setting', where they would heat the rock face with fire and then douse it with water. The rapid cooling caused 'thermal shock', making the rock crack and break apart. They would then pour on more water to wash away loose earth and rock, exposing the ore beneath, be it copper, silver or gold, which could then be extracted and smelted to separate the metal. Entire mountains were washed away in the process. This is visible in the spectacular landscape of Las Médulas. Pliny actually called this mining technique 'ruina montium' – ruin of the mountains. So vast is the scale of the devastation that in the eighteenth and nineteenth centuries, many geologists actually thought it a natural formation. There's evidence that the environmental pollution – on a scale not reached again until the Industrial Revolution – reached Greenland. In fact, there was controversy when Las Médulas became a UNESCO world heritage site, because the extraordinary landscape was created by human destructive activity.

Conquest and loot had proved, over the previous 300 years, a highly effective means of bringing wealth to Rome, but the empire was no longer expanding at the same rate. By the first century AD, taxation and tribute covered only around 80 per cent of the imperial budget, and the leadership showed no inclination to rein in their spending. The shortfall was met by mining.

When Augustus came to power, Rome already controlled the silver mines of Macedonia and southern Spain. The gold in the mountains of north-west Spain became his target. Resistance was fierce and the terrain hard, and it was Agrippa, Augustus' son-in-law, who finally took full control of the region. There followed the biggest mining operation the world had ever seen. Over 250 different Roman mine sites produced for 200 years, underpinning the Roman monetary system. (Roman gold coins were not debased as much as silver.) No other mining region was as sustained or prolific. Annual production is estimated at ten tonnes of gold, with ten times as much silver.[8] The mines were the emperor's; exploration was licensed out to contractors, with the army providing protection.

All that mining meant enormous engineering and geological challenges, not least getting the essential water supply to hard-rock open-cast mines. Going underground, the Romans encountered and overcame numerous problems – ventilation, lighting and drainage. For drainage they developed water wheels and Archimedean screws to lift out water. Extraordinary feats of engineering, all motivated by, as Pliny put it, 'the greed for gold'.[9]

But by 200 AD, the mines were depleting. Production was in decline. Treasury stocks were sapped to maintain an increasingly demoralised army. Then the debasement of the currency seriously accelerated.

Though debasement had begun as early as 64 AD with Nero, it was gradual. He reduced the purity of the denarius to 93.5 per cent, and 100 years later this fell to 83 per cent. But with the mines of Spain now running out, this would quickly become 50 per cent.

All sorts of ingenious ways to debase currency were found. Caracalla, who was emperor from 211 to 217 AD, introduced a coin that was one and a half times as heavy, but valued at twice as much. The result was an effective 25 per cent debasement.

Unlike the silver denarius, the aureus kept its near-100 per cent, twenty-four-carat purity throughout the debasement. The coins just got smaller, so the amount of gold was reduced that way. Gold was the sole anchor with deteriorating base currency all around, but as its supply waned, people began hoarding it. Many coins were melted down and refashioned as jewellery. Under Caracalla, the aureus slid to 6.46 g/0.21 oz. Twenty years later, under Severus Alexander in 235, it was 5.5 g/0.18 oz.

By 275 AD, denarius silver content was just 5 per cent. Citizens felt the effects. The decade 260–70 AD saw prices multiply tenfold, implying 25 per cent annual inflation.[10] In a breathtaking show of hypocrisy that even leaders today would struggle to pull off, the Roman authorities, despite the declining quality of the metal content of their denarius, refused to accept anything other than gold and silver in payment of taxes. Take in the good money; send out the bad.

By the time of Diocletian, who was emperor from 284 to 305 AD, there was so little precious metal in the money, the emperor had to resort to price controls. The idea of obtaining an aureus for twenty-five denarii was long gone, even if Diocletian had now clipped the aureus down a fraction more in weight. In 301, one gold aureus was worth 1,200 denarii. Average annual inflation was 12.5 per cent.[11] Imagine that compounded over time. It was under Diocletian that the last denarii were minted. Before long, not even 100,000 could get you an aureus, and the denarius was abandoned (though it remained as a unit of account). Diocletian also replaced the aureus with a new coin, the solidus, some 4.5 g/0.14 oz of gold. Yet another weight reduction.

Over 200 reasons have been offered for the decline and fall of the Roman Empire, ranging from climate change to the rise of Christianity to lethargy caused by too much time spent in hot baths to alien invasion. One hugely overlooked factor must be the depletion of its mines, and the resulting shortage of gold and silver. When the mines were depleted, the money ran out.

In these stories from the classical world, we see the cycle of civilisations. At their height, the currency is pure and golden. As they decline and fall, currency and gold part company. The Byzantine Empire, which followed Rome, went through just such a cycle.

By the time Rome fell in 476 AD, after a hundred years of struggle against Goths, Huns and other barbarians, the nucleus of the empire had long since moved east to Constantinople, today Istanbul. Constantine I had declared Constantinople 'New Rome' in 330 AD, and for 150 years the two cities had run in parallel, with a common gold coinage: the solidus introduced by Diocletian in 301 AD. Under Constantine I the solidus became widespread, as the principal coin of the Mediterranean and beyond.

Ultimately the two empires diverged. Rome crumbled, its resources drained trying to buy off Germanic tribes (at one point these payments reached 680 kg/22,000 oz per annum[12]), while the 'Eastern Roman Empire' would survive, thrive even, for another 1,100 years, a trading hub and military buffer between Europe and Asia, before it finally fell to the Ottomans in 1453.

The solidus remained essentially unaltered in weight, dimension and purity until the tenth century. It was the standard for Byzantine and European currencies. Most were minted in Constantinople itself, though some were minted in other cities of the empire as far afield as Thessalonica, Syracuse, Alexandria, Carthage and Jerusalem. In mediaeval Europe, one solidus would be worth twelve silver pennies (that 1:12 ratio again). Indeed, another Italian word for money, 'soldi', has its roots there. In Western Europe, the solidus also became known as the 'bezant' after its provenance.

We may call it the 'Byzantine Empire' today, but citizens called themselves Romans and their empire was, to them at least, the Roman Empire. Its zenith came during the reign of Justinian I (527–65), boosted by new mine supply as well as loot and plunder, when much of North Africa, Europe as far as Spain to the west and the Danube in the north, as well as Italy and Rome itself, had fallen under its rule. But Justinian sowed the seeds of demise with overspending, excess taxation, ill-discipline in his military and creeping corruption. Bubonic plague didn't help either. War with the Sassanians to the east in the early seventh century exhausted the empire's resources and paved the way for the rapidly expanding Islamic Empire to take many of its richest provinces from Egypt to Syria. The Arab conquerors minted their own coin, the dinar, 4.4 g/ $\frac{1}{7}$ oz of gold, similar in weight to the solidus, from captured gold supplies in Asia and East Africa. Control of Morocco and Algeria meant access for the Arabs to the plentiful gold of West Africa – Senegal and Mali, in particular.

Byzantine currency, meanwhile, followed the typical trajectory of empires: it started sound and ended worthless. As is so often the case, the debasement was gradual at first and then it accelerated. In the eleventh century, the debasement began in earnest. The carats in the solidus were reduced from twenty-four to twenty-one, then to eighteen; to sixteen, to fourteen, to eight and eventually below. The process took fifty years. The solidus was then abandoned and replaced with another coin, the hyperpyron. By the time Constantinople fell to the Ottomans, Byzantium had stopped issuing gold coins altogether.

Constantinople might have fallen, the Byzantine Empire might have gone, but the golden constant had not. It lived on elsewhere. It always will.

Touchstones: Separating True Gold from Fake

'O Zeus, why is it you have given men clear ways of testing whether gold is counterfeit but, when it comes to men, the body carries no stamp of nature for distinguishing bad from good?'

Euripides

Imagine you were a mediaeval trader selling something valuable. Your buyer turns up with some gold coins. An obvious concern of yours would be: are these really gold, or are they fake?

How did people check that the coins they were receiving were actually gold? They used touchstones.

A touchstone is a piece of dark stone – usually jasper, slate or lydite (which has its etymological roots in Lydia) – used to test the purity of gold or silver. When you rub metal against the touchstone it leaves a visible trace, like a streak. You can then compare this streak with other streaks made by metals of known purity, and thus get an idea how good the gold is.

Mixing gold with other metals was common, but a touchstone would give you a quick idea of purity and hence worth. Thus did touchstones facilitate trade and the widespread adoption of gold and silver as standards of exchange.

5

The Middle Ages, International Trade and the Changing Nature of Money

'If you can actually count your money,
then you're not a rich man'

Jean Paul Getty

Who is the richest person in history? Was Marcus Crassus richer than Elon Musk? Was John D. Rockefeller richer than Bill Gates? I enjoy running water, computers, electricity, aeroplanes and food from all over the world – am I richer than Marie Antoinette?

There is no way of knowing, because the metrics are uncertain and the contexts of the times so variable. It's an endless argument for the early hours of the morning.

Flick through the annals of history to find figures whose wealth was fundamentally tied to gold and one name stands out: German Jakob Fugger – also known as Fugger the Rich. He made his fortune in the sixteenth century, first by taking control of the gold and copper mines of Austria and Hungary, then by minting and trading those metals, then by lending them to kings and popes. Pope Leo was only able to pay off his debts to Fugger by selling absolution. By the time Fugger died, his net worth was equivalent to nearly 2.5 per cent of European GDP, tantamount to half a trillion dollars in today's money. Surely, he must rank among the richest.

Google the question, or consult AI, and the answer invariably given is Mansa (sultan) Musa of Mali. The source of this assertion, which now appears to have become fact, is a rather progressive article from the BBC, which deems his wealth 'indescribable',[1] placing him above the likes of Croesus, Genghis Khan, J. P. Morgan and Colonel Gaddafi. Fugger doesn't even get a look in. As with Fugger, Mansa Musa's enormous wealth was tied to gold. He controlled the gold mines of West Africa, not to mention an enormous number of slaves.

Musa was born in 1280 in Mali in West Africa. At some point in his early twenties, his brother Abu Bakr, the reigning mansa, had wanted to go and explore the edge of the Atlantic Ocean, and Musa stood in for him while he was gone. Abu Bakr never came back, and so did Musa become mansa.

Many argue that Musa actually saw to it that Abu Bakr never came back. The whole 'exploring the edge of the Atlantic Ocean' thing was just a ruse to get rid of him. Who knows? Perhaps Abu Bakr did make it to the edge of the Atlantic Ocean, also known as Brazil, and decided to stay. He wouldn't be the first.

At the time, the Mali empire extended through 2,000 miles of West Africa. With land ownership came ownership of the natural resources that lay within – and that's how Musa came to be so rich. Salt, gold and slaves. He sold millions of slaves to the Middle East, pioneering a pan-African slave trade that still continues today. Those slaves he didn't sell, he put to work in his mines, where they retrieved gold and salt for him.

West Africa has always been a prolific gold-bearing region. Today, Ghana is Africa's largest producer, having recently overtaken South Africa, whose premium deposit, the Witwatersrand Basin, was only discovered in 1886. Until then, West Africa had been top dog. Indeed, according to the British Museum, something like half of the Old World's gold came from the Mali Empire. Musa certainly enjoyed the trappings, and, like many of today's mega-billionaires, he also liked attention. He didn't have social media or TV appearances to get it, so Musa's means was *hajj* – a pilgrimage to Mecca, the spiritual home of Islam. In 1324, he set off with 12,000 slaves and a retinue of 38,000 others, including soldiers and entertainers – all of them dressed in gold brocade and silk. The 2,800-mile round trip took him some two years.

The slaves carried gold, the camels each towed as much as 300 pounds of gold dust, and there were heralds who bore gold staves, so that, in total, there were some eighteen tonnes.

When he arrived in Cairo, he went shopping. He did the same in Medina and Mecca. The sudden, dramatic rise in the supply of gold in those cities caused an inflationary episode that took some twelve years to recover from.

Ever the businessman, Musa perceived the devaluation of gold, so, on his way back from Mecca, he borrowed from money-lenders all the gold his retinue could carry. Some have argued that this was all a deliberate ploy to undermine the Cairo economy and relocate Africa's commercial centre out to Mali in the west – to Gao or Timbuktu. If so, it worked, if only briefly.

Over the course of his reign Musa conquered some twenty-four cities (and their surrounding districts) – among them Timbuktu, which he took on his way back from Mecca. Once back in Mali, Musa started throwing about his gold there too. For a reputed 440 lb / 200 kg of gold, he commissioned poet and architect Abu Ishaq al-Sahili to give Timbuktu a makeover. Universities and mosques were built, and Timbuktu became something of a cultural centre. The 'Paris of the Mediaeval World' some called it. One of Musa's buildings, the Sankore Madrassah, where maths, science, languages and the Koran were taught, is still operating today in the same capacity.

Musa died in 1337, at the ripe old age of fifty-seven, and the Mali Empire began to fall apart soon after.

The same laws of unsustainable spending applied then, just as they do now.

The Venetian Ducat and the First Printed Money

'Three thousand ducats, 'tis a good round sum'

William Shakespeare, *The Merchant of Venice*

In Britain, as the Roman Empire receded, gold made its way, quite literally, underground. The barbarian invasions caused many, judging by the numerous hoards from the period, to bury their money. Clipping – shaving off the edges of coins to steal some of the metal – was widespread. Very few new coins were minted. The previously vigorous late-Roman monetary system crumbled. As money, gold fell out of use almost altogether.

Several hundred years later, the Mercian king Offa (757–96), with his introduction of the silver penny, is generally credited as the originator of the British pound, though really his system was Roman. Twelve silver pence equalled a scilling. Twenty scillings (240 pennies) equalled a pound weight of sterling silver. Thus did the pound we still use today get its name. It was a unit of account rather than actual currency.

The Latin word for 'pound' is 'libra', and the pound sign, £, is a stylised writing of the letter L. Offa's Roman system remained standard until at least the sixteenth century and, in many ways, until decimalisation in 1971. But it was all based around silver. In Western Europe, gold had all but disappeared from circulation.

Further east, the Roman aureus had, as we have seen, been superseded by the Byzantine solidus as the leading gold coin. The solidus was supplanted by the Islamic dinar. Next, the Venetian ducat would enjoy several centuries of primacy.

Half land, half sea; half east, half west; between Christianity and Islam; one foot in Europe, but a short paddle to Africa and Asia, Venice was a true trading empire. Its merchants dealt in two currencies – the silver that was now standard in Western Europe and the gold circulating in Byzantine and Islamic lands.

Though Venice was founded in the fifth century by fleeing Romans, it would not strike any coins beyond a few silver pennies until the next millennium. It made do with the debased remnants of Charlemagne's coinage, itself inherited from Rome.

The Crusades proved one of the great money-makers in Venetian history, and Venice began building ships for the French. This led to a huge influx of French silver, with which it began minting its first significant coin in 1193: the grosso. About 4 g/⅛ oz in weight, it was soon copied across Italy and Europe. (It became the groat in Britain.)

The first gold ducat was minted almost a century later in 1285. With the final ducat minted 500 years later in 1797, shortly before the republic fell to Napoleon, the ducat had the longest production run in history of any gold coin from a single mint. Supply for the mint came via Africa and the Islamic Empire – the extravagance of Mansa Musa must have helped, with much of the gold spent in Egypt now making its way north – but also, and probably more significantly, via new mines in Hungary, where something of a gold rush was taking place. Gold coinage began to challenge silver and so did minting of the ducat speed up. It became the dominant coin of the eastern Mediterranean.

The Venetian Empire itself probably reached its zenith in the early fifteenth century, before the discovery of the Americas by Christopher Columbus and the new trade routes to Asia opened up by Vasco da Gama. Both would prove too much of a challenge to a Venice now bloating with bureaucracy. The influx of gold and silver from the New World, and the new mints in Spain, Belgium, Britain and Holland, meant the dominance of the ducat somewhat stuttered.

But while it was the world's most important gold coin, and Venice was the globe's foremost commercial power, one of the most important technological innovations in history – the printing press – took hold in Western Europe. In fact, at the dawn of the ducat, and hundreds of years before Johannes Gutenberg brought his invention to market, a young Venetian merchant-explorer named Marco Polo witnessed one of the very first examples of printed money.

In 1271, at the age of just seventeen, together with his father and uncle, Marco Polo made his way along the Silk Road to China, on a voyage that would end up lasting some twenty-four years. In China, he fell into the favour (and employment) of the Mongol Emperor Kublai Khan. On his way home, after a naval battle, he was captured by the Genovese, enemies of Venice, and imprisoned in Genoa, where he met a writer by the name of Rustichello da Pisa. Together they collaborated on a manuscript telling the story of Polo's adventures. They described the incredible things he saw in China: the palaces, the use of coal, eyeglasses, a postal service. One chapter has the most wonderful title: 'How the Great Khan Causeth the Bark of Trees, Made into Something Like Paper, to Pass for Money All Over His Country'.

Currency develops as technology develops, and the Chinese discovered they could use their presses to print money. It began in the seventh century with promissory notes from merchants to wholesalers. By the eleventh century, paper money known as 'jiaozi' was circulating alongside coins. Europeans had attempted something similar with pieces of leather or cloth, but it never really caught on. By the twelfth century, the Chinese government was issuing its own paper money. Polo marvelled at it: 'He hath the Secret of Alchemy in perfection,' he said, making money from the bark of mulberry trees, 'so numerous that whole districts are full of them . . . All these pieces of paper are issued with as much solemnity and authority as if they were of pure gold or silver.' Once various officials, as well as Kublai Khan himself, had put their seal on it, 'the money is authentic. Anyone forging it would be punished with death.' Indeed, anyone who dared refuse these notes faced 'pain of death' as well, 'however important he may think himself'. No surprise then that everyone took them 'readily, for wheresoever a person may go throughout the Great Khan's dominions he shall find these pieces of paper current, and shall be able to transact all sales and purchases of goods by means of them just as well as if they were coins of pure gold.'

We then learn that any merchant arriving into the kingdom with gold, silver or pearls was 'prohibited from selling to any one but the

Emperor', who then 'pays a liberal price for them in those pieces of paper'.[2] How easy it is to be generous with printed money that has no cost of production!

If the paper got damaged, merchants could take it into a mint and get a replacement piece – at a cost of 3 per cent. So Kublai Khan made good there as well.

The net result of Kublai Khan's money system was that he pretty much sequestered all the wealth of China and the surrounding empire, while everywhere else was left with his paper. 'His treasure is endless,' said Polo, 'whilst all the time the money he pays out costs him nothing at all.'

Merchants accepted Khan's money and his prices. What choice did they have? But here we also see the convenience of paper money. Fast – 'They are paid without any delay' – and portable, Kublai Khan's paper was 'so much lighter to carry about on journeys . . . ten bezants' worth does not weigh one golden bezant'.

Actions speak louder than words. When Polo left China, he didn't take the paper money with him. He took 4,000 gold coins instead. These got stolen from him in Turkey on his way home. Such are the perils of transporting gold.

Polo might have marvelled at Kublai Khan's enterprise, but it was one almighty racket. No wonder Kublai Khan had 'more treasure than all the kings in the world', and no wonder the Mongol Empire soon fell into irrevocable decline. Hyperinflation came to the Mongols, as it did their successors, the Ming, but Polo had already left, so he did not witness it. From the late fourteenth century, silver replaced paper in China.

The story never seems to change: this combination of centralised wealth, imposed fiat money and excess government control has led to many a collapse.

So, back to Europe and Johannes Gutenberg. Gutenberg established the basics of his printing press by 1440, and found some success by the mid-1450s, printing indulgences for the church. But he built up considerable debts and, according to one version of the story, died penniless, with his presses impounded by creditors: quite astonishing given the impact his work would eventually have. What he had lacked was a means of mass dissemination.

It was the Venetians, the great businessmen of the time, who turned Gutenberg's invention to profit. Venice, as one of the epicentres of European trade in the late fifteenth century, was a shipping hub, and news spread orally via their ships. You could print 100 copies of a pamphlet in Venice, give a handful to each ship captain, and their contents could be carried around the known world. In the destinations where the Venetian ships arrived, local printers could then copy the manuscripts and redistribute them internally, while the illiterate majority could gather and hear the news read to them.

Thus did Venice become the printing capital of Europe. It would not be long before Venice and the rest of Renaissance Italy discovered promissory notes, bills of exchange and paper money.

This new financial technology had come to Europe. But it would never be, despite many promises, as good as gold.

A Short History of English Gold Coins

The first English gold coin to be produced in quantity – during the reign of King Edward III, from 1327 to 1377 – was the noble. It was about 9 g in weight. A recoinage in 1465, during the reign of Edward IV, saw them replaced with a smaller, 5 g coin called the angel after a French design, the 'angelot'. That's why so many pubs have that name.

Sufferers of scrofula, a tuberculosis-type disease also known as 'king's evil', might have been given an angel coin to heal them, as it symbolised the 'royal touch' – the touch of a king, which was said to cure the disease. The last angels were minted during the reign of Charles I before the English Civil War – Oliver Cromwell, the puritan victor, would not have them minted. He did not want the heads of kings on his coins – bad propaganda while the issue of Divine Right was still raging, not to mention impious and idolatrous.

In 1663, after the Restoration, the new King Charles II replaced the angel with new milled coins – that is, coins struck by machine rather than by hand – with new designs. Scrofula sufferers would be given medals, known as 'touch pieces', instead.

This new gold coin was the guinea, named after the West African region where the gold came from – Mansa Musa's domain. It was about 8 g of twenty-two-carat gold (so it contained about 7 g/¼ oz of pure gold). It was originally intended to be twenty shillings, but its price fluctuated with silver availability (Samuel Pepys records the price at twenty-four shillings), until Isaac Newton, Master of the Royal Mint, set it at twenty-one shillings in 1716. The guinea was sometimes engraved with an elephant with or without a howdah (a small carriage on top), the emblem of the Royal African Company, which had been granted the monopoly of trade with West Africa.

The British stopped minting the guinea in 1799 during the Napoleonic Wars, and printed paper instead. Although in 1813, another 80,000 were struck to pay the Duke of Wellington's army in the Pyrenees, where the locals (wisely) would not accept British paper. The military guinea, as it was known, was the last guinea to be minted, aside from commemorative coins.

Even after the guinea was replaced by the sovereign in the Great Recoinage of 1816, and by the pound as the main unit of currency, it continued to be used as a unit of account. With its aristocratic overtones, it was used to pay for high-end goods and services: professional fees (from lawyers to tailors), land, horses, art and furniture. This remained the case until shortly after decimalisation in 1971. Many famous horse races still carry the name today. Effectively, a guinea was £1.05, and at racehorse auctions, even today, bids are made in guineas. The seller gets a pound, and the auctioneer gets the 5p as his commission.

There's even rather a nice but hard-to-find poem by an eighteenth-century comedian, George Stephen Kemble, called 'A Guinea'.[3] It reflects many of the themes of this book, from the magnetic power of gold and the desire it inspires to its use as propaganda. The poem begins thus:

> What is a Guinea? 'tis a splendid thing,
> Which represents our sovereign lord the King;

It goes on to describe how the guinea's power is as consistent as

> . . . the magnet's strong controul,
> Which always points the needle to the Pole;
> With equal truth, if used with equal skill,
> A guinea points the Passions to its will.

A guinea can even make the old and ugly look attractive to a young woman and 'make her love where she has no desires'.

> If bald, or toothless, line with gold his pockets,
> In spite of want of hair, or empty sockets,
> Let him but shew he's worth a brace of plums,
> Maugre his running sores, or boneless gums,
> To age shall blooming youth resign her charms,
> And clasp a withered mummy in her arms!

Plus ça change!

From the Dale: How the Dollar Got Its Name

'Pieces of eight!'

Long John Silver's parrot

Our story of gold deviates for a moment with a silver subplot, albeit an important one, because it tells of the origins of today's global reserve currency.

At the beginning of the sixteenth century, a mining prospector by the name of Stefan Schlick found silver in the Ore Mountains of Bohemia, not far from what today is the border between Germany and Czechia.

Many moved to the area in search of opportunity, and the mining camp became a village, which became the town of Joachimsthal – literally 'Joachim's Dale'. With that discovery, Stefan Schlick's family fortune was made for generations. We now know him as Count Schlick, and his descendants would be known for their military endeavours and for their amours, as well as for their silver.

Schlick started minting coins with his newly mined silver, similar in size and weight to the guldengroschen (shortened to 'guldener'), which were just gaining popularity across Central Europe at the time – each about ⅛ of a Cologne mark (roughly half a pound) of silver. (At this point in history, noble families could mint coins, as long as they had the precious metal with which to do it.) Schlick's coins weighed just under an ounce and were an inch and a half (4 cm) across. On one side was Joachim, father of the Virgin Mary, and on the other the Bohemian lion. Schlick called his coins 'Joachimsthalers'. German speakers to the north and west shortened this to 'thaler', while Czech and Slavic speakers to the south and east called them 'tolars'. Here lie the etymological roots of the dollar.

In time, the Holy Roman Empire adopted the denomination, and the Reichstaler, 401 grains of silver, became its standard from 1566 to 1750.

Large silver coins were becoming ubiquitous in the period; the corresponding English coin would have been the crown. The French had their écu, the Spanish their peso, the Dutch their daalder, the Scandinavians their daler and the Swiss the thaler. But, with the large quantities of silver discovered by the conquistadors in Mexico, Peru and Bolivia in the sixteenth century (more on this in a moment), it was the Spanish peso that would become the most widespread, a coin of worldwide importance, essential to trade between Europe, the Americas and even Asia.

The peso was more commonly known as the Spanish dollar, and many historians see the Spanish dollar as the first international currency, although Alexander the Great might have something to say about that, as indeed might Croesus.

It was a truly international coin, though. It made its way across the high seas through Spanish trading networks, which, thanks to the voyages of the Portuguese Vasco da Gama, among others, now extended around the Cape of Good Hope to Asia, as well as across the Americas and, indeed, the Pacific. The Spanish dollar became the basis for national currencies as far as Japan, the Philippines, China and India and all the way to Canada, not to mention the Spanish-speaking nations of South and Central America. Over the course of several centuries, millions of Spanish dollars were minted, made possible by the extraordinary silver discoveries in the New World, especially at Potosí, Bolivia.

Why did every pirate's parrot worth its salt greedily cry 'pieces of eight'? The reason was the Spanish dollar. There were eight reales to the dollar, so the coin was, literally, a piece of eight. It even had an 8 stamped on it. No wonder pirates craved it: from the sixteenth to the nineteenth century, it was probably the most stable and least debased silver coin in the western world. It became the most widely circulating coin in North America too. Spanish dollars made their way there via trade in the Caribbean.

There was, at the time, a shortage of English coins in North America thanks to England's typically short-sighted policies towards its colonies. English authorities refused to allow the colonists to mint their own money. With shortages at home, especially of silver, the English also limited the export of gold and silver coins. Settlers, who were not usually rich in gold and silver anyway – that's why they were emigrating – often ran out of hard money. Early on they found themselves adopting the wampum shells favoured by the Native Americans as currency. In 1637, Massachusetts even declared them legal tender.

Settlers also used commodities such as cod, corn, beaver skins, nails and tobacco as money, such was the shortage of coin. This led to all sorts of problems. Tobacco deteriorated quickly and so lost its value. Nails led to people burning down barns to get at the 'money' that held them together. Colonial governments also issued paper money to facilitate economic activities, but, despite Parliament in England passing several currency acts to regulate colonial paper money, it kept losing its value, even between states. No wonder Spanish dollars proved so useful and became so widespread. Colonists wanted them for the same reasons as their pirate cousins. They were good, hard money.

In 1704, a Royal Proclamation saw English Queen Anne introduce the West Indies to the gold standard, but the English tended to keep their gold and silver at home, away from the colonies, so even though prices might have been quoted in pounds, debts tended to be settled in Spanish dollars.

With the cry of 'no taxation without representation', the colonists rose up against their British overlords in 1775, finally winning independence in 1783. To fund their war effort, the colonists began issuing their own paper money – the continental. But that quickly lost its value too, mainly through overprinting to meet the cost of war. British counterfeiters also did their bit for the war effort, duplicating the notes to devalue them. (By no means the first or last example of financial warfare.) First issued in 1776, continentals had lost 80 per cent of their value by 1778. By 1780, the notes were worth one-fortieth of their face value. By 1781, they had become so worthless they ceased to circulate as money. Hence the expression, 'not worth a continental'.

The runaway inflation and the collapse of the continental is perhaps what prompted the Founding Fathers to include in their constitution that often-quoted phrase: 'No State shall ... coin Money; emit Bills of Credit; make any Thing but gold and silver Coin a Tender in Payment of Debts.' (US authorities broke that contract, of course, in 1870 and 1933, as we shall discover.)

After the revolution, Thomas Jefferson and Alexander Hamilton, had the task of forming a currency for this fledgling nation. They had a random selection of Spanish dollars weighed, and based on the findings, specified in the Coinage Act of 1792 that the US dollar would contain 371.25 grains (24 g) pure or 416 grains (27 g) standard silver – just under an ounce – so that it would have 'the value of a Spanish milled dollar as the same is now current'. The dollar, the basic unit of account for the United States, was modelled on the Spanish dollar. Even the '$' symbol was based on the inscription on one side of the Spanish dollar – the old p^s (for peso) which, to our modern eyes, looks like an S.

Spanish coinage remained legal tender in the United States until 1857. The pricing of equities on US stock exchanges in ⅛-dollar denominations persisted until 1997.

The global reserve currency of the world – built on a Bohemian name, a Spanish network and solid South and Central American silver.

6.

Lust for Gold Brings Violence to South America

'Get gold, humanely, if possible, but at all hazards, get gold'

King Ferdinand II of Spain

Covering some sixty square miles, the Yanacocha mine in the northern highlands of Peru is one of the largest gold mines ever known, and one of the most profitable. Cerro Rico – literally 'rich mountain' – at Potosí in Bolivia is the richest source of silver in human history. In the 200 years following its accidental discovery in 1545, it produced some 80 per cent of the world's silver. It was also known as the 'mountain that eats men' because so many died working in its mines.

There is a lot of gold and silver in the rocks of South and Central America. As Spanish and Portuguese explorers arrived in the fifteenth and sixteenth centuries, there followed a gold rush that changed the face of the continent for all time. The conquistadors, as they became known, showed incredible feats of bravery and ingenuity, but also similarly incredible cruelty and ruthlessness.

In South American myth, gold was the link between humanity and the cosmos. The Incas thought gold was the 'tears of the Sun'. Inti, the sun god, shed these tears upon earth so that people had a tangible connection to their divine origins. The Aztecs shared similar beliefs, as did the Moche people of northern Peru.

The myth goes that a young Inca warrior named Kuychi sought a lost temple which housed the tears of the sun. Guided by the constellations and by prophecy, he crossed treacherous landscapes, overcoming many trials and tribulations to find the temple, where he beheld a dazzling pool of liquid gold, its shimmering surface reflecting the brilliance of the sun itself. He understood the connection to the cosmos and, full of reverence, brought a single tear back to his people.

The earliest known use of gold in South America dates back 4,000 years – a necklace found in a tomb near Lake Titicaca, Peru, made from native gold.[1] Gold craftsmanship in Colombia, Ecuador and Peru evolved in almost complete isolation from the rest of the world, although techniques were similar – filigree (wire work), granulation, relief decoration and surface colouring.[2] The smiths' inventiveness went into enhancing gold's colour and its brilliance, usually using alloys. While they had the same instinct for gold, and rulers employed it as a symbol of power and divinity, the Precolumbians did not use gold as currency. The technology of coinage had not yet reached this part of the world and, as the Spanish invaders found, the European concept of money was almost incomprehensible. While the Aztecs of Central America used, among other things, coffee beans and beads, the Incas further south had a system based around barter and labour exchange, known as 'mita', with debts – especially taxes and tribute – recorded on knotted string devices called 'quipus'. But, across the continent, they were brilliant artisans nonetheless. If you are ever in that part of the world, the collection at the Museo del Oro in Bogotá is one of the most stunning you will ever see – diadems, helmets and crowns, rings, necklaces and bracelets, beads and breastplates, even fishhooks and penis covers.

Christopher Columbus and the Place Where Gold Was Born

'Gold is the most precious of all things. He who
has it can do in this world all he wishes'

Christopher Columbus[3]

When Christopher Columbus set sail in 1492, his goal was to find Cipango, the place where gold was born. He had read about it in Marco Polo's travelogues. Every three years, so the story went, King Solomon's fleet brought back gold, gems and spices from these legendary isles to Jerusalem.

Columbus landed first in the Bahamas to find natives, whom he described as both handsome and gentle, some of whom wore little pieces of gold suspended from their noses. He began asking where the gold came from. They pointed to the south, notably to a place they referred to as 'Cibao', which Columbus thought must be a rich, gold-producing region. This led him to the islands of Cuba and Hispaniola (the latter is today the Dominican Republic and Haiti). He had to find substantial amounts to justify his voyage when he returned home to Spain, so wherever he sailed, he asked about gold.

What Marco Polo had been referring to as Cipango was of course Japan, and when Columbus' ship ran aground in Hispaniola, Columbus thought that might be it. He was only a Pacific Ocean out. While his crew attempted to repair the ship, locals began arriving. They traded bits of gold for the small brass bells – hawk bells – which the sailors carried. The island chieftain gave Columbus a mask inset with large pieces of gold, and when Columbus asked him where the gold was, he told him about abundant gold supplies nearby. This evidence, and the prospect of much more gold, led Columbus to think that his shipwreck was providential.

He wrote to the Spanish king, ahead of his return, telling him about the people he had encountered, about the exotic birds, animals and plants, trees and fruits. But he also told him about the rivers that contained gold. Like just about every prospector in history, he was almost certainly hyping things up to vindicate his mission and raise funds for another. The letter was eagerly received, published and disseminated across the cities of Europe. Word of gold spread quickly. It always does.

But on his second voyage, Columbus discovered that there was in fact very little gold in Hispaniola. Indeed, gold mines, as such, were rare in the Americas: usually the metal was panned from rivers and streams. That didn't stop the rumours back in Spain though.

Contrary to popular belief, the conquistadors were often not trained warriors, just journeymen workers and craftsmen looking to better their lot. You could call it greed, you could call it self-improvement, but it is a powerful, enabling and motivating force. Whether soldier or artisan, gold is what they came for, as well as to spread the word of the Lord, of course.

One of them was Hernán Cortés, who landed in Mexico in 1519 with 600 men. He had heard tantalising tales of a powerful ruler with immense wealth.

The Night of Sorrows and the Vanishing Aztec Treasure

'We Spanish suffer from a disease of the heart
that can only be cured by gold'

Hernán Cortés

Cortés was the most famous of the early conquistadors, a persuasive speaker and a master strategist. As a teenager he wandered about the ports of southern Spain, no doubt excited by the stories he heard about Columbus, and, in 1504, at the age of just eighteen, he set sail for Hispaniola.

At first, he found work as a notary and a farmer. Illness meant he missed the doomed expeditions of 1509 to the South American mainland, but in 1511 he took part in the Diego Velázquez de Cuéllar expedition that conquered Cuba, where he remained, as an administrator, establishing himself, accumulating information about the region, accruing knowledge from the failed expeditions, as well as the successful. In late 1518, now thirty-three, almost fifteen years after he first landed, Cortés was appointed captain general of an expedition to Mexico by Velázquez. Cortés used his persuasive oratorical skills to put together a fleet: 11 ships, 500 soldiers, about 100 sailors and, significantly, 16 horses. The Aztecs had never seen horses before, and the Spanish were brilliant horsemen. It set off in early 1519.

In March he landed at Tabasco, where he remained, forging relationships with the locals and gathering information. They gave him a gift of twenty women, one of whom was La Malinche, a Nahua noble who had been kidnapped and sold into Mayan slavery. She became Cortés' lover, bearing him a son, perhaps the first Mexican 'mestizaje' (mixed race person). She also became his interpreter and advisor. Her understanding of local politics helped him form alliances with the many tribes that resented Aztec rule and the tribute they demanded. Such was the role she played in the Spanish conquests, she has become quite polarising: many see her as a traitor, others as a heroine and survivor. In any case, all this was to come.

From Tabasco, Cortés sailed west, declaring himself captain general and chief justice of Veracruz, answerable only to King Charles of Spain, effectively gaining total authority and freeing himself from bonds to Velázquez. He then did something extraordinary, so the story goes. He scuttled ten of his eleven ships, thus making escape for his men impossible. Success became their only option: the only way to survive was to win. Talk about incentive.

As he and his armies travelled inland, he avoided conflict where he could, encountering more and more unhappiness with the Aztec rule of Montezuma II. With La Malinche's help, Cortés began allying with some indigenous people, sowing discontent to turn them against their Aztec rulers. He soon had more than 200,000 allies.

The Aztec ruler, Montezuma II, did not want the Spanish in the capital city of Tenochtitlan, and he sent them emissaries with extravagant gifts, somehow thinking that would keep them away. He sent them elaborate garments, an obsidian mirror, a golden tray, a jar of gold, figures of gold, gold earrings and necklaces, armbands of silver, a shield made from mother-of-pearl, brilliant feather fans and head-pieces; then a large gold wheel six and a half feet across, weighing some sixteen kilos, decorated with glyphs, and a similar-sized silver wheel. One represented the sun, the other the moon.[4] Far from deterring the Spanish, as Montezuma hoped, the gifts only excited their desire. The Spanish sent a helmet to Montezuma, with a message saying they suffered from an illness which could only be cured with gold – perhaps not so far off the truth – and the Aztec ruler returned it filled to the brim with gold dust. Beats what you get at the GP, I suppose. Cortés and his men were now more motivated than ever.

The King of Spain was entitled to a fifth of any treasure found – a booty tax. What's more, Cortés was on shaky legal grounds: by declaring himself captain general and chief justice of Veracruz he had gone against Velázquez of Cuba. Cortés wanted the king onside, so he had the treasure carefully inventoried, then sent some of it back to Spain. We still have the inventory. One example of just how carefully precise it was: 'the other collar has four strings with 102 red stones and 172 apparently green, and around the two green stones are 26 golden bells and, in the said collar, ten large stones set in gold'.[5] The Spanish valued the gold and silver on weight alone (around 20,000 ounces), ascribing to the intricate pieces little artistic value, and melted down most of it. The list contained in total some fifty gold items, alongside many pieces of Aztec featherwork, clothing, jew-ellery, headdresses, animal skins and even two ancient manuscripts.

If we assume Cortés was honest with his accounting, and this list was a mere fifth of the booty, we can estimate that he and his men had at this point in July well over 200 gold and silver objects, weigh-ing as much as three tonnes.

In the following months, he and his men accumulated more treasure: from Montezuma; from the leader of the Tlaxcaltecs, longstanding enemies of the Aztecs, with whom Cortés formed an alliance; and from looting after Cortés and his troops massacred an unarmed crowd in the town of Cholula, whom they suspected of betraying them.

In November, Cortés reached the capital, Tenochtitlan, with his own army of 500 and some 1,000 Tlaxcaltecs. In accordance with custom, Montezuma received him with honour. Apparently, he was hoping to learn the weaknesses of the Spaniards to better crush them later.

But Cortés then took Montezuma hostage in his own palace.

The relentless plunder of the city began. The Spaniards demanded more and more gold. Their captive, Montezuma, told his people to bring it. Gold, silver, jewels and featherwork were laid at the feet of the invaders. 'Where was it all from?' Cortés asked, and Montezuma told him. There were several locations where gold could be found, panned in streams. Cortés immediately sent his men to those places to investigate.

In the palace where they were staying, they found a vast treasure hoard behind one of the walls: gold, jewels, idols, jade, feathers and more. This added to the invaders' ever-growing pile.

However, word of Cortés' discovery had also reached Velázquez in Cuba, who was deeply resentful, and in 1520, he sent a force to deprive Cortés of his command, under one Pánfilo de Narváez. Cortés left a garrison of just eighty in the Mexican capital, then marched against Narváez, defeated him, and enlisted his army in his own forces. But he returned to find that, in his absence, his hot-headed captain, Pedro de Alvarado, had massacred thousands of unarmed Aztec nobles at a festival. The Spanish version of the story is that Cortés then had Montezuma address the Aztecs to quell their anger, but the crowd, enraged by Montezuma's perceived betrayal and cooperation with the Spanish, attacked and murdered him. The Aztec version is that the Spanish killed him once they realised he was no longer useful in pacifying the population. Either way, Montezuma was no more, and the Spanish garrison was now under siege. Cortés decided they could not hold the city and should retreat.

But what to do about the treasure? One estimate is that the Spanish had amassed some 3.6 tonnes by this point, not to mention the feathers, clothing and jewels.[6] Cortés ordered the king's fifth and his own fifth loaded onto horses and the backs of Tlaxcaltec porters. He told his troops to take what they wanted. The smart ones took just a handful of gold and gems. The foolish took loads. Had they the gold, to paraphrase Ruskin, or the gold them?

As they fled, the Aztecs attacked them on the road out of Tenochtitlan. Those soldiers who overloaded either dropped their loot or were slaughtered because they could not run fast enough. The night became known as the 'Noche Triste' or 'Night of Sorrows'. Most of the treasures of Montezuma, including Cortés' share and the Spanish king's, were lost.

The following December, having reorganised his forces, Cortés returned and laid siege to Tenochtitlan, eventually taking it in August 1521. That marked the end of the Aztec Empire. Spain now controlled the territory from the Caribbean to the Pacific.

But what happened to the treasure?

The Spanish found some of it. They squeezed some more out of the defeated Aztecs when they tortured the new emperor, Cuauhtémoc. But most of it was gone.

Cortés again set aside the king's fifth and his own fifth, then began making suspiciously large payments to his closest cronies for weapons and services, so that when his soldiers got their share, they found they would have earned more by honest, less risky work elsewhere. The soldiers were furious. Cortés sent them off on other expeditions to the lands of the Maya in the south, promising them more gold. Others he granted large tracts of land. But those who served Cortés went to their graves believing Cortés had robbed them of their gold. Indeed, guests to Cortés' home reported seeing many bars of gold there.

One story is that Montezuma was not actually killed, and he and his people took their wealth north to seven separate locations in what is now the USA. For 500 years people have been searching for Montezuma's treasure – gold, silver, stones, jewellery, feathers, clothing and artefacts worth billions: the so-called seven cities of gold.

In 1981, a construction worker in Mexico City stumbled across a four-pound gold bar, 76 per cent gold, 21 per cent silver and 3 per cent copper, which archaeologists have confirmed was cast in 1519–20. That gold had likely been forged from melted Aztec artefacts, before being cast into a bar that was then dropped by a fleeing Spaniard on the fateful Night of Sorrows.

According to the Spanish who saw their work, Aztec goldsmiths were more skilled than their European counterparts. Such a shame that the Spanish preferred their gold in coins and bars: countless ornaments were melted down, leaving an incalculable cultural and artistic loss. But 'tis usually the way.

From Illiterate Swineherd to Conqueror of an Empire: The Incredible Journey of Francisco Pizarro

'If a son of Adam were to own a valley full of gold, he would desire a second one. And if he were to own two valleys full of gold, he would desire a third one'

The Prophet Mohammed[7]

Word of Aztec gold and Cortés' derring-do quickly spread. One ageing conquistador who wanted a piece of the action was a swineherd, the bastard son of a soldier and housemaid, who would go on to overthrow the largest empire in the world with just 168 men, 27 horses and a cannon. His name was Francisco Pizarro.

Some say it was his extraordinary bravery, ruthlessness and cunning. Others put it down to good fortune. But, given that the Incas had little to no resistance to European diseases – influenza, measles and smallpox especially – and that their civilisation functioned without money, markets, the wheel, writing, draught animals or any knowledge of iron or steel, perhaps the mismatch was such that, sooner or later, their demise was inevitable.

With little to no formal education, Pizarro was an illiterate and grew up tending pigs. Seeing that as a bastard he would get little or no inheritance, he became a soldier. He fought in Italy for a while, like his father before him, before hearing of the riches of the Americas, to which he sailed in 1502. He took part in various expeditions, especially around Panama, the Caribbean and Colombia, including one led by Vasco Núñez de Balboa which discovered the route to the Pacific, and eventually, after nearly twenty years, he reached the respectable status of mayor and magistrate of the newly formed Panama City.

In the early 1520s, as news of Cortés' lucrative conquest of the Aztecs spread, he formed a partnership with fellow conquistador Diego de Almagro, and they made two expeditions along the Pacific coast of South America in 1524 and 1526, though without great success. Harsh conditions and native attacks got the better of them. But on the second trip, they visited the mainland and the Inca city of Tumbes, where they saw llamas carrying silver and gold and local chieftains wearing it plentifully with, apparently, little idea of its worth. This was not an infrequent occurrence among the many communities they visited along the Pacific coasts of modern-day Colombia, Ecuador and Peru. They even came across miniature gardens made entirely of gold, according to one chronicler. They heard stories of a ruler in the mountains with pots of the stuff, and so was the idea of El Dorado, the mythical city of gold, planted in their minds. Pizarro became convinced that there was another rich empire to be taken and looted.

In 1528, leaving his partner Almagro in Panama, Pizarro went back to Spain to make his case to the king, who was impressed by this eloquent veteran. King Charles agreed to the mission, and the Queen of Spain signed a charter permitting him to conquer the Incas. Pizarro would be governor and captain of all conquered areas in New Castile, as the Spanish then called it. Pizarro secured no such title for Almagro, however, which would later prove a major bone of contention. He then returned to Panama, with four of his brothers, and in late 1530, together with Almagro, they set off for the western shores of South America, landing in what today is Ecuador, near Guayaquil.

While Pizarro had been in Spain, various epidemics of smallpox, influenza, measles and typhus, no doubt brought over by the Spanish and their livestock, had spread south from Central America. The natives had little or no resistance. Anthropologist H. F. Dobyns argues that 90 per cent of the population of the Inca Empire died in epidemics,[8] an argument that has been endorsed by other researchers. There is also evidence of severe drought in the Americas at that time. Among those who lost their life to the European diseases was the emperor Sapa Inca Huayna Capac, who died of smallpox. His great-grandfather had prophesied that white men with beards would one day destroy the Inca Empire. On his deathbed, Huayna Capac repeated the prophecy, saying the Inca empire would fall after the twelfth king. He was the twelfth Inca king.

As if disease was not enough, Huayna Capac left a bloody war of succession between his sons, Huáscar and Atahualpa. Pizarro arrived in 1532 just as the civil war was ending. The empire was exhausted, both by war and disease, Huáscar had been taken prisoner and Atahualpa was in charge.

Tumbes was a ghost town: deserted, like many along the coast, because of the spreading smallpox. On they marched to Cajamarca, where they met with a stroke of good fortune. The Emperor Atahualpa was there in the nearby thermal baths, relaxing after the recent victory over his brother. He met the Spanish the following day, who asked him to pay tribute to their king. 'I will be no man's tributary,' said Atahualpa, no doubt buoyed up by the fact that he had over 6,000 men and the Spanish had fewer than 200.

But in battle, technology is everything. So poor was communication in South America, the Incas had little to no idea what had happened to the Aztecs. Atahualpa did not even know who they were. Pizarro meanwhile had detailed written accounts which had been disseminated across Spanish territory. The Incas used weapons made of wood, stone, copper and bronze. None of them could pierce Spanish armour. Inca armour meanwhile was no match for Spanish steel. The Incas had no cavalry, nor any tactics to fight cavalry – let alone Spanish guns, swords and a cannon. But for so few to attack so many still required no small amount of bravery. The Spanish attacked, and the 6,000 men, many already weakened by disease, were slaughtered. Atahualpa was taken hostage. All in all, guns, germs, words and steel, to misquote historian Jared Diamond, destroyed the Incas.

Atahualpa then made Pizarro an offer. In exchange for his

freedom, he would fill a large hut in the town with golden objects, and then fill it twice with silver objects. The hut he chose was about 22 x 17 ft, the size of a large bedroom in a house today. The Incas then scoured their empire for treasure, which was brought back to Cajamarca, and the huts were filled as promised, stacked high with beautiful artefacts made of gold and silver. But this took time, and Atahualpa only fuelled Spanish gold lust, as he described the treasures in temples of the sun in Cuzco and Pachacámac. Pizarro dispatched troops to both locations, where they indeed found gold, and duly sacked the cities. They found life-size figures of men and women, great jars and pitchers half pottery half gold, vases sculpted in relief with birds, animals and insects, and more.

The country was stripped of its wealth, from rich temple fixtures to those fabled golden gardens: earth of gold granules, gold corn-stalks, and gold figures of men and llamas. The Spaniards melted most of it down. Five or six of the most beautiful pieces of metal-work were sent back to Spain intact, where they were displayed for a time, before being melted down there too. As well as the loss of life, there was a loss of beauty. 'Their only concern was to collect gold and silver and make themselves rich,' said a young priest travelling with Pizarro. 'What was being destroyed was more perfect than anything they enjoyed and possessed.'[9] Gold may last, but art made from gold rarely does.

Mindful of the power of the Spanish crown, and its reach, Pizarro's men audited the treasure meticulously. There were almost seven tonnes of twenty-two-carat gold and twice as much silver.[10] In the context of the times, this is a simply breathtaking number. (Remember: more than 80 per cent of the gold in the world today was only mined after 1900.)

A fifth was set aside for the king, and in 1534 Pizarro sent one of his brothers, Hernando, back to Spain with it. Pizarro took his share: almost 9,000 ounces of gold and twice as much silver. Plus extras, such as Atahualpa's throne, which was 183 pounds of fifteen-carat gold.[11] The rest was divided among the other conquistadors. There were different tiers according to rank, but even the lowliest soldiers took between 650 and 700 ounces of gold each, plus silver. Some reward. Forty years after Columbus found such modest amounts of gold in Hispaniola, the dream of endless gold had seemingly come true.

But then the betrayal. The treasure did not buy Atahualpa his freedom. Pizarro did not release him. Atahualpa's brother Huáscar, meanwhile, was assassinated, and the Spaniards maintained that this was at Atahualpa's order, so in August 1533 they used this as a pretext to have Atahualpa killed. Pizarro, it seems, opposed the execution and only went along with it to keep his discontented partner, Almagro, happy. To add insult to injury, Pizarro then fathered two sons by Atahualpa's widow.

While Pizarro, on his 1528 trip to Spain to secure royal charters for their mission, had acquired for himself the governorship of all lands conquered and a royal title, Almagro only got a title and the governorship of the small town of Tumbes. Significantly discontented, Almagro had almost refused to participate in the third joint expedition, which had brought them the wealth of Atahualpa: only the promise of the governorship of as-yet-undiscovered lands made him come around. He joined up with Pizarro shortly after the Battle of Cajamarca. Next, they marched to Cuzco, the heart of the empire, fighting and winning four battles along the way. Cuzco put up no resistance: Atahualpa had recently been an enemy, so many viewed the Spanish as liberators. Indeed, it seems this was the case for many of the diverse groups ruled by the Incas – over 100 different languages were spoken across the empire. They might not have stuck with this opinion after they were put to work in Spanish mines, but many chiefs served the Spanish and paid taxes (often in labour), just as they had done to the Incas, while the Spanish left many existing social structures in place.

But these quests for gold rarely seem to end well. Almagro never quite shook the suspicion that the Pizarro brothers were trying to cheat him out of his fair share of the loot. The crown ruled that the northern half of Peru belonged to Pizarro and the southern half to Almagro: both thought, however, that Cuzco belonged to them, and they nearly came to blows over it. It was some city, it seems. 'This city is the greatest and the finest ever seen in this country or anywhere in the Indies . . . We can assure your Majesty that it is so beautiful and has such fine buildings that it would be remarkable even in Spain,' Pizarro wrote to King Charles of Spain. Hoping he would find more gold and drop his claims, they agreed that Almagro could lead an expedition to the south (into present-day Chile).

Despite his affection for Cuzco, it being so far inland and at such altitude meant it was relatively inaccessible to the Spaniards. Pizarro's scouts reported a better site close to the Pacific Ocean, with good water supply, plenty of wood, fertile land and clement weather. So did Pizarro found the city of Lima in 1535.

In the following years, between 1535 and 1537, the Pizarros then found themselves under attack from Manco Inca, the puppet ruler they had installed, who had raised an army and laid siege to Cuzco. In Lima, too, they came under attack from another Inca general.

Cuzco was rescued by Almagro, returning from Chile, who lifted the siege and drove off Manco, only to take the city for himself, capturing two of the Pizarro brothers in the process. He hadn't found the wealth he was hoping for in Chile, and had come back to claim his share of Peru.

Almagro had the support of the many Spaniards who had missed out on Atahualpa's gold, but Pizarro sent his brother Hernando to take him on. In 1538, at the Battle of Las Salinas, Hernando was victorious and Almagro was captured, tried and executed. The story was not over. Resentment towards the Pizarros and the early conquistadors, who had left slim pickings, was strong among latecomers. They rallied around Almagro's son, Diego, and in 1541 they took Lima, murdering Francisco Pizarro in his home.

A year later, a force led by another of the Pizarro brothers took Lima back, capturing and then executing the young Almagro.

Despite newfound riches, lust for gold never abates.

Lost Treasure of the Incas
and the End of the Spanish Empire

> But he grew old—
> This knight so bold—
> And o'er his heart a shadow—
> Fell as he found
> No spot of ground
> That looked like Eldorado.

Edgar Allan Poe, 'El Dorado'

Wherever there is lots of gold, there always seems to be a story of lost gold. Legend has it that some of Atahualpa's ransom escaped the Spanish. A group of Incas were on their way to Cajamarca with gold and silver when they heard the emperor had been murdered. They hid the treasure in a cave in the mountains, where it lay for fifty years until it was found by a Spaniard named Valverde. But it was lost again until one Barth Blake, a Canadian adventurer, found it in 1886. He died suspiciously and nobody now knows where the treasure is, except that it is somewhere in the Andes.

Another Inca warrior, called Rumiñawi, led an uprising in 1533 in Quito in the northern part of the Inca Empire. The story goes that he ordered the city's treasure to be hidden and the city burned. He was captured and tortured, but he never revealed where the treasure was. It had been thrown, says one version of the story, into one of Ecuador's many lakes – in the Llanganati Mountains, eighty miles south-east of Quito, a strange, inaccessible, cloud-forest-covered mountain range beneath the volcanoes, but above the jungle basin.

Pizarro's story – and more importantly the story of his wealth – was soon being told across Europe. For the next 200 years, thousands of adventurers made their way to South America in search of gold and silver. Rumour spread of a land where the king coated himself in gold dust. This legend became known as El Dorado. South

America was turned upside down. Among the many taken in by the story was the English explorer Sir Walter Raleigh, who made two trips to South America in search of the fabled city. There were expeditions to the jungles, the deserts, the plains and the mountains. Adventurers endured hunger, bloodshed, disease and countless other hardships, yet many died without handling so much as a single nugget of gold. The lure of El Dorado persists to this day.

The 'royal fifth' sent by Cortés in 1519 was the first in what would become a steady stream of precious metal shipments flowing from the Americas to Spain. When they got the mines producing, the amount of gold and, especially, silver was extraordinary. The destination was the House of Trade in Seville. Elaborate precautions prevented smuggling. Fishermen were forbidden to take their boats out to meet the incoming treasure fleets on pain of 200 lashes and 10 years a galley slave. A copy of the register of everything on board was sent with another ship. When officials went on board, all had to swear an oath that they had no gold, silver or pearls that were unaccounted for. No doubt gold was still smuggled – it always has been and it always will – silver, being bulkier, was harder to conceal. Once at the House of Trade, the precious metal was weighed by the 'balanzario' and placed in the vaults in triple-locked chests, before being sent to the refiners for resmelting, eventually to be sold by public auction.

Spanish ships returning to their homeland, groaning under the weight of their gold and silver cargoes, became targets for English pirates, leading to hundreds of years of conflict between the two maritime nations. One famous shipment, carried by the Spanish galleon *Nuestra Señora de Atocha*, sank in a hurricane, carrying an estimated 47 tonnes of silver, 100,000 gold coins and additional gold and silver artefacts. (It was finally discovered in 1985 by American treasure hunter Mel Fisher after a sixteen-year search.) Another ship, the *San José*, which was sunk by the British off the coast of Cartagena in 1708, and discovered in 2015, is said to contain as much as 200 tonnes of gold and silver,[12] although that estimate seems on the high side to me.

With the influx of this newfound gold and silver came an ironic twist in the tale – inflation. The enormous amounts of precious metal from the New World meant a meteoric rise in the money supply, which affected the whole of Europe, though Spain especially. The Price Revolution, as it became known, spelt the end of the Spanish Empire.

The supply of goods could not keep pace with the increased supply of money, and so prices went up. Over the course of the sixteenth century, prices in Spain increased by about 300 per cent. As is often the way, wages did not keep up, making life extremely difficult for Spain's middle and lower classes. Instead of investing in their own industry, the Spanish used their gold and silver to buy goods from other European countries (thereby exporting their own inflation), while overstretching militarily especially in wars with the Ottomans and the Protestant countries of Northern Europe. The empire was too vast to maintain as the crown and the country fell into debt. A sharp drop in imports in the seventeenth century compounded the financial woes, and by the end of the Thirty Years War in 1648, the Spanish Empire was well and truly in decline.

Irony of ironies, the gold (and silver) that the Spanish set out to find would ultimately destroy the Spanish Empire. They had the gold – and the gold had them.

Why Olympic Athletes – and Pirates – Bite Coins

'They don't give you gold medals for beating somebody.
They give you gold medals for beating everybody'

Michael Johnson, sprinter

Why do Olympic winners bite their gold medals? The short answer is: for no other reason than that a photographer just told them to. But the tradition of biting gold goes back a long way.

You might have seen pirates in movies biting their coins too. Such hard-toothed individuals might inspire excitement, but once upon a time, anyone handling money would bite their coins: it was a rude test of purity.

As well as scraping (to look for plate) or indenting to test softness, biting might involve a little bending too, using the teeth as a clamp. If the metal was soft and malleable, it was likely pure gold or silver. Hard and brittle, it could indicate that the coin was counterfeit or mixed with other metals. The biting test probably worked best in mediaeval times, when coins, such as Florence's florin, were twenty-four-carat, thin and soft.

This method might expose crude forgeries, but it would by no means have been foolproof. Copper was added to gold coins from the Tudor period onwards, which would have made them harder, and the bite test that much less reliable. For the prospectors of the gold rushes, however, who only required a simple differentiation between actual and fool's gold, the bite test would have been relatively dependable. We have always used our bodies to measure things.

Today's Olympic winners needn't bother biting their gold. The last time an Olympic gold medal had any significant amounts of gold in it was over a hundred years ago.

The gold medals at the 1896 Olympics in Athens, when the Games were first revived, and then in Paris in 1900, were silver gilded with a thin layer of gold. Things perked up for the athletes in 1904 at the St Louis Olympics, when the gold medals were made of twelve-carat gold (50 per cent gold, 50 per cent copper), and even more so in London in 1908, when the gold medals were twenty-two-carat gold, and weighed almost an ounce (25 g).[13] This proved the peak. (It was probably Britain's peak too.) There were 109 gold medals handed out: 100 oz of gold, give or take. Expensive.

At the 1912 Stockholm Olympics, the gold content was reduced to eighteen-carat, and from 1920 in Antwerp onwards the medals were back to gilded silver. The declining gold content is not so dissimilar to the trajectory of the currencies of empires.

Today, the International Olympic Committee stipulates that modern Olympic gold medals must weigh at least 500 g and contain at least 6 g of gold. Olympic gold medals remain largely of silver (93 per cent) and copper (6 per cent), plated with about 6 g (a bit more than ⅕ oz) of gold. A gold medal is thus roughly 1 per cent gold.[14]

At the 2021 Olympics in Tokyo, the metals came from a recycling initiative. The Japanese handed in nearly 80,000 tonnes of electrical gadgets, including laptops, digital cameras, gaming devices and 6 million phones. The appliances yielded 32 kg/1,000 oz of gold, 3,500 kg/113,000 oz of silver and 2,200 kg of copper. This would be equivalent to a low-grade gold mine but a high-grade silver mine – there is a lot of silver in electrical gadgets.

7.

The Birth of Central Banking and the Accidental Gold Standard

'Gentlemen, I'm an honest man but unfortunately
I am unable to pay my debts back on this occasion.
Sorry – will see what I can do'

Charles II

If you needed somewhere safe to store your gold in late-mediaeval London, the vaults of the goldsmiths were the obvious place. You paid a fee, and the goldsmiths issued you with a receipt certifying the quantity and purity of the metal stored. It took several hundred years, but these receipts, which the Bank of England calls 'running cash notes', became the first British bank notes, eventually changing hands as though they were gold itself.

Rather than leave your gold in a vault doing nothing, goldsmiths began to lend it out. They lent at one rate, and paid another, lower rate of interest to you (as well as giving you all sorts of guarantees). The difference in the two rates of interest was their profit. Thus did goldsmiths become the forerunners of the City of London's great tradition of banking.

Not surprisingly, the rates of interest payable on the gold the smiths lent were high, often as high as 20 per cent. They got so high that in 1624, King James I, whose relationship with money-lenders was a constant source of contention, declared they must not exceed 8 per cent. In 1660, Parliament went further, passing 'An Act for restraining the taking of Excessive Usury', and reduced the maximum rate to 6 per cent.

Charles II was a big spender, almost constantly fighting the Dutch during his reign from 1660 to 1685, and a notorious bon viveur – hence his nickname 'the Merry King'. He fathered at least twelve illegitimate children. The Royal Household, he said, 'needed' an annual income of £1.2 million. But, after years of civil war over the issue (1642–51), Parliament now had a tight grip on the amount of money the king could raise through traditional means. Not a man to be held back, however, he persuaded Parliament to impose hearth taxes on the English. Twice a year, tax inspectors would demand entry into your home, rather in the manner of a BBC licence-fee enforcer today, to count the number of fireplaces. You then had a tax imposed on you based on how many you had. No surprise, the English hated it. But it became the crown's largest single source of income. Charles then secured a pension for himself by secretly promising his cousin, King Louis XIV of France, that he would convert to Catholicism.

But above all, he borrowed like mad – from the goldsmiths of London.

Charles, effectively, sold them 'tax futures' – future tax income at a discount, in exchange for gold now. (These debts were often recorded on sticks of wood – tally sticks.) The goldsmiths then sold the king's debt into the secondary market. It worked at first. The smiths thought the crown would never default on its loans, and the king could raise funds for his wars against the Dutch. But there was a limit to this debt expansion: the amount of gold in the goldsmiths' vaults. Eventually, it ran out.

By 1671, the discount on the king's tax debt had reached 10 per cent. In other words, people were starting to doubt it would be repaid. New funds barely covered maturing loans. Then the 1660 Usury Act was cited: interest rates above 6 per cent were against the law – thus all those loans made to the crown were illegal. The king's tally sticks became worthless. The goldsmiths and their customers had 'got the short end of the stick', as the saying derives. They owned the king's debt, which was illegal for him to repay. Charles wrote to the goldsmiths, the Bank of England tells us, and effectively said:

'Gentlemen, I'm an honest man but unfortunately I am unable to pay my debts back on this occasion. Sorry – will see what I can do.'[1]

This was the Great Stop of 1672. Most of London's goldsmiths were ruined. Ten thousand wealthy families in England were 'financially embarrassed'.[2] Just as the Third Anglo-Dutch War was beginning, the goldsmith bankers of London ceased all further credit to the crown, and Charles II was forced to recall Parliament to plead for funds for the eighty-two ships he wanted to attack the Dutch with. Messy.

But it only got messier. Largely for diplomatic reasons, Charles had his niece – his brother James's daughter – Mary marry the Protestant King of Holland: William of Orange. When Charles died in 1685, James came to the throne, only to be overthrown by Mary and William in the Glorious Revolution of 1688. To ingratiate them, and 'to erect a lasting monument of their Majesties' goodness in every hearth in the kingdom', Parliament repealed the loathed hearth tax. Now William and Mary had the same problem Charles had had. Not enough money. The crown's largest source of revenue was gone – and the crown had wars to fight, against France this time, and in Ireland and Scotland, not to mention that £1.2 million cost of the Royal Household.

William approached the goldsmiths of London. Unsurprisingly, they said no.

Then in 1691, a Scottish businessman by the name of William Paterson came up with a plan for a new type of bank. Members of the public could lend the crown £1.2 million in exchange for 8 per cent interest (this exceeded the legal limit of 6 per cent, but the usury laws were circumvented because it was considered a state loan rather than a private loan). A royal charter would enable the bank to operate as a joint-stock company with limited liability, and those who signed up to the scheme to become shareholders. No other joint-stock banks would be permitted to issue bank notes, so the bank would have special status and considerable competitive advantage. In 1694, the Chancellor of the Exchequer, Charles Montague, enacted Paterson's plan, and the Governor and the Company of the Bank of England were incorporated. The £1.2 million William needed was raised in just eleven days from 1,268 different people.[3]

The bank was established in an old Roman temple where Mithras had been worshipped. Mithras was, among other things, the Roman god of contracts.

The bank could lend the full amount of its deposits to the government. It could also issue notes against that same capital, which depositors could spend. The alchemists' dream of creating money out of nothing had been realised – ironically at a time when counterfeiting was rife. The intrinsic value of the paper might have been close to nil. Its token value, however, was much more. In many ways it was the birth of both fractional reserve and central banking. If only we could turn back time . . .

The Scourge of Counterfeiters and the Father of the Gold Standard

'Gentlemen, in applied mathematics, you must describe your unit'

Isaac Newton[4]

With groundbreaking contributions to mathematics, optics, mechanics, philosophy, astronomy and alchemy, including the laws of motion, the theory of gravitation and the reflecting telescope, Isaac Newton, along with William Shakespeare, Leonardo da Vinci and Aristotle, must be considered one of the cleverest individuals to have ever lived. As if that isn't enough, he is credited with the design of the gold standard, the primary monetary system of the world for over 200 years.

But this brilliant system was an accident.

Let's go back to where the problem began.

In 1695, counterfeit coins accounted for at least 10 per cent of English money.[5]

Why use a good coin if you can offload a counterfeit? This was especially so when it came to paying taxes, and that's what many English used them for. The Exchequer that year reported no more than ten good shillings for every hundred pounds of revenue.[6] Bad money was driving out good.

There were two types of coinage in circulation – coins struck by hand prior to 1662, and machine-struck coins thereafter – when the Royal Mint first installed machines to mint coins. Clipping was a major problem, especially of old coins.

Silver coins, meanwhile, were disappearing from circulation altogether. Silver was worth more on the continent as bullion than it was in England as tender, so arbitrageurs melted down the coins, shipped the silver abroad and sold it for gold. Everyone from the Jews to the French was blamed, but by 1695 it was almost impossible to find legal silver in circulation.

This led to a shortage of money, which, of course, inhibited trade. More damage was caused to the English nation in just one year by bad money than 'in a quarter of a century by bad Kings, bad Ministers, bad Parliaments and bad Judges', said the nineteenth-century historian Thomas Babington Macaulay, who was also Paymaster General.[7]

King William, meanwhile, needed stable currency if he was to continue his wars on the continent, and in 1695 he all but begged the House of Commons to respond to the currency crisis. The Secretary to the Treasury, William Lowndes, then wrote letters to the wisest men in England, seeking their advice: philosopher John Locke, architect Sir Christopher Wren, political economist Charles Davenant, bankers Sir Josiah Child and Gilbert Heathcote, lawyer John Asgill and scientist Sir Isaac Newton. Quite the roster.

Newton was in his early fifties and not far off the peak of his powers. He had published his most famous work, *Philosophiæ Naturalis Principia Mathematica*, just eight years earlier in 1687, and it had established him as the smartest man in the country. He would now put his great mind to money. Indeed, his interest would land him a rather good job.

With the formation of the Bank of England, Newton had become aware of the possibilities of paper money. 'If interest be not yet low enough for the advantage of trade,' he wrote, 'the only proper way to lower it is more paper credit till by trading and business we can get more money.'[8] He could see that token value and intrinsic value were not necessarily one and the same.

It was also obvious to Newton that the currency criminals were rational actors. They would continue to clip, counterfeit and sell abroad while there was profit in it. Bullion smuggling carried the death sentence, yet still it went on. Coercion alone would not be enough to stop it. The market itself needed to be changed.

He came up with two measures. First, to deal with the clipping: all coins minted prior to 1662 should be called in, melted down and remade into coins that had a single consistent edge. With no more hand-hammered coins in circulation, clipping coins would become that much more difficult. Reminting the entire country's coin, how-ever, at a time of such primitive machines, was no small undertaking.

Second, to deal with the silver issue: the amount of silver in coins should be lowered so that the silver content equalled the face value.

Newton's second proposal was not widely welcomed, and espe-cially not by John Locke. There were twenty shillings to a pound, so a shilling should contain a concomitant amount of silver. Newton may have thought that the token value was more important than the silver content, but landowners and Parliament, which was largely made up of them, thought that by lowering the amount of silver by 20 per cent they would lower effective net worth by 20 per cent. In 1696, Parliament approved the recoinage, but stipulated the new coins maintain the old weights. Newton warned the silver out-flow would continue, and it did.

Locke and Newton, despite their disagreement on this issue, were friends, and Locke had been for many years trying to find Newton a job. He nudged one of his protégés, Charles Montague, the Chancellor of the Exchequer, who, in March 1696, sent Newton a letter notifying him that the king intended to make him Warden of the Mint. Two days later, Newton left his home in Cambridge for London. So began his new career.

As Warden of the Mint, Newton was responsible for overseeing the production and circulation of England's currency, as well as ensuring the quality and accuracy of the coins that were minted. Newton took his new role very seriously, when perhaps it was only intended to be a sinecure.

Putting his chemical and mathematical knowledge to good use, Newton got the machines working and the coins minted at a speed that defied the predictions of even the boldest optimist, and as an industrial operation his recoinage was an enormous success.

Newton would also have to learn the skills of a policeman – both investigator and interrogator – and he proved masterful: a ruthless enforcer of the law, who oversaw numerous investigations, exposing frauds, and then prosecuting perpetrators. Poor counterfeiters had no idea of the intellect they were up against, and many were sent to the gallows for their crimes. He even pursued and caught the most notorious of all the counterfeiters, one William Chaloner, a confidence trickster who had been operating for years with apparent impunity.

When Newton began his great recoinage, Chaloner brought attention to himself by loudly and publicly criticising mint practices, claiming he could do it better. At this point, Newton had no idea who Chaloner was, but the criticism got under his skin. The ambitious Chaloner's goal was to get a job at the mint from where he could perpetrate his frauds on a nationwide basis, but he had underestimated Newton, and the unintended effect of his criticisms was not only to prick Newton's considerable pride, but to draw attention to himself. Newton set about getting his own back, and it was only in his subsequent investigations that he discovered Chaloner's extensive operations. Eventually, Newton brought him to trial, but Chaloner managed to get acquitted. Newton could not let it go, however, and pursued him to the last, often operating almost as deceitfully. Finally, after more than two years of pursuit, Newton got his man. Chaloner was prosecuted and found guilty of high treason, for which, in 1699, he was hanged at the gallows.

So good at the job of warden was Newton that, in 1699, he was promoted and made Master of the Mint, and after the union between

England and Scotland in 1707, Newton directed a Scottish recoinage that would lead to a new currency for the new Kingdom of Great Britain.

He had solved the clipping issue, and the counterfeiting issue was vastly improved, but silver was still making its way across the Channel, just as Newton had said it would. By 1715, almost all the coins that Newton had struck between 1696 and 1699 had left the country.

Newton's studies moved on from tides, planetary motions and pendulums to the gold markets. He drew up an extensive table of assays of foreign coins and in doing so realised that gold was cheaper in the new markets opening up in Asia than in Europe, and thus that silver was not just being sucked out of England, but out of Europe itself to India and China where it was traded for gold.

Meanwhile, the world's next great gold rush had started.

A Huge Gold Discovery in Brazil – and Most of It Ends Up in England

'We hardly have any money, but Portugal gold'

A man from Exeter, 1713

In 1694, Portuguese deserters found alluvial gold 200 miles inland from Rio de Janeiro in Minas Gerais in Brazil.

There soon came 'white, coloured, black, Amerindian, men and women; young and old; poor and rich; nobles and commoners; laymen and clergy',[9] said a priest, one of the many flocking there. By 1724, within just three decades of the discovery, world gold output had doubled. By 1750, 65 per cent of global gold production was emanating from Brazil.[10] Production only began faltering after 1765.

To avoid the king's fifth, smuggling was rife. Itinerant friars were carrying so much gold dust in hollowed-out statues of saints that a decree was issued forbidding the establishment of religious orders in Minas Gerais. Even so, the local governor estimated that the king was missing out on over 60 per cent of his 'quintos reals'. Legitimately or otherwise, the gold made its way to Lisbon, along with sugar, tobacco and other Brazilian products – similar amounts to those which had come to Spain in the previous century – and with it the Portuguese minted their moydores coins. Those minted after 1722 are regarded as some of the finest gold coins ever minted and, along with English guineas, replaced the Venetian ducat as the go-to coin of international trade.

The Portuguese used their gold to buy goods from England, which was becoming something of a commercial powerhouse: cereal crops, beef and fish, woollen goods, manufactured articles and luxuries. Portugal imported five times as much from England as it exported to it, and it used its newly acquired gold to settle the difference.[11] The moydores, which weighed slightly more than an English guinea – they were worth twenty-eight shillings – actually became currency, especially in the west country, where there were more of them than local coins. 'We hardly have any money,' wrote an Exeter man in 1713, 'but Portugal gold.'[12] In London, the Mint began minting guineas from the moydores. There had never been as much gold coinage minted before, and while the silver was leaving for Asia, the gold was coming and staying.

Newton was called on to investigate.

He came up with a new system, which he outlined in a report to the Treasury in 1717. Within three months, there was a Royal Proclamation forbidding the exchange of gold guineas for more than twenty-one silver shillings and another Great Recoinage. The ratio of gold to silver was effectively set at 1:15.[13] It did not make much difference. Twenty-one shillings of silver still got you more than a guinea's worth of gold on the continent, so the export continued. In the Chinese and Indian markets which were now opening up, thanks to the efforts of the East India Company and others, silver was even more valuable. The result was that silver was used for imports, and so left the country, while exports were traded for gold, which came into the country.

The Bank of England itself was also buying vast amounts of gold, 'to be coyned as it comes in'.[14] By 1715, it had 800 kg/25,700 oz, a nascent central bank reserve. By 1730, it had 15.5 tonnes. London overtook Amsterdam as the foremost precious metals market. All in all, some two-thirds of that Brazilian gold is thought to have ended up in England, hundreds of tonnes in total.[15] Brazil was the supplier for Britain's great gold standard.

Britain had always been on a silver standard. A pound was a pound of sterling silver. 'In all men's minds the only true money of the country was the silver coin,' said Sir John Craig, historian of the mint.[16] The Royal Proclamation suggested a bimetallic standard, but in practice, with so much silver going abroad, it moved Britain to the gold standard. Gold was more dependable than clipped silver, and Newton's system proved the bedrock of Britain's money, and thus its domestic and international trade through the eighteenth century, helping it to become a trusted and formidable commercial power. But it was an accidental gold standard. Nobody – not the institutions nor the persons involved – had had the slightest intention of basing a new monetary system solely on gold. Most wanted to sustain silver as the prime coinage of the land. Newton had tried to create a functioning bimetallic standard. Market forces had other ideas, and over the next 200 years Newton's accidental standard gradually became the system not just of Britain, but of every major nation in the world bar China.

In the 1770s, there was another recoinage in Britain, which, in terms of sheer scale, was unprecedented. Some 155 tonnes of gold in total were minted, perhaps thirty times more than Newton's recoinage of 1696–9, and greater than anything undertaken by the empires of Spain or Venice, or even Rome. No attempt was made to recoin silver. In effect, it was an admission that Britain was now on a gold standard (though what silver coinage there was remained legal tender). The accidental gold standard was formalised.

It didn't last.

Less than twenty years later, British Prime Minister William Pitt the Younger, who on no account wanted the revolutionary fervour that had gripped France taking hold in Britain, began pouring funds into the continent to support European monarchs. His money was known as the 'Golden Cavalry of St George', because of the image of St George on the golden guineas he sent. But the gold soon ran out, and the Bank of England asked the prime minister to free it from having to redeem its notes for bullion. Pitt obliged. Britain abandoned Newton's gold standard, and the currency of the crown became unconvertible. Inflation raged and Napoleon, who had just seized power, got war.

In 1816, as those wars ended, there was another Great Recoinage in Britain. The twenty-one-shilling guinea was replaced with Britain's famous sovereign: a twenty-two-carat coin that is still struck today. Worth twenty shillings, it was a one-pound coin, adorned with Italian engraver Benedetto Pistrucci's famous image of St George and the dragon. From 8 May 1821, Britain was back on a gold standard: anyone could walk into the Bank of England with a paper note and exchange it for gold sovereigns. Some 9.8 million sovereigns were struck that year.

This new gold standard would last almost 100 years, and it would be copied the world over.

8.

The Mysterious World of Alchemy

"Tis mere opinion that sets a value upon money'

Isaac Newton[1]

Never mind his little-known achievements at the Royal Mint, what is even less well known about Isaac Newton is his fascination with alchemy and biblical prophecy.

From a modern perspective, this might seem odd. Newton was a scientist. Science means respectable, rational investigation. Alchemy means strange, mystical magic. The two are worlds apart. However, this distinction is relatively recent.

From its ancient origins to its association with the occult today, alchemy has captured the imaginations of millions. It is a cross-cultural phenomenon with influences from Europe, Asia and North Africa. Its practitioners have sought spiritual enlightenment, immortality and the secrets of the universe. Above all, they have sought to turn base metals into gold. Nobody has yet succeeded. That doesn't stop them trying.

Why this need to make gold? There are two explanations. As the purest and most perfect of metals, gold symbolises enlightenment, immortality, divine perfection even. The ancient Chinese thought that, through this transmutation, they could gain a deeper understanding of both the universe and the self. The ancient Egyptians believed that the gods actually created the world through a process of alchemical transformation, and they developed elaborate rituals and practices to mimic this process in the physical world, though the

82

physical reality of their experiments did not quite match up to their lofty goals: they tried to make gold by painting lead with egg yolk, for example.

The second, more prosaic explanation is that same urge to create wealth and power that drove some of history's bravest explorers, its most ruthless conquerors, its mightiest leaders and its lowliest thieves: greed.

At alchemy's heart is the legend of the Philosopher's Stone, a universal substance that could cure all diseases, grant eternal youth and, of course, transmute base metal into gold. At one point, Newton thought he had found it, though modern chemistry shows that true transmutation (changing one element into another) requires nuclear reactions, something far beyond Newton's capabilities at the time. Some, in the quest for inner transformation and enlightenment, sought to transmute their own souls and consciousness into higher states of being. They believed that their experiments and operations had symbolic and allegorical meanings that could reveal hidden truths about nature, humanity and the universe. Maybe so.

Ancient Greek philosopher Empedocles introduced the theory of the four elements – air, water, earth and fire – which was then advanced by, among others, Plato, Aristotle and Hippocrates. The theory attempted to explain life, change and the complexity of all matter. It found its way into geology, cosmology and medicine, and it became the theoretical basis of alchemy for centuries.

We might mock it, but alchemy was a systematic discipline, based on observation, experimentation and documentation. Chemistry would not exist in the same way were it not for alchemy: the alchemists developed methods for distillation, sublimation, precipitation and crystallisation – methods still important today. They contributed to the discovery of new substances – phosphorus, sal ammoniac and aqua regia. They developed scientific method, emphasising empirical verification, and scientific equipment. Maria the Jewess, for example, who lived in Alexandria in (probably) the second century and is seen as the first true western alchemist, is credited with the invention of several kinds of chemical apparatus, including the bain-marie, a double boiler that is still used in modern chemistry and cooking today. Never mind Newton, even the great Leonardo da Vinci dabbled in alchemical practices.

Alchemy flourished during the Islamic Golden Age, roughly between the eighth and fourteenth centuries. Jabir ibn Hayyan, aka Geber, often referred to as the 'father of chemistry', for example, wrote numerous works on the subject in the eighth century, describing processes such as calcination and reduction, and developing several laboratory techniques, including crystallisation, distillation and sublimation. It also flourished in Europe in the Middle Ages, where, in 1550, one of alchemy's definitive texts, the *Rosarium Philosophorum* ('Rosary of the Philosophers'), was published. But as we shall discover, many alchemists were also viewed with suspicion and mistrust.

While Newton kept his findings to himself, many alchemists were boastful showmen. Frauds were so common that Ben Jonson even wrote a play about it. *The Alchemist*, first performed in 1610 and to considerable success, tells of a trio of con artists who set up shop in London and convince their wealthy clients that they can turn base metals into gold. It ridicules not only the scammers but also the gullibility of those who believed that the power of alchemy could make them rich.

But you can't deride the persistence or the creativity of alchemists. Both are driven by that same 'greed for gold', as Pliny put it. After hunger, thirst and lust, greed is surely mankind's greatest motivator.

Horse Manure, Mercury and the Invention of Meissen Porcelain

'One sometimes finds what one is not looking for'

Alexander Fleming[2]

As many a life coach will tell you, failure is crucial to success. For every brilliant joke you hear, there are a hundred others the comedian tried that are forgotten or were dropped. For every genius scientific discovery, there are a thousand fruitless experiments.

Nevertheless, from grinding gems into dust and then mixing them with blood, urine and dung to combining human or animal sperm with herbs and chemicals to create a small, sentient being that would serve as a source of wisdom or power (aka a homunculus) – many of the paths that alchemy took seem just daft.

They heated quicksilver with horse manure and then distilled the resulting mixture thinking you could turn mercury into gold. One group of alchemists trying to create the Philosopher's Stone left a mixture of various chemicals and metals in a sealed container for forty days. When they opened the container and found a chicken alive inside, they were convinced they had done it, as the chicken was a symbol of transformation.

Often, alchemists are ascribed their abilities posthumously. In the fourteenth century, Nicolas Flamel, a French bookseller and manuscript illuminator, who had married a rich heiress and philanthropist, devoted much of his time to understanding the text of a mysterious twenty-one-page book he had acquired. A Jewish sage on the road to Santiago de Compostela, so the story goes, told him it was a copy of the original *Book of Abramelin the Mage*, which contained the recipe of the Philosopher's Stone. Thus did Flamel disappear down the rabbit hole of alchemy.

Over 200 years later, the story began to circulate that Flamel had indeed cracked it. Not only had he figured out how to turn base metals into gold; he had found the elixir of life. The trigger was a tomb discovered in Paris in the graveyard by the church of Saint-Jacques-de-la-Boucherie, which bore Flamel's name. Inside the tomb, an alchemical book was found along with a note that read, 'This book is made to the glory of God and to the profit of the common good. Herein is contained the science of the Philosophers, with many admirable things of the said science, which God hath given to the children of men.' It is now thought that someone added the book later,[3] while Flamel and his wife's well-publicised philanthropy probably helped support the rumours about his wealth.

Treasure hunters began to search for his buried fortune, devising all sorts of elaborate schemes. Among them was the great Victor Hugo, best known as the author of *Les Misérables*, who, in the 1840s, became obsessed with the idea of finding Flamel's treasure, and spent months studying alchemy and deciphering clues. He was convinced that the treasure was hidden in the abandoned tower of Saint-Jacques-de-la-Boucherie, and he and a group of fellow treasure hunters eventually broke into the tower only to find nothing.

Even so, Flamel has acquired near legendary status among alchemists. He even made it into J. K. Rowling's *Harry Potter and the Philosopher's Stone*.

Sixteenth-century Swiss physician and alchemist Paracelsus, who was particularly admired by Newton, is another example. On the one hand he was a groundbreaking physician, a pioneer of the medical revolution of the Renaissance, known as the father of toxicology: one of the first to recognise the hazards of metalwork and the toxic nature of mercury. On the other hand, he was anti-establishment and contrarian: 'the universities do not teach all things, so a doctor must seek out old wives, gipsies, sorcerers, wandering tribes, old robbers, and such outlaws and take lessons from them. A doctor must be a traveller . . . Knowledge is experience.'[4]

He too thought he had discovered the secret of the elixir, though at least he tested it on himself (many physicians of the time were great self-experimentalists), rather than perpetrate some fraud. He prepared a potion made from gold, pearls and other ingredients and drank it, convinced that it would grant him immortality. Instead, he became violently ill and had to spend several days in bed recovering.

Despite his failure, he persisted with his experiments. His work, in particular his belief in the power of experimentation and his willingness to challenge established ideas, paved the way for many of the scientific breakthroughs of the centuries that followed.

Alchemical experimentation often had unexpected benefits. The story of Johann Friedrich Böttger is one such example.

As a teenager at the turn of the eighteenth century, the young German locked himself away to devote his time to the pursuit of the Philosopher's Stone – known in German as the *Alltinktur* or *Goldmachertinktur* (gold-making tincture). But word got out, as it so often seems to, that he could produce gold from base metals, and he caught the attention of both King Frederick I of Prussia and King Augustus II of Saxony, known as Augustus the Strong – both of whom had spending problems and hankered for gold. They both tried to arrest him. Augustus the Strong won out. Böttger was imprisoned for attempting to create gold through alchemy, a practice forbidden by law because it was fraudulent and a threat to the stability of currency. Then, once imprisoned, they put him to work creating gold, which he couldn't do, and became rather an object of ridicule and scorn.

But during his imprisonment, he came under the supervision of another alchemist, Ehrenfried Walther von Tschirnhaus, who had been tasked with finding a way to make porcelain. Chinese porcelain was highly valued in Europe – known as white gold – and European artisans had been trying for centuries to replicate it with little success. Böttger had negligible prior knowledge of porcelain-making, but, fearing for his life, he began experimenting with different materials and techniques and eventually discovered a formula for a type of hard-paste porcelain that was comparable to the finest Chinese ceramics. To be able to produce this prized substance locally was a major business breakthrough. Augustus the Strong founded the Royal Meissen Porcelain Factory in Meissen, granted Böttger his freedom and made him director. The factory still produces high-quality porcelain to this day – indeed Meissen porcelain is considered some of the finest in the world – and Böttger became something of a legend among porcelain and ceramics aficionados.

How often does the pursuit of one thing lead to the discovery of something else.

On that note, let's go back to the alchemical studies of Sir Isaac Newton.

The Search for the Philosopher's Stone, and How Sir Isaac Newton Went Mad

'You are an alchemist; make gold of that'

William Shakespeare, *Timon of Athens*[5]

Newton's interest in alchemy began during his undergraduate years at Cambridge University, where he came into contact with the works of Paracelsus. Newton spent many years of his life dedicated to its study, but he conducted his experiments in private, and so his interest was largely unknown to contemporaries. Only in the twentieth century were some of his alchemical manuscripts discovered and published.

This collection, now known as the *Newton Papers*, contained over a million words, many of which were in Latin, and included works by prominent alchemists of his time, as well as his own notes and observations. His studies were complex and obscure, often using cryptic codes, symbols and allegories. They reveal a side of him that contrasts with the rational, empirical physicist, though he will have seen alchemy as a noble pursuit and a complement to his scientific research, rather than as a contradiction or a distraction. There is one story of his becoming so absorbed in his alchemy that he forgot to eat for several days, and did not even notice that he had been fasting until a colleague pointed out his emaciated appearance.

Newton's treatise *Praxis* reveals his belief in the transmutation of metals, the Philosopher's Stone and the attainment of spiritual purification and illumination. Newton also believed that alchemy had a deep connection with biblical and prophetic texts, and he saw his own work as a continuation of the alchemical traditions of ancient wisdom. Newton's *Index Chemicus*, containing over 900 entries, was, says his biographer Thomas Levenson, 'the most comprehensive listing of alchemical ideas, writers and concepts ever composed'.[6]

In the early 1690s, at the peak of his scientific career, Newton wrote of his success in making gold, that he had forged the legendary stone of the ancients, the Philosopher's Stone. Here was the alchemist's dream realised at last – as he put it, the 'quintessential matter or Chaos out of which man and all ye world was made'.[7]

We know he was conducting experiments with mercury, sulphur and other metals, which can react in such a way to produce gold-coloured alloys or compounds. Perhaps these confused him, especially as he believed what he was attempting was actually possible.

The realisation of failure seems to have sent him into delirium and depression. Perhaps alchemy intensified his existential and spiritual anxieties – his writings on the subject betray a sense of frustration, confusion and disappointment, says Levenson, not so readily apparent in his other work. Perhaps the depression came because his experiments involved extensive use of mercury and lead, which may have had negative effects on his health and mood. In a letter to Samuel Pepys in 1693, he said he was 'extremely troubled by the embroilment I am in, and have neither ate nor slept well this twelvemonth, nor have my former consistency of mind'.[8] Newton's hair, examined during a later exhumation, was found to contain four times as much lead, arsenic and antimony and fifteen times as much mercury than is normal – levels indicating chronic poisoning.

He never completed *Praxis*; he kept his findings to himself, and his interest in alchemy waned. After his depression, he never came back to it again with anything like the same vigour. Shortly before he died in 1727, he burned important papers in his fireplace. Many think these might have been related to his alchemical investigations, and even perhaps some discoveries.

Newton's interest in alchemy was intertwined with his scientific pursuits. He believed that the universe was governed by a set of fundamental laws and principles, which could be uncovered through careful observation and experimentation. His alchemy may not have led to any significant breakthroughs, but it played a role in shaping both his worldview and his scientific practices.

One final insight into Newton's predilections comes from his investment in the South Sea Company – the company that precipitated the South Sea Bubble, often seen as the world's first financial crash. He was an early investor and had the wisdom to sell his stock in 1720, after a good run. But the stock kept rising, so Newton bought back in. It proved close to the top of the market. His eventual losses totalled £20,000 – forty years of his base salary as Master of the Mint. He later said he 'could calculate the motions of the heavenly bodies, but not the madness of people'.[9]

His speculation – and his need to get back in – perhaps reveals something about his nature, which would also explain his interest in alchemy: he was as greedy as the rest of us.

Alchemy Gives Way to Chemistry, but Voldemort Brings It Back Again

'Everyone seems to have a clear idea of how other people should lead their lives, but none about his or her own'

Paulo Coelho, *The Alchemist*

Newton's change of heart pre-empted a decline in the science of alchemy more generally. Starting probably with Robert Boyle, a contemporary of Newton generally regarded as the first modern chemist, distinctions began to be drawn between alchemy and chemistry. By the 1740s, alchemy was restricted to the realm of gold-making, so quickly became associated with charlatans. The scientists of the Enlightenment, looking to legitimise their own practices, distanced themselves and their chemistry. Ever since, alchemy has been associated with pseudoscience, quackery and the occult.

But it still entrances us, as evidenced by its considerable influence in popular culture, from Marvel supervillain Diablo to Japanese manga series *Fullmetal Alchemist*. Paulo Coelho's *The Alchemist* has become a modern classic, selling millions of copies in over eighty languages, while J. K. Rowling's *Harry Potter and the Philosopher's*

Stone was the highest-grossing book in history, never mind the film and the six sequels.

Modern alchemists are still seeking to unlock the secrets of the universe through the study of ancient texts and practices. *The Book of Aquarius* was published anonymously in 2011. It explains 'how to make the real Philosophers' Stone, capable of healing all disease, reversing the aging process and transmuting lead into gold'. What can I say? It has good reviews on Amazon – 4.4 out of 5. Elsewhere, author Mark Stavish views alchemy as a form of personal transformation and self-improvement.

But pseudoscience or not, the many concepts and practices developed by alchemists, such as distillation, purification and transmutation, are still used in modern laboratories.

I find it fascinating that in alchemical legend, gold should be so closely associated with the elixir of life. We are back to that theme of gold and eternity.

At the same time, many of those who pursued alchemy wanted, simply, to get rich.

The Genius Gold-Maker Who Conned Himmler

In 1914, a young German named Heinz Kurschildgen started his first job as an apprentice in a dye factory in his hometown of Hilden. He became fascinated by the chemicals he was working with and built a small laboratory at home to conduct experiments.

Before long, he thought he had found a way to make gold, and even persuaded several investors to give him money. However, it soon became clear that he couldn't make gold, and he found himself prosecuted for fraud. The courts let him off on the grounds that, mentally, he was not all there, but only on condition that he solicited no further investments with schemes to make gold.

He was soon claiming he could make other transmutations and became something of a joke figure in his hometown, where a bust was even erected in his honour, albeit ironically, inscribed with the words: 'For the genius gold-maker, from his grateful hometown.'

But in 1929, he returned to his first calling: kidding people he could make gold. He approached German President Paul von Hindenburg and the Head of the Reichsbank, Hjalmar Schacht, with a proposal to make the gold they needed to pay off Germany's First World War reparations, which amounted to almost all the gold that had ever been mined in history by that time. That would take quite some alchemy.

But Kurschildgen was not a man to be deterred. He raised a load more money, defrauded his clients and ended up with eighteen months in jail.

After his release, he was soon at it again. This time, he approached the newly installed Nazi government with a plan to make petrol from water.

Chief Scientific Advisor Wilhelm Keppler paid him a visit, and Kurschildgen agreed to reveal his methods and surrender the rights to the government. Meanwhile, his claims about being able to make gold piqued the interest of SS leader Heinrich Himmler, who had a notoriously superstitious streak and a fascination with alchemy. Himmler started generously funding Kurschildgen to conduct his experiments.

But Reichsanstalt physicists soon declared his contraptions useless, and Kurschildgen ended up in a concentration camp.

'Himmler has fallen for a gold and petrol maker,' said Joseph Goebbels in his diary. 'He wanted to defraud me, too. I knew what he was about straight away'.[10]

After two years, Kurschildgen was released early for good behaviour. Himmler had him put straight back in the camp. On no account did he want this embarrassing story becoming public.

After the war, Kurschildgen tried to get recognised as a victim of Nazi persecution so he could claim compensation. 'The Gestapo would stop at nothing to get my invention,' he told the courts.[11]

As with most of his ventures, his petition was unsuccessful.

Even so, you can't fault the man's ambition.

9

Gold Fever Everywhere

'Eureka! Boys, I believe I have found a gold mine'

James Marshall, carpenter

Aside from taxation (see my excellent book, *Daylight Robbery*), it is difficult to think of anything that has had a more understated yet profound influence on the course of human history than the gold rush. Nations, indeed civilisations, have been formed on the back of them.

The twenty-fourth of January 1848 stands out amongst them as a watershed moment, the dawn of a new golden age.

On that day, James Marshall – a carpenter from New Jersey – was conducting a routine inspection of the tailrace, the channel carrying the water outflow from the lumber mill which he was helping build. The mill was on the western slopes of the Sierra Nevada in California, a semi-arid wilderness, largely inhabited by native tribes. (The fertile land of Oregon to the north was, at this point, more attractive to pioneers and other migrants.) Marshall saw something shining at the bottom of the ditch. 'It was about half the size and shape of a pea,' he said. 'It made my heart thump, for I was certain it was gold. Then I saw another.'[1]

'Eureka!' He ran back to the mill shouting. 'Boys, I believe I have found a gold mine.'

His find triggered a gold rush that captivated the world, bringing hundreds of thousands from across America, Australia, Europe, South America, Central America and China to California.

You could even say that the year, 1848, is the dividing line between two distinct histories of gold – one before and one after, akin to BC and AD.

Some 370 tonnes are believed to have been mined in the first five years – then 100 tonnes annually until 1860, when the best years were over. But Marshall's discovery sparked gold rushes in Australia, New Zealand, Canada and, most significantly of all in terms of future gold supply, South Africa, causing mass migrations of people and more. his cry of eureka would become the California state motto. His discovery changed the course of civilisation.

Across the world, the scale of the gold business changed out of all proportion. The amount of metal available was unprecedented. World gold supply more than doubled in a decade. The Paris Mint, for example, minted 65 million napoléons d'or between 1800 and 1850, then 150 million in the eight years from 1850 to 1857. The US Mint's output of gold eagles rose fivefold.

Just as the mines of northern Spain had enabled Roman money, so the gold rushes of the nineteenth century enabled the classical gold standard.

On the day that Marshall found those golden peas, California was still legally part of Mexico. Nine days later, after two years of war with the US, Mexico ceded the land west of Texas and south of Oregon: California, Nevada, Utah, most of Arizona, half of New Mexico and Colorado, and the south-west corner of Wyoming. If only Mexico had known!

Right from the beginning, Marshall had tried to keep his discovery a secret, with only a handful of people in the know. He ran some rudimentary tests on his peas: he bit them and hit them with a hammer. Sure it was gold, four days after his discovery, he rode out to his boss, German-born John Sutter.

'It was a rainy afternoon when Mr. Marshall arrived at my office in the Fort, very wet,' Sutter recalled. 'He told me then that he had some important and interesting news which he wished to communicate secretly to me, and wished me to go with him to a place where we should not be disturbed, and where no listeners could come and hear what we had to say. I went with him to my private rooms . . .

Marshall took a rag from his pocket, showing me the yellow metal; he had about two ounces of it.' Sutter then got out his *Encyclopedia Americana*. 'After [reading] the long article "gold" . . . I declared this to be gold of the finest quality, of at least 23 carats.'[2]

Sutter swore his workers to secrecy, but he couldn't hold them to it. Word spread to the nearby homesteads along the American River. That May, after several months digging through the rainy months, a Mormon from a nearby settlement went to San Francisco (which had only just had its name changed from Yerba Buena) with a bottle of gold dust, and waved it about, crying, 'Gold! Gold from the American River!'[3]

Pandora's Box had been opened. An ordinary man could pick up more gold in a day than he could earn in a year. San Francisco emptied. By mid-June, at least three-quarters of San Francisco's male population had left the city for the rivers and streams of the Sierra Nevada to look for gold. Sutter's workmen had long since abandoned him. 'Even my cook has left me,' he complained. His mill was left uncompleted and now his property was swarming with prospectors, squatting his land. 'The whole country from San Francisco to Los Angeles, and from the seashore to the base of the Sierra Nevada, resounds with the sordid cry of gold! GOLD!! GOLD!!!' said the *Californian* on 29 May. 'The field is left half planted, the house half built, and everything neglected but the manufacture of shovels and pickaxes.'[4]

On 1 June, the military governor wrote to his superiors in Washington DC. There were some 4,000 miners on the river already, half of them Indian, he estimated. 'No capital is required to obtain this gold, as the labouring man wants nothing but his pick and shovel and tin pan, with which to dig and wash'.[5] That is why so many flocked to California: no capital was required. It really was a gold rush for every man. Only later did partnerships and corporations push out the small men and mining become big business.

Like so many, Benjamin Kloozer, a soldier stationed in California, was torn between duty to his country and the lure of gold. He wrote to his brother in Boston, 'I hate to desert [but] I am almost crazy . . . I have the "gold fever" shockingly bad.'[6] Soldiers were paid

$6 per month. Prospecting he could make $150 per day.[7] He was one of many who left their posts.

By late summer, especially thanks to a story in the *Baltimore Sun*, news had reached the east coast of the extraordinary fortunes being made. Even wealthy professionals began heading west, leaving wives and families behind to fend for themselves. 'Poets, philosophers, lawyers, brokers, merchants, farmers, clergymen – all are feeling the impulse,' said the *New York Herald*.[8] Shops and schools closed. 'The whole population are going crazy . . . Old as well as young are daily falling victim to the gold fever,' said one man.[9]

It's thought that in 1849, some 90,000 – almost all of them men – set out for California, two-thirds of them American. They became known as the '49ers'. From the east coast, some 40,000 went by land, often forming joint-stock companies to buy wagons and provisions and for security. The perceived threat was Indians, but the big killer was disease: cholera, diphtheria, 'mountain fever' (typhoid) and pneumonia. It was a treacherous three-to-seven-month journey of nearly 3,000 miles, full of incredible hardship: lost belongings, broken-down wagons, pack animals dying from exhaustion, and weather that ranged from freezing-cold blizzards to torrential rain to dust storms to scorching heat. The route was marked by numerous graves.

The more expensive, safer route took as long as eight months: 15,000 miles by overcrowded ship around Cape Horn, the freezing tip of South America. More popular was the shorter, 7,000-mile, two-to-three-month 'Panama shortcut'. A sail down the east coast to Panama, a thirty-five-mile jungle trek across the fever-ridden Panama isthmus and another boat up to San Francisco.

'Neither the Crusades nor Alexander's expedition to India can equal the emigration to California,' wrote a Michigan doctor.[10] Men abandoned everything to risk this perilous journey and then spend their days up to their waists in freezing-cold water, moving rocks and stones searching for gold, their fingers numb, their boots rotting and their clothes permanently drenched. In the evenings, their clothes still damp, men had to scrape off poisonous mercury, to which gold adheres, and heat it until it vaporised. That did little good for their health.

As I keep saying, gold is quite the motivator.

A Shortage of Women

'Go West, young man, go West and grow up with the country'

Horace Greeley, US politician and publisher

By 1850, San Francisco's population had gone from below 1,000 to 30,000 people.[11] Some 700 ships docked in 1849. Many crews did not hang around for the return journey – they deserted their ships to go digging.

Prices skyrocketed, especially for food and commodities, with supplies so sparse. A plot of land which cost $16 in 1847 sold for $45,000 eighteen months later.[12]

The 500-mile front was becoming crowded. The easy gold had been picked off. As is now famously known, the big money was made by those selling picks and shovels: selling goods and services to miners rather than actually mining.

So many domestic servants abandoned their jobs that there was a shortage, and for a period, a domestic servant could earn as much as congressmen. In California, there was a huge shortage of women, so 'female services', from washing, ironing and cooking to prostitution, commanded fortunes. It would cost fifteen ounces of gold to spend the night with a lady ($40,000 in today's money).[13]

There was a lack of dollars too, so gold became the principal currency, with prices denominated in weights. Men carried a leather pouch of gold dust as their wallet.

With no authority present, justice fell to fellow prospectors, and it could be swift. A man who stole $300 had a T branded on his cheek and his ears cut off.

Significant technical advances began to be made, especially in hydraulic mining, enabling a dramatic reduction in workforce and the harvesting of low-grade deposits. Canals, tunnels and aqueducts were built – 4,400 miles of waterway by 1857 – on a scale comparable to the Romans in Spain, meaning that mining output increased. There was an explosion in manufacturing for mining machinery and equipment for hydraulic operations. Previously this was an industry dominated by the East, but the newer, more immediate demand changed that.

Assay offices soon started up as the gold began to be shipped. The US Mint opened an office so that gold coins could be struck on the spot. Much of the gold paid for the Union military effort in the Civil War.

The Gold Rush had a profound impact on the settlement of the western United States, California especially, changing both its demography and its destiny. Before the discovery at John Sutter's lumber mill, there were around 160,000 people in the entire territory, mostly Native American or Mexican, and just 2,700 settlers.[14] It was not even a recognised state yet. By about 1855, more than 300,000 people had arrived.[15] Towns and cities rose up as a result: Sacramento and San Francisco gained particular prominence. California now constituted a state.

Transportation transformed. There were new roads, bridges, wagons, ferries and steamships, either to help prospectors, equipment and supplies reach California or to get them and their product home again. In 1852, California's first railroad company, the Sacramento Valley Railroad, was incorporated, and in 1856 the railroad opened for business, carrying lumber, ore, food, goods and passengers along the twenty-three-mile line between Folsom and the river docks in Sacramento. Numerous other rail lines quickly emerged across the state. In 1863, construction of America's first transcontinental railroad, the Pacific Railroad, began, a 1,911-mile track connecting San Francisco to the eastern US rail network in Iowa. Transportation infrastructure across the Panama isthmus was improved, and eventually, in 1881, construction began on the canal.

Lumber production increased dramatically. Many new sawmills

started up. There were numerous new flour mills too. The need for clothing increased, and the leather industry especially saw dramatic growth. There was rapid development of agriculture. Many who did not find the yellow metal turned to California's 'green gold'. The region's favourable climate enabled production of fruit, grain and vegetables to feed the growing population. As well as farms and orchards, vineyards were planted too, and California would soon become a wine exporter. The economic expansion meant a need for financial services, and so many new banks started up.

Trade along the Pacific coast exploded. Chile, for example, suddenly had new markets to export to and buy from. Across the ocean too – China began exporting sugar, and even Norway expanded its shipping industry (particularly taking Europeans to California around Cape Horn).

The Gold Rush was also colossally damaging to the environment. Forests were torn down to provide lumber. Habitats were destroyed. Biodiversity was lost. Rivers became clogged with sediment, especially with the pressured water jets of hydraulic mining, which eroded gravel hillsides. Entire landscapes were washed away and waterways blocked. Goodness knows what damage was done to aquatic life. The mercury to extract gold from ore led to widespread mercury pollution, contaminating rivers, soil and ecosystems, poisoning both wild and human life.

While many thrived, many ended up penniless, not least John Sutter himself, who, in 1852, with his property overrun and his goods and livestock stolen or destroyed, went bankrupt. Many lost their families and their lives. There were lots of clashes between the various racial groups, which sometimes got bloody and violent. The Chinese young men were particularly unwelcome, thought to be taking employment opportunities away from locals. Never mind the settlers, what about the indigenous people? Tens of thousands are thought to have been killed.

History is not black and white. The California Gold Rush is one of the most amazing episodes, the American dream in real life. It attracted people from all over the world. It made many new and wonderful things possible. It also did many terrible things. Like gold itself, there is contradiction at its very heart.

I marvel at the effect it had on mass psychology, the behaviours gold fever inspired: the energy, the creativity, the courage, the determination, the innovation, the imagination, but also the ruthlessness, the greed, the violence, the crime, the destruction.

What is so amazing is the speed at which everything happened. California was transformed. Friedrich Engels wrote to Karl Marx saying the new economy and markets arising from the Gold Rush seemed to 'come out of nothing'.[16] He was right. Bubbles accelerate investment, so do gold rushes. We have seen it time and time again in the great infrastructure booms, the tech booms, Dutch Tulip Mania, the South Sea Bubble and, here, the Gold Rush.

'Complete Mental Madness': The Gold Rush in Australia

When finds of wondrous treasure
Set all the South ablaze,
And you and I were faithful mates
All through the roaring days!

Henry Lawson, 'The Roaring Days', 1889

In 1849, a ship moored in Sydney Harbour with news of the California Gold Rush. Persuasively, it had 1,200 ounces on board. A man by the name of Edward Hargraves, who had been wandering Australia for some twenty years, was instantly taken with gold fever, and he got himself on the next boat to San Francisco.

On board, he found himself sharing a cabin with another 'sufferer', a sheep farmer with an interest in geology by the name of Simpson Davison, who had come to Sydney to sell his wool, only to find himself similarly taken with the fever. Over the journey, the two spent many hours discussing the geology of New South Wales, and how the rivers running off the Blue Mountains might also contain gold, so that by the time they arrived in the US they couldn't wait to get back to Australia and put their theories to the test.

They had some success in California, but Hargraves was soon on a ship back to Sydney, where he arrived in January 1851. Within a few weeks, he was scratching around in the gravel of a creek north-west of Sydney, which ran off the Macquarie River, exploiting some of the techniques he had learnt in California. His hunch was proved right. He had a difficult time convincing people of his find, meeting with both disbelief and accusations of fraud, but before long others soon started finding gold in the area. Hargraves named the place of his discovery 'Ophir', and within four months there were more than 1,000 prospectors.[17] 'A complete mental madness appears to have seized almost every member of the community,' said the local rag, the *Bathurst Free Press*. 'There has been a universal rush to the diggings.'[18]

Unlike California, which was a free-for-all, colonial authorities in Australia had more control. They appointed 'Commissioners of Land' to regulate the diggings and collect licence fees for each claim. In the Victoria discoveries which followed, there were limits on how much river frontage diggers could have (eight metres for two to three men) and how much open ground they could dig.

Gold had been discovered in New South Wales and in the Blue Mountains several times before, but the government suppressed the news. It did not want gold fever causing the 'destruction of all discipline' among the soldiers and convicts.[19] This time it could not keep a lid on things.

In the year of Hargraves' discovery, 1851, New South Wales would produce 4.5 tonnes, rising to 25.5 tonnes in 1852. This was chicken feed compared to what would be discovered in Victoria.

There, the authorities, fearing a population exodus to the gold frenzy of New South Wales, offered a reward of £200 for any gold found within 200 miles of Melbourne. Within six months of Hargraves' Ophir discovery, gold was found in the streams coming off the coastal mountains near Melbourne, first at Ballarat, then at Bendigo Creek off Mount Alexander. By December, almost every man in Melbourne was digging. As much as two tonnes per week were recovered.[20] Within two years, Australia was producing as much gold as California.[21] Over the course of the 1850s, Victoria produced 650 tonnes, around one-third of global output, while New South Wales produced 90 tonnes. The extraction techniques were different to California, requiring deeper digging into tenacious clay, for which new methods were developed.

Hargraves took a reward of £10,000 plus a life pension for his discovery and was appointed a Commissioner of Land. He changed the course of Australia's history. Now, Australia attracted immigrants by the boatload. By 1852, 30,000 diggers were arriving each month. Ships from Britain, Europe and California were packed.[22] Australia's total population quadrupled from 430,000 in 1851 to 1.7 million by 1871. Victoria's grew from 77,000 to 540,000.[23]

The demography of the convict colonies changed for good. As well as many from Britain, Europe (French, Italian, German, Polish and Hungarian especially) and the US, thousands of Chinese prospectors came digging too, bringing their own mining techniques known as 'paddocking'. As in California, they were not particularly welcome. In 1855, Victoria enacted the Chinese Immigration Act to limit the number of Chinese passengers allowed to arrive on each vessel. To evade the law, many Chinese simply sailed elsewhere in Australia and then completed their journey by land. By 1861, Chinese immigrants made up 3.3 per cent of the population, and most of them were men: 38,337 to just eleven women.[24] Many seem to have been in some kind of indentured servitude, under contract to Chinese and foreign businessmen. In exchange for the boat fare, they worked on the goldfields until their debt was settled. Most eventually returned to China.

The immigrants brought new skills and professions, but the gold meant wealth. It was shipped to London and a huge flow of imports returned. There were investments in infrastructure – Australia got its first railways and telegraphs – banking and industry. New towns and cities sprang up. In 1855, the Royal Mint set up a branch in Sydney and started minting sovereigns there. It was a veritable economic boom. The rush also accelerated the push for democratic reforms and self-governance.

'The discovery of the Victorian Goldfields has converted a remote dependency into a country of worldwide fame,' said the Victorian Gold Discovery Committee in 1854. 'It has attracted a population, extraordinary in number, with unprecedented rapidity; it has enhanced the value of property to an enormous extent; it has made this the richest country in the world; and, in less than three years, it has done for this colony the work of an age.'[25] That's what a mining boom can do for a community.

Like in the California Gold Rush before it, there was also environmental damage, destruction, violence, crime and bankruptcy. Many of Australia's Aboriginals found themselves displaced from their land. The degradation of natural resources harmed their way of life, as did the intrusion of miners on their cultural practices and social structures. The introduction of alcohol and new diseases, for example, sometimes had devastating effects.

By sending convicts down under, Britain was effectively giving diggers free transit and the opportunity to make a fortune. One final impact of the Australian Gold Rush was the end of convict transportation.

Multiple gold rushes created a force of professional prospectors who were ready to travel anywhere at the hint of gold. At a new discovery, first-mover advantage is everything, and prospectors, therefore, move quickly. Surface and alluvial gold are easy to mine. When mining gets deeper it gets harder and more expensive. There followed gold discoveries in every other Australian state except South Australia: first, Western Australia (though its big discoveries, Kalgoorlie and Coolgardie, did not come until the 1890s); then Queensland in 1853; Northern Territory in 1865; and Tasmania in 1877.

In May 1861, gold was discovered in New Zealand. Gabriel Read, a veteran of both California and Australia, was in a stream beneath the Dunstan Mountains of the South Island. 'I shovelled away two and a half feet of gravel, arrived at beautiful soft slate and saw gold shining like the stars in Orion on a dark frosty night,' he said.[26] He panned seven ounces in ten hours. Soon, 2,000 prospectors a week were arriving at the port of Dunedin, whose male population had already gone inland digging. The Molyneaux and Arrow Rivers were particularly rich in pickings. Further discoveries were made in 1864, and immigrants came from Britain and the US, France, Italy, Germany, Greece and, of course, China.

Australasian output matched American into the 1870s. Total global production, boosted also by supply from Russia (40 tonnes per annum in the 1860s), was over 200 tonnes.[27]

What would be the consequence of this huge increase in global gold supply?

The Biggest Casualty of the Gold Rushes

'The road to the City of Emeralds is paved with yellow brick'

L. Frank Baum, *The Wonderful Wizard of Oz*[28]

'There will be considerable surplus,' warned *The Times*. 'The price must fall,' declared *The Economist*, wrong about everything even then.[29] French economist Michel Chevalier wrote an entire book, *On the Probable Fall in the Value of Gold*, in 1857. He was wrong too. What they had failed to see was gold's increased use as money, and what it would replace.

The biggest victim of the gold rush was in fact silver. Its price halved. And it would lose its role as money.

In 1850, only Britain, Portugal, Brazil and a handful of other nations were on pure gold standards; by the end of the century, every major nation bar China was. There was now so much more gold, and paper, silver was no longer necessary.

It might seem strange to the modern mind that the silver-to-gold ratio should have been so important from Newton's time at the Bank of England to the turn of the twentieth century, but it was a huge issue. There was even a famous allegory written about it – a children's story, which would become one of the most popular feature films of all time: *The Wizard of Oz*. I'll come to that in a minute.

The history of bimetallism in the US began in 1791 with the proposals that gold and silver be the basis for the nation's currency at a ratio of 15:1. But like what had happened with silver in the UK, the economic disruption created by the Napoleonic Wars caused the value of US gold coins to be worth more as bullion than as currency, and they vanished from circulation. So, in 1834, with a new coinage act, Congress adjusted the gold-to-silver ratio to 16:1, close enough to Europe's ratio of 15.8:1, and effectively disincentivised the export of coins.

Scarcely had the discoveries in California been made when the US began minting $1 and $20 gold coins, in addition to the $10 eagle. Before the discoveries, the US Mint had struck $4 million worth. In 1851, after the discoveries, it minted over $62 million.[30] Gold is 'virtually the only currency of the country', said a congressman proposing a $3 gold coin in a debate in 1853. The year 1853 would also prove the last time silver dollars were struck, though they still circulated. In practical terms, if not nominal, the US was moving to a gold standard.

By 1857, global gold circulation had increased by almost a third. There was talk at international monetary conferences of an international gold standard from as early as the 1860s. The issue was the impact on the price of silver and the consequences. It had been money for thousands of years. The word even means money in a plethora of different languages. But the move from silver to gold gathered pace. In 1872–3, Germany launched its new gold mark, followed by Denmark, Sweden, Norway and the Netherlands. France, Belgium, Switzerland and Italy had signed up to a Latin bimetallic monetary union in 1865, but this was undermined by the tumbling silver price, so they largely abandoned the silver part of the equation after 1874.

In the US, the Coinage Act of 1873 eliminated the standard silver dollar altogether and with it bimetallism. The act became known as the Crime of 1873. A rearguard action followed, a 'silver crusade', championed by the Populist Party, to get silver reinstated. There was, thought some, a 'deep-laid plot' engineered by a foreign conspiracy to increase the national debt, which would have to be paid in gold.

But in the absence of coinage, silver's usefulness declined. The Panic of 1873, which led to the so-called Long Depression, saw the silver price drop rapidly. Many, especially in the silver-producing states, such as Nevada, Colorado and Idaho, argued that bimetallism was necessary for prosperity and called for a return to pre-1873 laws. These required the mint, which was currently refusing silver, to take all the silver offered and then return it into the economy struck as silver dollars. The increase in the money supply would boost trade, they argued. Critics said that workers' wages would not keep up with price rises, and that the cheap silver would drive gold out of the economy. A watered-down act eventually passed in 1878 that saw the Treasury buying some silver, though not enough to satisfy the free-silver advocates. Twelve years later, the Sherman Silver Purchase Act was passed, which saw increased government purchases of silver and the dwindling of government gold reserves. In 1893, there was another financial crisis: the Panic of 1893. Many, including the president himself, Grover Cleveland, said the panic was caused by inflation resulting from the increase in silver supply and the act was repealed. Economic conditions did not improve, however. In fact, they deteriorated. This was the US's first Great Depression (it would be called that until the 1940s), and it ruined many Americans. Unemployment reached 25 per cent. Farmers went bankrupt, their farms sold to pay their debts. Many died of disease or starvation, many from suicide.

No surprise, the 1894 mid-term elections saw the ruling Democrats obliterated. They suffered the largest loss of seats by a majority party in congressional history. The Republicans gained control of both the House of Representatives and the Senate. Many thought the party would be wiped out in the west in the 1896 presidential election if the Democrats did not support silver. One who thought this way was an ambitious young Democrat by the name of William Jennings Bryan. An impressive orator and champion of bimetallism, he thought the issue could carry him to the presidency.

But to do that, he would have to win the nomination at the Democratic National Convention in Chicago. There, on 9 July 1896, he gave what is widely regarded as one of the greatest speeches in American political history, now referred to as 'the Cross of Gold'.

Bryan had begun the convention with little support, and his speech started softly. 'I would be presumptuous, indeed, to present myself against the distinguished gentlemen to whom you have listened if this were a mere measuring of abilities,' he said. 'But this is not a contest between persons. The humblest citizen in all the land, when clad in the armor of a righteous cause, is stronger than all the hosts of error. I come to speak to you in defense of a cause as holy as the cause of liberty—the cause of humanity.'

But it grew. 'Upon which side will the Democratic Party fight; upon the side of "the idle holders of idle capital" or upon the side of "the struggling masses"?' he asked.

There are two ideas of government. There are those who believe that if you will only legislate to make the well-to-do prosperous, their prosperity will leak through on those below. The Democratic idea, however, has been that if you legislate to make the masses prosperous, their prosperity will find its way up through every class which rests upon them. You come to us and tell us that the great cities are in favor of the gold standard; we reply that the great cities rest upon our broad and fertile prairies. Burn down your cities and leave our farms, and your cities will spring up again as if by magic; but destroy our farms and the grass will grow in the streets of every city in the country.

Then he spoke his final sentence. 'You shall not press down upon the brow of labor this crown of thorns; you shall not crucify mankind upon a cross of gold.'[31]

As he said it, he placed his hands to his temples, and then extended his arms as if crucified and held the pose. There was total silence as Bryan lowered his hands, walked down from the podium, and back to his seat. Then 'bedlam broke loose', as the *Washington Post* reported. 'Delirium reigned supreme.' Delegates threw their hats, coats and handkerchiefs into the air; they knocked aside the policemen who flanked Bryan, raised him to their shoulders, and carried him around the floor. It took twenty-five minutes to restore order. It must have been some speech, and it won him the nomination.

But Bryan lost that 1896 presidential election to William McKinley. He stood again in the next election in 1900, where war with Spain, which had begun in 1898, replaced silver as the dominant issue. Bryan, who took an anti-war stance, lost that election too.

The United States formally adopted the gold standard in 1900. With Austria, Russia, Japan and India now also on gold standards, and only China still bimetallic, the roll call was complete.

But sat in the audience, listening to that Cross of Gold speech, was a forty-year-old author who had previously attended some of Bryan's rallies. His name was L. Frank Baum.

The Wonderful Wizard of Oz

'"I am Oz, the Great and Terrible," said the little man,
in a trembling voice'

L. Frank Baum, *The Wonderful Wizard of Oz*[32]

L. Frank Baum lived for many years in a prairie town in South Dakota working for a local rag, where he witnessed first-hand the plight of farmers in the late nineteenth century. In 1891, the rag went bust and Baum moved to Chicago, where he would later see the effects of the fateful depression of 1893 on urban lives. He was allied to Bryan and the cause of Democratic Populism, but though he went on marches and rallies, he was not a political writer. His desire was to write stories that would 'bear the stamp of our times and depict the progressive fairies of today'.[33]

The result was *The Wonderful Wizard of Oz*, America's 'best-loved homegrown fairy tale'.[34] It tells the story of Dorothy, a young

Kansas girl who is whisked away in a tornado to a strange magical land, where she must follow the Yellow Brick Road to Oz and find the wizard, in order to be able to return home.

The Wonderful Wizard of Oz is, first and foremost, a story, not an allegory as overt as *Candide* or *Animal Farm*. What's more, it is a story aimed at children, not adults. Among the reasons it has been such a success is that any allegory is subordinate to the story. Indeed, the allegory disappears altogether in the sequels – though the original story was not written with a sequel in mind. The sequels only came after demand from readers.

Nevertheless, the story was born out of the raging depression of the time, and the arguments that were circulating around it. Many of the landmarks were inspired by the area where Baum lived in South Dakota, where the prairies were grey and endless – like those outside the house where Dorothy lives. Even Dorothy's Aunt Em's eyes had turned to 'the same gray color to be seen everywhere'. Her Uncle Henry 'was gray also, from his long beard to his rough boots'. Everything was grey with depression. Colour only comes – and lots of it – when Dorothy is magicked away to Oz.

In the film version of the story, Dorothy's slippers were ruby. This was to parade the new technology that was Technicolor. But in the original, the slippers are silver, given to her by the Good Witch of the North, to wear as she sets out on the Yellow Brick Road to the Emerald City, the capital of Oz. The symbolism is obvious once you see it: silver shoes 'tinkling merrily' on a gold path. The Yellow Brick Road is the gold standard, the silver slippers the Populists' desire for free silver, which they believed would bring prosperity to the farmers and workers. The green of the Emerald City, to which the Yellow Brick Road leads, represents the greenback – the US dollar – which proves a facade. The allegory becomes even more explicit at the end of the story when Glinda, the Good Witch of the South, explains to Dorothy that the shoes could have taken her back to Aunt Em on the very first day she came to Oz, if she had known their power: such is the power of silver.

Just as James Bond was named after the author of a birdwatching book that Ian Fleming saw on his shelf when he was trying to come up with a good name for his character, Baum is reputed to have said that the name 'Oz' came from his filing cabinet, labelled 'O–Z'.[35] It has been suggested that Oz might have referred to Australia. But Oz is also an abbreviation of 'ounce', the standard measure for gold and silver bullion. The dollar once was an ounce of silver.

The characters each represent a different group in American society, with Dorothy herself the typical American, plucky and positive in the face of adversity. The Scarecrow, who seeks a brain, represents the farmers and rural communities, dismissed as ignorant and uneducated. The Tin Woodman, who seeks a heart, is the industrial worker. Once independent and hard-working, he had been put under a spell by the Witch of the East (probably the bankers of New York). The Cowardly Lion, who seeks courage, might be the military, or he might be Bryan himself, who was smeared for his anti-war stance during the Spanish–American War, which had begun two years before the book was first published.

The Wizard of Oz himself represents the US President, perceived as all-powerful but really just an ordinary man behind the smoke and mirrors. He is unable to solve the problems of the common people. The green glasses that everyone must wear in the Emerald City symbolise the way in which people are blinded to the truth by the illusions of power.

Once you start looking for symbolism, it is quite easy to find it, even perhaps where none was intended. *The Wonderful Wizard of Oz* is a children's story, but it also sought to champion the common people and challenge the political establishment in the late nineteenth century. That same desire for political and economic reform still pervades today.

The Worst Business Deal in History

'I tell you there wouldn't be any South Africa
at all if it weren't for the mines'

Alan Paton, *Cry, the Beloved Country*[36]

In Johannesburg, South Africa, almost 6,000 feet (1,850 m) above sea level, there is a thirty-one-mile geological formation, a reef some two and a half miles deep, known as the 'white water ridge': the Witwatersrand. Figures vary, but this ridge, which gave the South African currency, the rand, its name, has produced as much as 62,000 tonnes of gold,[37] perhaps 30 per cent of all the gold that has ever been mined (at one point it was almost half, but the deposits are depleted now). In the late 1960s, it was producing 1,000 tonnes per year.[38]

One theory of the Witwatersrand's origin is that it was a meteorite, but the underground basin where the gold is deposited is generally thought to have been a huge inland lake. Ancient alluvial gold settled in the basin to form the deposits.

A Welsh mineralogist by the name of John Henry Davis discovered gold in the region in 1852 and reported his findings to the leader of the new South African Republic, who feared what would happen if the discovery became known. He ordered Davis to sell his gold, worth £600, to the Transvaal Treasury and had him escorted out of the country. Pieter Jacob Marais, a veteran of the California Gold Rush, then found gold in late 1853 on the Jukskei River. Seeking a licence for further exploration, he was told should his findings lead to any disturbance in this new republic's existence, he would be punished by death. No surprise, he soon left the country. Others would also find gold, but the main discovery is generally attributed to an Australian prospector by the name of George Harrison, in 1886. He sold his claim for what would prove the greatest gold deposit of all time for just £10, then disappeared into history. If a worse business deal has ever been done, I should like to know what it is.

Though prospectors seemed to know gold was there, they had failed to understand the geology. Suspecting it to be similar to California and Australia, they had been following streams looking for conventional placer deposits. But here the gold was below the 'veld', as the Boers called it. Field is the literal translation, but savanna is probably more accurate.

Following the rivers, many struck lucky with diamonds instead, with the best pickings on a large farm belonging to two brothers called Johannes and Diederick de Beer. Their name would of course become almost synonymous with diamonds, and the Kimberley mine built on their property one of the deepest open-pit mines ever dug. Hence the name Big Hole. Many mining giants were already nearby, among them Cecil Rhodes, Alfred Beit and Barney Barnato.

Within months of Harrison's discovery, prospectors were arriving from all over the world, including many from Wales and Cornwall. The main mining camp, Ferreira's Camp, became a settlement, which would evolve into the city of Johannesburg. Within ten years it overtook Cape Town to become the largest town in South Africa. Within fifty years, it was one of the largest cities in the world.

Extracting the gold from the rock proved problematic, however, and many of the fine particles were getting lost. Then in 1887, two doctor brothers by the name of Forrest and a chemist by the name of MacArthur, all from Glasgow, found a method of crushing the rock to a powder and then using cyanide to dissolve the gold (and any silver) within (rather as you could separate sugar from sand by dissolving the sugar in warm water). The MacArthur–Forrest process had recovery rates of 96 per cent. Their method suddenly made South Africa viable. The Kimberley diamond magnates quickly circled. The problems of extraction meant that, unlike in California, which was an opportunity for every man, in South Africa the capital-rich mining finance houses dominated, four of them. Output surged. By 1892, annual production was thirty-two tonnes. By the end of the decade, those numbers had quadrupled.

In 1899, the Second Boer War put a stop to production for three years. In fact, the Witwatersrand Gold Rush was a major cause of the conflict.

The Boers were concerned about the large numbers of foreigners, whom they called Uitlanders, migrating to the Witwatersrand. President Paul Kruger of the South African Republic, pursuing his policy of Africa for the Afrikaners, worried Boers would be outnumbered. He began to impose heavy taxes, especially on the sale of dynamite to foreigners, to slow the momentum. The miners then protested to the British, who were glad for an excuse to claim the goldfields as their own. So began the three-year conflict that ended in 1902 with the Treaty of Vereeniging. Control of the Witwatersrand fell to the British.

Production soon resumed, and by 1913, as the First World War loomed, South Africa was producing 280 tonnes – 40 per cent of global output.[39] Eventually, South Africa would produce 50 per cent. It would pay for much of Britain's efforts in the two world wars.

London was the big beneficiary, getting the gig to refine and distribute the gold. Sixty per cent went to the Rothschilds' Royal Mint Refinery and 40 per cent to Johnson Matthey. Even after the Rand Refinery opened in 1921, South Africa's gold still made its way exclusively to London for distribution until 1968. While that relationship lasted, London was the world's premier gold market.

The Witwatersrand Gold Rush brought development, employment and wealth. This part of Africa saw its first railways. Its roads and infrastructure improved beyond all recognition. Employment and opportunity were created for millions of people, whether African, Asian or European. Johannesburg would grow into one of the most important cities in the world. South Africa was unified in 1910. The fortunes made by a few created the super-wealthy class of miners and industrialists known as Randlords. It also brought the most devastating war in the history of South Africa, economic inequality, social uprooting, negative health impacts, pollution and ecological destruction. The pattern of the gold rush repeats.

Today those deposits are thought to be 95 per cent depleted. Some mines now run over two miles underground, the deepest on earth, as the mining companies chase ore. Imagine getting the lift to work in the morning.

The final great gold rush of the nineteenth century began in

1896. A gleam of gold caught the eyes of two prospectors fishing for salmon in 1896 on a tributary of the River Yukon in Northern Canada. They called it Bonanza Creek, and the two managed to pan out some eighty ounces over the next eight days. Though they tried to keep their discovery a secret, when they returned by ship to San Francisco, staked claims and sold their gold, word quickly got out. The papers even reported on it. A stampede followed. Between 1897 and 1898, an estimated 100,000 people set out for the Klondike goldfields, some risking the deep midwinter, trying to get that first-mover advantage. Every steamer on the American west coast was overloaded with diggers. The prospectors were followed by suppliers and outfitters, even writers and photographers. The author Jack London set many of his most famous books, including *The Call of the Wild* and *White Fang*, there.

A few got rich. Many lost their lives. Only 30–40 per cent are thought to have actually made it over the mountains to Klondike. Many died from malnutrition or hypothermia or even in avalanches along the route.

It was the last of the great migrations of gold diggers, and it came just as the United States went on the gold standard. Currencies were now convertible into gold on demand. Shipments of gold were the ultimate means to settle a balance. The central banks of the world cooperated with each other.

For a bit.

10.

The First World War and the End of Sound Money

'The first panacea for a mismanaged nation is inflation
of the currency; the second is war. Both bring a temporary
prosperity; both bring a permanent ruin. But both are
the refuge of political and economic opportunists'

Ernest Hemingway[1]

On 31 July 1914, with ultimatums of war flying around Europe, 5,000 people queued patiently outside the Bank of England, waiting to swap their five-pound notes for sovereigns. After all, gold is safer than paper money. The Bank of England 'promptly exchanged' their notes.[2]

Elsewhere, however, banks had panicked and stopped paying out in gold. Economist John Maynard Keynes accused them of 'a fit of hoarding'. 'The future position of the City of London as a free gold market will be seriously injured if at the first sign of emergency specie payment [payment in coin rather than paper] is suspended,' he told Chancellor David Lloyd George, who agreed. The country was not 'ready for the suspension of specie', Lloyd George said.[3]

In 1913, total central bank holdings amounted to 8,000 tonnes, more than twice private holdings.[4] However – and not for the last time – Bank of England holdings, at just 300 tonnes, were complacently low, less than a third of French holdings, or a seventh of American. 'Our position as a lending nation', it had said a few months before to justify its small position, 'gives us the power of attracting gold from abroad whenever we require it'.

Thus, at the onset of war, was the Bank of England under considerable pressure. But the empire produced over 60 per cent of the world's gold, so arrangements were quickly made to buy the entirety of South African and Australian production. Germany, however, had no links to mine supply and had to buy the gold it needed. It did so secretly from, of all places, London, though with growing numbers of submarines, mines, destroyers and aerial patrols, shipping gold became a dangerous business.

The Largest Recovery of Sunken Gold in History

On 23 January 1917, SS *Laurentic* set sail from Liverpool for Halifax, Nova Scotia, with a crew of 475 and cargo that included mail, supplies and commercial goods. When four on board were found to have yellow fever two days later, it docked on the north coast of Ireland, disembarked them and then, in a bitterly cold blizzard, set off again. There were reports of a German U-boat sighted not far offshore, and *Laurentic* was due to rendezvous with a destroyer escort, but Captain Reginald Norton chose to proceed without it. Why did *Laurentic* need an escort? And why did Norton feel such an urgent need to proceed? It was carrying the largest cargo of gold bullion ever to have crossed the ocean – 39 tonnes, 3,211 gold bars in total[5] – to buy munitions and supplies from North America.

Norton's decision would prove calamitous. About three miles off the coast, *Laurentic* ran into a mine, then another twenty seconds later, listed and began to sink. Forty-five minutes after the explosions, Norton made a final search of the ship for survivors, then boarded a lifeboat, the last man to leave. The crew of 475 had abandoned ship.

Temperatures dropped overnight to minus ten. Some 351 of the 475 died in their lifeboats of hypothermia, soaking wet and freezing.

Some were picked up by fishermen, dead or alive. For weeks afterwards bodies kept washing ashore. One was eventually found 150 miles away in the Outer Hebrides.

The 3,211 bars of gold sank to the bottom of the sea.

'Get Guy and Dusty' came the order from the Admiralty. Guy was Guybon Chesney Castell Damant, a retired Royal Navy officer and a renowned deep-sea diver, also known for his research on preventing decompression illness. Dusty was Ernest Cecil Miller, a younger 'diver of superlative courage',[6] who would go on to become a rear admiral. They and their crew were known as the 'tin can openers' for their work breaking into sunken German vessels to salvage their code books and other valuable intelligence.

Over the next six years they worked every summer at depths of 120 ft (37 m) to retrieve the gold, braving gales, minesweepers exploding mines nearby and numerous cases of the bends. Each box, one foot by one foot by six inches, weighed 140 lb (64 kg). One year they retrieved just seven bars, another 1,255 bars.

In total, Damant and his crew recovered all but twenty-five of the 3,211 bars of gold. For every £100 of gold a diver recovered, he got a half-crown (equivalent to 12.5p). The cost of the operation was about 2.5 per cent of the value of the recovered gold. Damant got a CBE for his trouble.

In the 1930s, three more bars were found. Since then, nothing. It means there are still some 8,500 ounces of gold lying somewhere on the ocean floor in treacherous waters three miles off the coast of Donegal.

The Human Cost of Leaving the Gold Standard

As the First World War began, France, Germany and Russia stopped convertibility of paper into gold within days. The Bank of England did everything but. It increased the paper money supply, especially low-denomination notes, and reduced the coin supply. In 1916, for example, it minted just 2 million sovereigns, compared to 13 million in the year before war broke out. Extensive propaganda campaigns urged people to buy war bonds and savings certificates, while discouraging withdrawal of gold and hoarding. Its campaign to persuade citizens to trade in their coins for notes was so successful that, of the 115 million sovereigns in circulation at the onset of war, 100 million of them were soon in its vaults. The government placed limitations on the export of gold, and there were exchange controls to prevent gold leaving the country to settle international debts. It also declared a temporary moratorium on payments at the onset of war, allowing banks to delay settling certain types of financial transactions. This all helped prevent a run on gold.

France did something similar, calling in 160 million of its napoléons and banning the private export of gold, so that France also ended the war with high reserves. Germany's reserves got depleted by three quarters. The US also cut back on the minting of coins and banned exports to husband reserves, though, domestically, dollar bills remained redeemable.

Thus did most governments, Germany aside, actually end the war with more gold than when they started it. They issued paper, and took in gold. It was their people who ended up with so much less. The US was the big winner, of course, emerging from the war with almost half of all central bank gold. It quickly became the world's leading economic power with its dollar the supreme currency.

But the bottom line is this. None of the Allied Powers, led by Britain, France, Russia, Italy and the United States, nor the Central Powers, led by the German, Austro-Hungarian and Ottoman Empires, had the gold to pay for the war to go to the extent that it did.

With gold alone as money, the war would have had to end when the gold ran out. It really would have been over by Christmas. Debt and paper made that war and all its terrible consequences possible. How about that for a thought?

Some 50 million people lost their lives in the war or to the Spanish flu that followed. Almost an entire generation of young men was wiped out. All that grief, destruction and ruin. The consequences were terrible. Europe's golden age was over, and, relative to the rest of the world, it has pretty much been in decline ever since. The stage was set for Weimar hyperinflation, the rise of Nazism and another war. With the discipline of gold, it simply could not have happened to anything like the same degree. There was not enough gold to pay for it all. Paper and debt – not gold – were the enablers.

If ever there was an argument that money should be independent, and governments should not be allowed anywhere near control of its supply, this is surely it.

After the War and the Return of a (Bogus) Gold Standard

'All that glisters is not gold'

William Shakespeare, *The Merchant of Venice*

After the war, almost everyone in the UK, left and right, agreed that wartime controls should be eradicated as quickly as possible. The desire was to get back to 1914 and build a better country at the same time. An 'effective gold standard should be restored without delay', said Lord Cunliffe, Governor of the Bank of England. Many, especially policymakers, seemed to think Britain could afford extensive social reform, without having to change the economic system, that they could, simply, revert to the gold standard and British imperial might would return. They failed to appreciate just what damage the war had done.

Under a gold standard, with paper money convertible to gold at a fixed rate, and vice versa, it effectively meant foreign exchange rates were fixed, except for the small movements resulting from the costs of exchanging money and transporting gold. But Britain actually came off the gold standard after the war in order to preserve its gold reserves. There was considerable economic pressure. The Bank of England was relieved of its duty to sell gold at a fixed price. The £5 note was still exchangeable for five sovereigns, but, of course, there were hardly any sovereigns now in circulation. Sterling was allowed to float against the dollar, and it promptly fell from $4.76 in 1918 to $3.66 in 1920.[7] That did not please the South African producers, who were now mining half the world's gold tied to their wartime price of £3.89/oz. Their costs had risen, and they were losing out on a better price which they could get for their gold in New York. To prevent outflow, Britain also banned gold exports in 1919. In June of the same year, the US, on the other hand, lifted its ban on gold exports.

The gold market itself slowly returned to business as usual. The Rothschilds, who operated the Royal Mint Refinery (a lease they acquired in 1852), agreed a new price with the South African producers. The daily ritual of the gold fixing was established, where the five principal traders and refiners – Nathan Mayer Rothschild & Sons, Mocatta & Goldsmid, Pixley & Abell, Samuel Montagu & Co. and Sharps Wilkins – met at the Rothschild offices in the City of London and agreed the price for the day. (Today there are fourteen participants at the fixing.)[8] It meant buyers and sellers of size – mining companies, gold-producing nations, central banks – could buy and sell large volumes at an agreed price. London was again the hub of the global gold trade. The only blight on that status was when South Africa established its own refinery, the Rand Refinery, in 1922. Even so, most of their gold was still sold through the Rothschilds and London, even if it wasn't refined there. With the gold market functioning again, now, perhaps, the gold standard could be restored. The narrative gathered pace.

While the currencies of Switzerland and the Netherlands depreciated by about 20 per cent against the dollar, the currencies of Italy, Belgium and France fell between 60 and 80 per cent. Some of that depreciation occurred during the war, some shortly after with all the currency interventions that followed.[9] The German mark collapsed altogether. Russia, meanwhile, had succumbed to revolution. The US, the only country properly on the gold standard, had 45 per cent of central bank gold, compared to France with 8.6 per cent, Britain with 7 per cent and Germany with 3 per cent.[10]

The US was striking coins: 540 tonnes of coins were struck between 1920 and 1924. France struck a minimal amount. Britain and Germany struck no coins at all.

International conferences, in 1920 and 1922 respectively, all resulted in resolutions recommending a return to gold standards. But at a League of Nations conference in 1922, it was agreed that existing gold reserves and stagnant mine supply meant that there was not enough to finance world trade. The solution was to limit gold circulation and use pounds or dollars instead. Returning to proper international gold standards would be no easy feat.

Britain experienced price increases, first because of the war, then with the removal of rationing, but post-war deflation reversed this. Prices fell 50 per cent between February 1920 and December 1922. This strengthened the currency, and it rallied against the dollar. To rebuild its gold stock, the Bank of England kept interest rates high and continued to block gold exports. Helpfully, the Federal Reserve in the United States had cut its interest rates and allowed credit to expand in America, prompting gold to stop flowing there in any meaningful quantities. By 1924, Britain was through its post-war slump, and Montagu Norman, Governor of the Bank of England, was determined to return to gold. It was a matter of principle. For him gold was, as financial historian Liaquat Ahamed put it, 'one of the pillars of a free society, like property rights or habeas corpus, which had evolved in the Western liberal world to limit the power of government'.[11] Norman wanted to restore the City as the world's leading banker and sterling as the leading currency. If they did not restore gold payments on the pound, even the German mark would become a more popular currency, he said to the Treasury Committee. Moreover, he wanted first-mover advantage: other countries would surely do the same. Switzerland, South Africa, the Netherlands, Sweden and Australia were all making noises. Norman did not want to be beaten to this objective, and he worried that further delay in readopting gold would lead to outflows of the metal from London with reduced confidence in both the country and the pound. What's more, with the pound close to its pre-war level,

Britain could return to gold at the same, pre-war rate, something other countries in Europe could not accomplish. It would be a return to how things were.

Keynes, however, and other advisors besides, believed the restored pre-war valuation would be too high to sustain. Overvaluing sterling, he warned – rightly as it turned out – would create 'many difficult and injurious things' for British industry'.[12]

At a dinner given by the chancellor, Winston Churchill, on 17 March 1925, the course was set. The political pressure was too great. 'There is no escape,' said Reginald McKenna, chairman of Midland Bank. 'You have got to go back, but it will be hell.' The following month, Churchill announced that gold and the pound would once again be interchangeable. But there was a big but. 'We are [not] going to issue gold coinage,' he explained. 'That is quite unnecessary for the purpose of the gold standard [and] would be an unwarrantable extravagance.' Really?

Under Newton's gold standard, not only were notes exchangeable for gold, but there were plenty of gold coins in circulation. This new gold standard was going to keep gold in the vaults of central banks, not in the pockets of the people. Notes would only be exchangeable for gold with the permission of the Bank of England, though it would be obliged to sell bars of no less than 400 oz against legal tender notes (amounts no ordinary citizen would ever have). Churchill justified it, saying if Britain did not return, 'the whole of the rest of the British Empire would have taken it without us and it would have come to a gold standard, not on the basis of the pound sterling, but a gold standard of the dollar.'[13] The gold was all but removed. The system was bogus. No wonder it failed. A gold standard in which ordinary people don't handle actual gold is like a library that won't let you touch the books.

Within five years of Britain's return, virtually the entire world was using a gold standard once more. Yet while the US minted another 925 tonnes of gold, Britain minted none.

With interest rates so high and sterling so overvalued, Britain's exports suffered. There was economic stagnation. Unemployment rose. Industrial strife followed. Sterling became an easy target for speculators.

But this new international gold 'standard' was rebuilt country by country. Germany did so as part of reforms intended to end hyperinflation, as did Austria in 1923 and Hungary in 1924. In all three countries, the restored gold standard coincided with, or was followed up by, the introduction of new currencies. Italy returned to the gold standard in 1927, like Britain at a rate judged too high. The high exchange rate, or 'quota novanta', was something of a vanity project for its head of government, Benito Mussolini. Like the British pound, the Swiss franc and Dutch guilder also returned to their pre-war exchange rates. Other currencies stabilised too, if at lower levels. Many European nations, the French included, restored their standards at lower valuations, reflecting the larger intervening depreciation they had experienced.

Whereas about 10 per cent of nations were on the gold standard in 1921, and 20 per cent by 1924, 70 per cent were by 1928 and 90 per cent by 1929. In 1930, Japan was one of the last large economies to return to gold, and the number of countries on this new gold standard peaked in 1931.

But, as I say, this was not a true gold standard. Britain, France, Germany and the US held 70 per cent of central bank gold stock, but only 10 per cent of that gold circulated, compared to 56 per cent in 1900.[14] Gold flows had vanished, along with gold coinage. It was only halfway to a gold standard, if that.

Moreover, the amount of foreign currencies held by central banks was on the increase – from around 19 per cent on the eve of the First World War to more than 40 per cent by 1929[15] – though this varied considerably from country to country. Austria for example, though a gold-standard country, had very little gold and 97 per cent of its assets in foreign currency. Indeed, one goal of the new standard was to suppress the gold price so that nations could build their reserves. But without the gold rushes of the previous century, mine supply was dwindling, and production was disincentivised by the suppressed price. Mining output in 1929, at 600 tonnes, was 15 per cent lower than it was in 1915. South Africa alone was responsible for 53 per cent of it. (The British Empire yielded 71 per cent of world output.) At over 50 per cent, monetary gold was the mainstay of international demand. Jewellery accounted for less than 25 per cent.

It was all about to change.

The Wall Street Crash 'came with a speed and ferocity that left men dazed,' said *The New York Times*, 'the bottom, simply fell out of the market.'[16] It quickly exposed the fragility of the new gold standard. World trade slumped by a third. Unemployment skyrocketed. Agricultural and commodity prices collapsed, leading exporters to suspend debt repayments. That led to problems in bond markets. Scrambling for cover, companies and investors withdrew gold from London, precipitating devaluation and default. In Austria in May 1931, one major bank, Credit-Anstalt, collapsed, followed by another, Darmstädter, in Germany, triggering a banking crisis in Europe. Germany lost 40 per cent of its gold reserves just in May and June. In July, Britain lost 20 per cent in two weeks. Nobody could find a way to prop things up. Montagu Norman, key architect of this revived gold standard, collapsed from exhaustion. Then, in August, Britain's Labour government fell. In September 1931, the Bank of England suspended its 'obligation to sell gold at a fixed price . . . For the time being'. This was one of many temporary government measures that became permanent. Montagu Norman, who was convalescing, got a cable from his deputy, Ernest Harvey, saying, 'Sorry we have to go off tomorrow and cannot wait to see you before doing so.'[17] Britain never went back to gold.

Britain's departure caused further panic. The fear was that the US would follow Britain and stop redeeming its notes. While they still could, the central banks of Europe, never mind large institutions, moved quickly to trade their dollars for gold at the Federal Reserve. Between August and October, the US sold 1,100 tonnes, 17 per cent of its reserves, mainly to the central banks of Belgium, France, the Netherlands and Switzerland. In all, in May to December 1931, Britain and the US lost 1,800 tonnes, 90 per cent to those four countries, whose reaction was quite understandable: the value of their sterling holdings had gone from $4.86 to $3.25 overnight.

In all of this, London's role as trading hub continued. Indeed, the market saw great activity. The Bank for International Settlements (more on this in a moment) calculated that between 1931 and 1936, some 3,110 tonnes, equal to 70 per cent of all the gold mined in that period, fell into private hands, where it was hoarded. By this point, Britain, Austria, Canada, Finland, Germany, Japan, Norway, Sweden and Portugal had all left the gold standard. Belgium, France, Italy, Switzerland and the US remained. They now had 77 per cent of central bank gold stocks.

But it was the economies of those that devalued that revived quickest. Their exports got cheaper.

Meanwhile, America got a new president.

The Greatest Theft in American History

'This is the end of Western Civilization'

Lewis W. Douglas, Budget Director[18]

Between the stock market crash of 1929 and the inauguration of Franklin D. Roosevelt in March 1933, US money supply fell by a third, the stock market fell by 80 per cent, unemployment rose to 25 per cent, and over 9,000 banks (as many as half the US total) disappeared. Depression was visible everywhere: homes and farms foreclosed, people queuing in bread lines, parks in New York now full of tents to shelter the homeless. From his election win to his inauguration, Roosevelt had 115 days to assemble a team and work out the details of his policies, which had been vague during the campaign – just some promise of a 'New Deal'.

Now America's gold was fleeing the country. Indeed, on the very day of his inauguration, some 164 tonnes were reserved by foreign accounts. Ordinary citizens, because of the many bank failures, started hoarding gold at home rather than keep their money in dollars in the bank. In the four days before he took office, the public turned over $200 million in paper dollars.

Roosevelt had barely mentioned the gold standard during the election, or the devaluation of the dollar. But, with so many countries dropping out – just France, Belgium, the Netherlands, Italy, Poland and Switzerland now remained – the issue was a huge one. How would America support it? Many clearly doubted its ability to do so.

Roosevelt was inaugurated on Saturday 4 March. On the Monday, he rushed through legislation, declaring a bank holiday on tenuous legal grounds to prevent 'further hoarding of coin, bullion or currency or speculation in foreign exchange', which he deemed 'heavy and unwarranted'.[19]

He villainised both hoarders and speculators. Surely the former, with banks collapsing everywhere, are just protecting what's theirs, while the latter are equally justified: foreigners getting their gold while they can, before devaluation.

His declaration was almost inevitable, though. The banking system was in crisis. The Federal Reserve had advised the outgoing president, Herbert Hoover, to declare a bank holiday on his last day in office, but he left the decision to Roosevelt. Then, on the Saturday, Roosevelt's inauguration day, the stock exchange in New York announced it was suspending operations on the Monday, because of a lack of bank credit for brokers.

On Thursday 9 March, there followed the Emergency Banking Act, which allowed the government to inspect the health of all banks, ensuring that only the institutions it deemed financially sound could reopen. This restored public confidence by reassuring citizens that their deposits were safe. It granted the president the authority to regulate banking transactions and foreign exchange. It also allowed for the Treasury, if necessary, to require 'all individuals, partnerships, associations and corporations to pay and deliver to the

Treasurer of the United States any or all gold coin, gold bullion, and gold certificates'.

There was no legal or political precedent. There had not been any discussion linking private ownership of gold to the banking crisis. Roosevelt had only held office for five days. On the sixth, he issued an executive order temporarily suspending the convertibility of the dollar into gold by prohibiting all domestic gold payments and restricting international gold movements.

Then the banks were allowed to reopen. But 2,000 of them, still running at the time the bank holiday was declared, never opened their doors again.[20]

On 5 April 1933 came Executive Order 6102, 'Forbidding the Hoarding of Gold Coin, Gold Bullion, and Gold Certificates'. It declared, 'All persons are hereby required to deliver on or before May 1, 1933, to a Federal Reserve Bank . . . all gold coin, gold bullion and gold certificates now owned by them.' Failure to comply would be punishable by 'fine, imprisonment, or both'.[21]

Suddenly owning gold was a serious crime. 'This is the end of Western Civilization,' said Budget Director Lewis W. Douglas. Some of that gold might have been US minted gold coinage, but much of it was personal property. Nuggets, medallions, bars, collectibles, foreign coins: the act made no distinction. All gold was confiscated, not just legal tender gold. FDR did so to restrict 'unjustified enrichment'.[22] He must have known he was going to devalue, but it is this conflation of gold coin and gold property that makes Roosevelt's confiscation so alarming an episode.

In the next few months, citizens handed in some 500 tonnes of gold,[23] as well as certificates, some issued as long ago as the Civil War. They thought this was a temporary measure, a national emergency, and the exchange was seen as a civic duty. They would not be allowed to own gold again for over forty years, until 1975. Exports at $20.67/oz were briefly allowed to continue, but those to France and the Netherlands quickly escalated, so a month later Roosevelt banned these as well. 'Congratulate me,' he said on 18 April. 'We are off the gold standard.'[24]

The dollar dropped 28 per cent almost immediately, while the gold price, which had been $20.67/oz for ninety-nine years – since 1834 – rose to $27/oz. American exports, however, became more competitive, and within months factory employment began to improve.

Many bonds had been agreed – issued by states, municipalities, railroads, utilities, industrial concerns – with the standard clause 'in gold coin of the United States of America of or equal to the present standard of weight and fineness'. With the dollar devaluing, if these obligations were paid off in gold coins (now worth significantly more), the transfer of wealth would have been staggering. So in June, legislation was passed to nullify contractual obligations for payment in gold.

It's one thing devaluing the currency. This is a common crime committed by leaders against their citizens. But Roosevelt's intention by confiscating gold was to make sure that citizens did not enjoy any of the increase in the value of gold. Only the Treasury would get that.

Roosevelt slid further down the slippery political slope in August with another executive order which redefined the crime of 'hoarding' to 'holding'. We see just how devious, Orwellian even, the use of language was in politics, even then.

Meanwhile, Roosevelt, taking Treasury Secretary Henry Morgenthau's advice, would decide the gold price each day, while he ate his breakfast, usually raising it by a few cents. One day he decided on a 21c rise. The reason? 'It's a lucky number, because it is three times seven.' By January 1934, the price had reached $34/oz. At the end of the month, Roosevelt issued a proclamation fixing the price at $35, which lasted until 1968. The devaluation of the dollar was complete. From $20 to $35, a devaluation of 70 per cent, confiscated from American citizens. The process took eleven months. His spending plans were enabled. There had not been a single mention of it in the manifesto on which he was elected. 'The whole world will be put into bankruptcy,' Montagu Norman had warned, but Roosevelt just laughed at old 'pink whiskers', as he called him.

Stalin Sends Spies to Study American Mining and the US Builds Fort Knox

'Gold is not everything, but everything needs gold'

Russian proverb

Over the next fifteen years, US gold reserves would increase to unprecedented levels. But the large part of that increase did not come from American citizens handing their gold in. Roosevelt and Morgenthau announced they would buy all US mine supply (sixty tonnes annually). Then they said they would buy any gold imported to the US Assay Office. The US even began buying gold on foreign markets to protect the price at higher levels.

But the devaluation first of sterling, then of the dollar, kick-started a mining boom. Until then, worldwide production had been sliding, costs had been rising and no new significant discoveries had been made. But now, effectively, the gold price had risen 70 per cent. Suddenly, mining was a lot more profitable, and it boomed. Homestake, America's largest gold producer in the 1930s, saw a 20 per cent increase in output at its South Dakota mine, with more investment in deeper shafts and better pumps. It became perhaps the best-performing stock in the US. Americans might not be able to own gold – but they could still own Homestake.

Many went to California, searching for the gold the 49ers had missed. Not quite a second gold rush, but thousands of previously unemployed became gold prospectors. In all, US production doubled. Output in Canada and Australia increased too. It even increased in Russia.

Joseph Stalin wanted to revive the glory days of Russian gold mining. Until the California discoveries of 1849, Russia had been the world's largest gold producer, and its output gradually increased until the revolution of 1917 disrupted things. Now Stalin, who had read books about the California Gold Rush, wanted to inspire something similar in Siberia.

He even sent an agent to the US, masquerading as a professor from the Moscow School of Mines, to study American gold mining, and then recruited an American mining engineer to mastermind a Soviet Gold Rush. Prospectors who found deposits were richly rewarded, and special stores were set up with food, equipment, clothing and luxury goods, which only accepted gold as payment. Meanwhile, Stalin's purges provided plenty of cheap labour.

By the mid-1930s, the Soviet Union was producing 155 tonnes annually. Only South Africa produced more. The Soviet Union remained the world's second-largest producer until 1990. Between 1940 and 1980, the two nations were responsible for 80 per cent of global output.

The Soviet Union kept some of its gold. Estimates are that its reserves were around 500 tonnes in the mid-1930s, rising to 2,050 tonnes in 1952. But we also know it sold lots, both before and after the Second World War. In 1937, for example, it sold 187 tonnes through London. Between 1952 and 1964, it sold 2,900 tonnes through London and Paris.[25]

South Africa's leaving the gold standard in 1932 led to a 22 per cent rise in output over the next three years, because it now became profitable to process lower-grade ore. But other nations were now producing so much that South Africa went from producing 51 per cent of global output in 1930 to 33 per cent by 1935. That percentage would rise above 50 per cent again by the end of the war.

The US government did indeed buy every ounce that came into the US Assay Office. The Bank of France met with an army of arbitrageurs trying to buy gold at the old French fixed price and sell it into New York. France lost 180 tonnes in the first month of $35 gold. Not only did French stock make its way back across the Atlantic but so did Belgian, Swiss, Dutch and Italian, as they tried to cling on to outdated fixed prices: an incredible 2,000 tonnes by 1936.[26] Eventually, these nations were forced off their gold standards. In 1936, the new Popular Front government of France took

France off, promising greater spending and higher wages, and devaluing the franc. It placed an embargo on gold transactions, and citizens were given one month to declare their holdings or surrender gold at the pre-devaluation price. Unlike in the US, few did. They had less trust in their leaders, it seems.

US reserves rose meanwhile by 50 per cent to 9,000 tonnes, accumulating so much gold that in 1936 a special depository had to be built to store it. It decided on a location safely inland, far from the more vulnerable coastal cities, next to the Fort Knox military installation in Kentucky. It would become a symbol of American power.

The gold flows were only going one way. The US could support $35 gold almost indefinitely, it seemed. Its official holdings by 1939 on the eve of the Second World War were 15,679 tonnes. They were going to get higher still. The US continued buying through the Second World War and after, as European central banks sold what little gold they had for the dollars they needed to rebuild their shattered economies.

The high watermark of US reserves came in 1949: 22,000 tonnes, a figure not far off half of all the gold that had ever been mined.

So much gold had come to the US that Roosevelt's confiscation was really not necessary.

In ancient Egypt, gold was a royal prerogative: ordinary citizens could not own it. Something similar had happened in the US. The government could own gold, but not citizens. Roosevelt called this new system a 'managed standard'.

It was another bogus standard, and so doomed to fail.

The Greatest Investment in Prospecting Ever Made

Here's one for the geologists. In the 1930s, a young German geologist by the name of Rudolf Krahmann suggested that Gold Fields, one of the biggest mining companies in South Africa, try out a magnetometer to locate new reefs. Gold Fields offered Krahmann a fee of $840 plus $560 expenses, which Krahmann accepted. It had just made the greatest investment in prospecting ever.

Krahmann discovered the West Wits Line, where many mines, including the world's largest (West Driefontein), were built. Geologists came back with two of the greatest holes ever drilled: 5,430 and then 8,000 grams per tonne of rock. The four new mines built there yielded 6,000 tonnes of gold over the next forty years. Extraordinary.

II.

The Nazis and the Greatest Hoard
of Treasure Ever Discovered

'We'll be building a solid state . . . without an ounce of gold behind it'

Adolf Hitler[1]

On 4 April 1945, as US forces advanced into central Germany, in the dense forests of Thuringia, an area nicknamed 'the green heart of Germany', they took a little-known village by the name of Merkers. As was normal, they then imposed a curfew on the locals.

At dawn the following morning, two women broke the curfew. One was about to give birth and needed to see a midwife. Two US officials stopped them. Satisfied with their answers, they then gave them a lift. Driving past the entrance to a mine, they asked the women what it was. 'A salt mine,' said the women. Just a few days before, they added, the Nazis had stored the Reichsbank gold there.

The story was soon corroborated by escaped slave labourers and a British prisoner of war, who had helped unload the trains carrying the loot. Soldiers went to investigate. Inside, not far from the entrance, they found several hundred bags, each containing about a million Reichsmarks. Deeper into the mine, they found several hundred more, as well as hundreds of woollen coats, before, some 2,000 feet underground, coming up against a steel door.

They blew a hole in the wall next to the door to find a room packed with bag upon bag of gold coins – 3,326 bags in total – neatly arranged in rows. There were bags of gold rings, of silver, a bag of platinum even, and fifty-five boxes of bullion bars.[2] In total, some 200 tonnes of gold alone, more than 3,600 bales of foreign currency

133

and thousands of works of art – priceless paintings and sculptures – among them the 3,000-year-old bust of Egyptian Empress Nefertiti.

The BBC reported the find the following day. Reichsbank president Walther Funk was listening. 'Everything is finished,' he said to his wife, heartbroken.[3] The mine was supposed to have been blown up if enemy forces ever got close. Then it would have taken years to excavate, during which time Germany could restabilise itself under Hitler's leadership. The gold could then be used to rebuild the country. The plan had failed.

This was the largest treasure hoard ever discovered. Even so, the British Ministry of Economic Warfare estimated that Merkers represented only a fifth of all gold held in Germany at the end of the war.[4] Another 134 hoards would also be discovered and sent to Frankfurt for sorting, though none on the same scale as here.[5] Tonne after tonne had long since left Germany. Merkers was just a fraction of what the Nazis stole. We'll never know quite how much they did.

Gold was a centrepiece of Nazi strategy. They accumulated as much of it as they possibly could, by whatever means necessary. They confiscated it, they stole it, they looted it, they ripped it from the mouths of those they exterminated, and they robbed the central bank of every country they invaded. Hitler, who, in the words of historian George M. Taber, 'knew nothing about economics and cared little for gold',[6] thought he could fight the war without it. But those close to him – his number two, Reichsmarschall Hermann Göring, his private secretary Martin Bormann, head of the secret service Heinrich Himmler, and Reichsbank president Hjalmar Schacht – felt differently. Schacht later even argued in his book *Gold for Europe* that the solution to Europe's economic problems in the 1930s was to establish a new gold standard.

'In wartime', Georg Thomas, one of Hitler's senior economists, told him, 'Germany will need a considerable reserve of gold and foreign exchange for propaganda, espionage and other purposes.'[7] Thomas was right. Gold enabled the Nazis. By 1942 they had it in abundance.

Some of that gold was used to finance the war machine, some to ensure their survival after the war was over. There might have been 200 tonnes or so of Nazi gold hidden in Merkers, but they stole three times as much from Europe's central banks,[8] not to mention the private and institutional gold that ended up in their hands (likely almost as high a figure). In exchange for raw materials from abroad, between 1939 and 1945, Germany shipped roughly 790 tonnes[9] of stolen gold. Just the gold transactions of the Reichsbank between 1939 and 1945 were north of 810 tonnes.

Where did the gold go? To Switzerland. To Portugal. To Sweden. To Spain. To Turkey. To the Vatican. And to South America. Official Argentine gold reserves, according to one source, went from 346 tonnes at the beginning of the war to 1,173 by the end. Brazil's went from 50 to 346 tonnes.[10] That's just the official stuff. Vast quantities made their way to South America to sit in private hands, to ensure the future of fleeing Nazis and build the next Reich. Vast quantities have never been found.

Hitler's Secret Gold Reserves

After the First World War, Germany's reparations were set at 132 billion gold marks. That would be 47,300 tonnes of gold.[11] As already noted, it was an amount not far off all the mined gold in the world at that time. In total, the Allies only ever received some 15 per cent of that.

The Dawes Plan brokered by the US government allowed American money to finance German industrial reconstruction, so the Germans could then pay reparations to Britain and France, who could then repay the US for its war loans. One of the reasons the US was slow to join the Second World War was the investments of Ford, General Motors and other US industrial giants. As Britain fought for its life in 1940, some 300 US companies continued business as usual in Germany, heavily invested in the country's industry. No wonder Germany was not fully shut out of the international financial system until 1941.

In the inter-war years, a select group of bankers wielded significant influence over the global financial system, among them Montagu Norman of the Bank of England, Benjamin Strong of the Federal Reserve and Hjalmar Schacht of the Reichsbank. They helped set up the Bank for International Settlements (BIS) in 1930 to manage the world's gold reserves and oversee reparations payments. Ironically, just after the BIS was founded, the reparations issue faded, and by 1932, they were cancelled altogether, as the new international gold standard fell apart – though that was considered a passing phase.

The BIS held gold for member countries. Even though gold might change hands, in the vaults of the BIS, the Bank of England or the Federal Reserve, it was simply that the stored gold changed ownership. Hard to believe but sometimes it was just a note on top of the bullion that signified who owned it. On one trip to the US, where Federal Reserve Chairman Benjamin Strong decided to show Schacht the Berlin gold stored in its vaults, they couldn't find it. 'Never mind,' said Schacht. 'I believe you when you say the gold is there. Even if it weren't, you are good for its replacement.'[12]

When Hitler assumed power in 1933, his two main priorities were rearmament and reducing unemployment. Schacht created several phantom accounts to hide Reichsbank gold reserves, so the rest of the world would not realise the extent of German rearmament. In 1934, hidden gold amounted to about 40 per cent of published holdings. By 1938, it was four times published holdings.[13]

As Germany was forced out of the international financial system, gold provided the solution. Established in 1940 and controlled by Göring, the Devisenschutzkommando (DSK) – literally 'currency protection commando' – was a Nazi unit of handpicked SS soldiers whose purpose was to loot. In newly invaded countries they went to banks and, accompanied by an employee and a notary, took gold, currency, diamonds, bond certificates, anything of value. The sole mission of the DSK was to search and locate assets, but not to administer them. That responsibility lay elsewhere. Göring retained personal control over stolen art and his preferred works were sent to his retreat in Carinhall. The gold, mostly, went to the Reichsbank.

Stolen gold was carefully weighed, catalogued and stored, but to disguise its provenance it was often resmelted and then stamped with pre-war German markings. Transporting and transferring gold was a problem, however. For this the Nazis required banks.

Neutral Switzerland provided the solution.

How Switzerland Served the Nazis in Exchange for Its Freedom

'It's not enough to have money. You need to have it in a Swiss bank account'

German quip[14]

Tonnes of gold and precious gems were processed through the neutral countries, such as Sweden, Spain and, most notoriously of all, Switzerland.

On the one hand, Switzerland upheld the integrity of its banking. But in doing so it enabled one of the most abhorrent crimes in history. A key part of the western war strategy was to restrict German trade. Partly to save their own skin, the Swiss undermined this, making possible so much of what the Nazis did.

In the early stages of the war, Switzerland provided extended credit to Germany. It also processed payment for critical resources – rubber from Japanese-occupied Malaya, iron from Sweden, chromium from Turkey, tungsten from Spain and Portugal. As Germany's gold holdings grew and the war progressed, as much as 70 per cent of stolen Nazi gold – not to mention currency, silver, platinum, gems, stocks and bonds – passed through Swiss hands.[15] In return for enabling the war machine, the Nazis didn't invade, and the Swiss kept their freedom.

Portugal swore to remain neutral, and then sold vast amounts of tungsten, often at inflated war prices, to both sides. At first, Germany paid Portugal with cash, but then, in 1941, the Central Bank of Portugal discovered the Nazis had been using counterfeit money, so it insisted all further payments be in gold. By some accounts, Portugal became the second-largest recipient of Nazi gold: its holdings increased from 63 tonnes in 1939 to 356 tonnes in 1945.[16]

Spain was nominally neutral too, and an important source of tungsten and other minerals, not to mention foodstuffs. It owed Germany for its support during the civil war and proved strategically important as a conduit to Argentina, Paraguay and Chile. (Portugal did the same for Brazil.) By the end of the war, Spain's debts to Germany were settled and its gold holdings had almost trebled.[17]

Spain and Portugal were both under dictatorships, but liberal Sweden was also a source of essential goods, in this case iron ore. Northern Sweden – Lapland – supplied about 90 per cent of European ore. In total, Sweden received some sixty-six tonnes of gold from Germany, of which an estimated 10 per cent came from Holocaust victims.[18] Only after 1943, when the war turned against the Nazis, did Sweden try to improve relations with the Allies.

The Gold Declaration of January 1943 was supposed to mark the point at which the Allies, especially the US, took a harder line towards the neutrals, but Switzerland continued receiving consignments of gold from Germany as late as 1944.[19] Privately, Nazi officials and SS leaders also secreted millions of dollars' worth of gold, currency and artworks in Switzerland, hidden in numbered accounts, immune to scrutiny thanks to banking laws, enacted, ironically, in 1934 to provide anonymity to Jews escaping the Nazis. The Reichsbank was still selling bullion to the BIS as late as 1945.

The Nazi March on Gold

'One blood demands one Reich'

Adolf Hitler, *Mein Kampf*

Austria was the first country to fall to the Nazis. At daybreak on 12 March 1938, German forces marched unopposed into Austria, derailing a referendum scheduled for the next day to decide on whether to unite with Germany.

Knowing invasion was coming, the Austrians had packed their gold to be sent to the Bank of England, but they hadn't actually dispatched it. There were some sixty-nine tonnes. (German official holdings at the time were just twenty-five tonnes – though it had another four times that hidden.) On the day of the invasion, two commandos and an official entered Austria's central bank and took possession of its gold. Schacht then gave the order to transfer the gold to Berlin.

Austrians then saw the value of their currency halved: such manipulation of exchange rates was a tactic the Nazis would repeat practically everywhere they conquered. Occupying soldiers could then acquire stuff on the cheap and send it back to Germany. This made the Nazis popular at home.

The following month, the referendum took place, and union with Germany met with 99.7 per cent approval.

Austria also had six tonnes stored with the Bank of England and another seventeen tonnes with the BIS. Cables were sent instructing the banks to transfer the gold to Germany's account and the orders were carried out. Germany now controlled all Austrian gold: ninety-two tonnes in total.

The Czechs were better prepared: they had shipped most of their ninety-five tonnes abroad to the Bank of England and the BIS. It didn't make much difference.

As with Austria, the day they invaded, Nazi troops went straight to the central bank and, brandishing guns, ordered officials to sign documents putting the six tonnes they hadn't shipped under German control. They then sent orders to the BIS and the Bank of England to sign over Czech gold to the Reichsbank, and the banks carried out the orders. When the *Financial Times* broke the story, there was national outcry. Prime Minister Neville Chamberlain – who by now had acquired the nickname 'J'aime Berlin' on the continent – met with a torrent of anger, as did Montagu Norman.

The Poles were next, and they were less well prepared than the

Czechs. They still had seventy tonnes in Warsaw and other regional locations. As the Germans closed in, with the Luftwaffe strafing the capital with bombs and the roads packed with people fleeing the city, fifteen anonymous-looking buses loaded with gold departed the National Bank of Poland and made their way on the long journey south to the village of Sniatyn, to meet with trucks and trains carrying gold from other locations around the country. From Sniatyn the gold was taken by train to the Romanian port town of Constanța, and then shipped to Istanbul. From there it was trained to Beirut, then taken to Toulon in ships which zigzagged their way across the Mediterranean to avoid U-boats, before being moved up to Paris. When Germany invaded France the following year, the seventy tonnes were shipped to Senegal before finally ending up in New York. What a journey!

Even Britain was no longer considered safe, let alone France, and in 1938–9 thousands of tonnes were shipped across the Atlantic – even Mussolini's Italy sent gold there. There was a risk the international monetary system could be destabilised, said an angry Britain, before eventually shipping its own gold: 1,499 tonnes, perhaps the largest transfer of wealth ever. The Nazis claimed the US was trying to grab Europe's gold. In fact, the US was helping the Nazis by providing their trading partners Portugal, Spain, Switzerland and Sweden with somewhere to keep gold they had received from Germany. 'We now have 85 per cent of the world's monetary gold,' said Treasury official Harry White in 1940.[20]

As nations spent heavily on the war effort, the US, which could turn over weapons and planes quickly, was happy to take their gold in exchange. No wonder it was so slow to get involved in the war.

Jewish Gold: Seized, Stolen and Resmelted

The Nazis were not the only ones to make use of Switzerland. Throughout the 1930s, many Jews did the same. In August 1939 alone for example, just before the Nazi invasion of Poland, there were 17,000 transfers from Poland to Switzerland.

From as early as 1934, tax laws in Germany discriminated against Jews, one of the richest socio-economic groups in the country. They were required to declare their worth, and then had a 20 per cent wealth tax imposed on them. If it emerged that they had concealed anything, the penalty was ten years in jail and all wealth confiscated. Those who fled the country also had to pay an exit tax, though eventually they would not be able to take any capital with them at all, or indeed even leave.

In 1938, the Nazis nationalised all Jewish-owned property. In return, Jews were issued war bonds that would only be honoured if Germany won the war. The Nazis then sold their possessions. They also sold the possessions of those Jews who had already fled the country, those from nations they conquered and those sent to concentration camps, with the profits of any sales forwarded to the Reichsbank in Berlin. Their gold, however, the Nazis did not sell: that they took and resmelted.

The search for Jewish wealth was relentless. The Nazis knew the Jews had lots of it. They thought nothing of violence or torture, as houses were turned upside down in search of valuables. It went on everywhere they conquered. In France, Belgium and the Netherlands, the Devisenschutzkommando was ruthless, supported by informers and collaborators known as 'Vertrauensmänner' or 'V-männer' (confidential agents). Himmler issued orders to extract dental gold – fillings, caps or dentures – as victims entered camps, and the practice continued until the war's end. Forty-eight dentists stood trial after the war, but many more likely participated.

Concentration camp loot arrived in Berlin in battered suitcases or canvas bags. One shipment from 1944, for example, listed as case 71, contained 1,536 gold or silver bracelets, 2,656 watches, pearl necklaces, gold cufflinks, tiaras, Passover cups, silverware and currency.[21] The Reichsbank realised the market value, and the proceeds were then deposited to an SS account under the name Melmer. From there it was transferred to an account under the name of Max Heiliger, a slush fund for the SS leadership. The name Heiliger means 'holy one'. Overall, it's thought around eleven tonnes were stolen from concentration camp victims in this way.[22]

Where it ended up is not entirely known, because of the chaos of those final days of war. But there is little doubt that resmelted bars of concentration camp gold sit in the vaults of the world's central banks today, bearing false pre-war stamps, their origins erased.

Whether by theft, confiscation or tax, precisely how much wealth was taken from Jews, whether in Germany or in the conquered territories, is unknown, but a 2010 study by the German Ministry of Finance found that stolen Jewish wealth paid for roughly one-third of Germany's Second World War effort.[23] A staggering sum.

The Incredible Flight of Norway's Gold

On 9 April 1940, the Nazis launched a simultaneous invasion of Denmark and Norway. Denmark had long since sent its gold to the US and its vaults were empty, but Norway had kept back about a fifth of its gold – fifty tonnes – to back the currency. Anticipating invasion, Norway packed it all into crates – 1,542 in total – ready to be moved at a moment's notice.

As German ships approached on 8 April, the central bank ordered the gold to be moved north from Oslo to Lillehammer. As the last of the trucks were leaving the Norwegian capital, the Nazis arrived to discover there was no gold in the bank. Threatening that everyone would have 'der kopf kaputt' (their heads smashed in), the Nazis discovered the gold had gone to Lillehammer.

In Lillehammer, an official by the name of Fredrik Haslund was given the responsibility of overseeing the transport of the gold. He went out and found some men, and told them to bring picks and shovels, as they would be doing road work. One of them was poet Nordahl Grieg, a relative of composer Edvard Grieg.

They packed the gold onto a train to be moved further north to Åndalsnes on the coast. They arrived in the middle of the night to find Åndalsnes was being heavily bombed. Haslund met with British expeditionary troops, who had landed a few days before, on their way south to bolster Allied defence at Lillehammer. They were agitated because of the bombing and loss of men. Haslund told them about the gold, and also declared Norway was ready to turn over its entire merchant marine fleet of 1,100 ships. The English Captain Vian was astonished. 'I think it is the first time in our history', he said, 'that a captain has been woken up in the middle of the night and offered more than 1,000 ships and £16 million in gold.'

On 21 April, Lillehammer fell. Berlin treasury officials accompanied by the Gestapo arrived at the Bank of Norway, had a locksmith open the vault and found just a few bank notes scattered like tumbleweed.

By now Åndalsnes had been bombed to ruins. Three British cruisers arrived with fresh troops, and the first of the ships was loaded with about nine tonnes of gold. Haslund was awaiting orders to load the other two ships, when he received intelligence that German soldiers would soon be marching down the valley. He should vacate the railway area at once. It took all night to load the remaining crates from the train carriages onto twenty-five trucks. In a convoy half a mile long, bombarded by the Luftwaffe, the trucks made the journey down into the harbour. Miraculously, none took a hit. In the harbour, they met with more bombing, though there the Germans' main targets were moored ships.

The bombardment was so bad that Haslund decided to move to another harbour, Molde, some thirty-five miles away. The trucks made the journey by unpaved country roads. Crossing a fjord by night on a ferry, the trucks arrived at Molde the following morning. The drivers had now gone forty-eight hours without sleep. The gold was hidden in a factory, while the men bunked down to sleep in a nearby school.

Two days later, the British ship HMS *Glasgow* arrived at Molde. They began loading gold as quickly as they could, managing to get 756 crates – some twenty-three tonnes – on board before German bombing forced the captain to cut the ropes and set sail. That left 547 cases – eighteen tonnes – behind.

Haslund had found a steam ship on the other side of town that hauled freight among the islands. The exhausted men navigated their way there through the debris of war and loaded up the steamer, the *Driva*. But the Germans were bombing every ship in sight. Again bombing disrupted loading, before the *Driva* set off leaving thirty crates behind.

The *Driva* was attacked relentlessly, and it eventually ran aground. But some quick thinking got the ship out of the sand: they shifted the gold to the other end of the ship, and the change in weight got it floating again. They took the *Driva* into a nearby fishing village for repairs. How to move the gold without getting bombed? The village police suggested using local fishing boats – puffers – to move the gold north. They would surely not attract Luftwaffe attention, and they could travel by night, piloted by local fishermen who knew the waters.

Under cover of night, the crates were loaded onto four puffers, with Haslund and some guards on the fifth. His escape plan, should the Germans stop them, was to sink the vessels in shallow water. But the puffers passed through the fjords and up the coast without notice. At Gjemnes, they met with the trucks carrying the other thirty crates and loaded them aboard. Two days later, in an uninhabited bay on the island of Inntian, the crates were transferred to two bigger, more seaworthy fishing boats. They continued their journey north, now sometimes travelling by daylight because of the shortening nights. They were sighted by a German pontoon plane, encountered a battle between British and German destroyers and almost ran into a U-boat submerging thirty yards away, before finally anchoring in a small bay near Tromsø – on the ninth day since setting off in the puffers. There they would wait for the British.

In Tromsø, officials from the Bank of Norway audited the gold. It was all there. But the cook on Haslund's boat became ill. A doctor diagnosed her with scarlet fever. Haslund explained that he too had felt ill for several weeks: he then learnt that throughout this entire journey he too had been suffering from scarlet fever.

The British arrived and the cargo was loaded onto their ship, HMS *Enterprise*. At anchor it survived a Nazi air attack and, with Haslund on board, set off for Britain. They arrived at Scapa Flow three days later and from there travelled down to Plymouth, from where the gold was transferred to the Bank of England, with Haslund demanding a receipt. Norway then decided London was not safe, and, never mind the risk of U-boats, two weeks later the gold was shipped to the US.

All in all, only one bag of gold was lost. A sailor on board HMS *Glasgow* stole a bag of Hungarian gold coins from a box that had got damaged. He then went on a drinking spree on the Glasgow waterfront paid for with his newfound wealth. He was given a ninety-day detention.

In August 1940, Haslund wrote an official report on the operation. Its success, he said, 'would not have been possible without the energy and devotion to duty of so many persons'. He recommended that everyone who helped him should receive a gold twenty-kroner coin with a picture of the king on one side and a 'suitable inscription' on the other. Nothing was ever given to those incredible Norwegians who saved the country's gold. The gold in the US was eventually sold to fund the government in exile. Only ten tonnes were returned to Norway – and that was in 1987.

But Fredrik Haslund was some kind of hero.

The Turning of the Tide

Though Stalin showed little interest in gold after the death of Lenin in 1924, by the late 1920s he had changed his mind. Production increased almost fivefold in the seven years after 1929. By the time of Operation Barbarossa, Hitler's invasion in 1941, the Soviet Union had almost 2,500 tonnes earmarked to be sold to the west, as well as its own holdings of 375 tonnes. It put it all – not to mention diamonds, artworks and Lenin's embalmed body – on a train to the other side of the Urals.

Hitler's invasion began a month later than planned, because he detoured into Yugoslavia and Greece to secure the region. A costly strategic mistake. The Nazis' plan was to starve the local population, kill 30 million people, eliminate the country's Jews and then settle this empty and fertile land. By October, after victories in Smolensk,

Uman and Gomel, some 2 million Soviet soldiers had been captured. Russian citizens were not as rich as Western Europeans, but German soldiers still looted them. Soldiers could send home any plunder that would fit into a postal bag tax-free. German soldiers shipped some 3.5 million bags of stolen property. According to studies carried out for the Nuremberg trials, looted Soviet citizens lost some 1.54 tonnes of gold bars and another twenty-three tonnes of coins and jewellery.

Hitler's second deviation, to take Crimea and Ukraine's coal-mining regions, meant the drive towards Moscow began only in October. They reached the suburbs of Moscow by December. The Kremlin's towers could even be seen through field glasses – the Nazis were that close. But the temperature was −50°C, and they weren't fully prepared for the cold. Equipment started to malfunction. Frostbite kicked in. Supply lines were stretched. The Russians had had time to organise themselves, and a counterattack forced the Germans into retreat. Their momentum was now gone. Casualties began to mount. The Battle of Moscow marked the turning point. By the time of Stalingrad and Kursk, the Soviet Union was resurgent. The Nazis were no longer expanding. Now they were in retreat. Like the Romans centuries earlier, there would no longer be the gold of the newly conquered to fund their war machine. And unlike the Romans, Hitler did not have the bountiful mines of northern Spain. The tide of the war had turned.

Hungary: Two Trains Carry the Wealth of the Nation – Most Is Still Missing

Hungary was caught between a rock and a hard place: Hitler one side, Stalin on the other. Initially, it sided with Hitler, but in early 1944 Hitler got wind of the fact that Hungary had secretly been negotiating for peace with the Allies. Needing Hungarian oil, he called the Hungarian head of state, Miklós Horthy, to Austria for a series of meetings and then, while he was out of the country, invaded. The tried-and-tested rounding up of valuables from the citizens soon followed, especially the Jews, of whom there were some 800,000. They were forced to hand over their possessions, and over 500,000 of them were sent to concentration camps.

The following November, as Soviet troops advanced on the Hungarian capital of Budapest, the national gold was moved west, first to a bunker, then onto a train: thirty tonnes were packed into 600 crates, along with other valuables such as the Post Office's stamp collection, the Holy Crown and coronation insignia. After many weeks on the Austrian border, the train ended up at Spital am Pyhrn, a small village in Upper Austria, where the valuables were then stored in the crypt of a church. Escaped Soviet prisoners of war made several unsuccessful attempts to steal the gold, before American troops, led by General Patton himself, took control of the 2,669 bars. They would eventually be returned to Hungary.

But there was a second Hungarian gold train, carrying the stolen wealth of Hungary's people. Its story is the tip of a much bigger iceberg, the widespread scramble for loot in the chaotic days at the end of the war.

SS official Colonel Árpád Toldi was put in charge of the operation to get the treasure back to Germany, safe from Allied hands. He commandeered a forty-six-wagon freight train and had it loaded with gold bullion and jewellery, diamonds, pearls and other gems, watches, cameras, over 200 paintings, Persian and Oriental rugs, silverware, china, furniture, fine clothing, linens, porcelain, stamp collections and currency (mostly US dollars and Swiss francs).[24] Estimates are that over $5 billion in today's money was on that train.

There were over 200 people on board too: Hungarian and Nazi soldiers to provide an armed escort, and dozens of Hungarian civil servants to audit everything. There were even seven carriages of coal miners, there to bury the treasure should the need arise.

In December 1944, with the Soviets closing in, the train set off for Austria, stopping several times en route to pick up more looted treasure. Then, close to the border, it stopped for Toldi and other officials to take an inventory of everything on board. It took them three months. In late March 1945, the train started moving again and passed into Austria. The Russian army was, at this point, just ten miles behind.

Once in Austria, the train stopped occasionally to offload some of its contents onto trucks, especially the gold. What happened to those trucks is a secret that has been carried to the graves of those who took it. At one of the first such stops, Toldi himself got off, taking his family and forty crates of gold with him, saying he would rejoin the train later. No surprise, he never did.

Toldi showed up in Austria a year later, was detained, interrogated, then released and never heard of again. One of many from that period who have disappeared from view with their ill-gotten gold.

The train came to a final halt in Werfen, Austria, where US forces took control. Despite demands from the Soviets, who now occupied Hungary, and the Central Board of Jews, representing what was left of the nation's Jewish population, for the contents of the train to be returned, the US sent the majority of the loot to a military warehouse in Salzburg.

Ownership of the valuables was impossible to ascertain, US authorities decided, so they gave it to refugee aid organisations, or sold it and gave them the proceeds. Auction receipts totalled $152,000, perhaps 2 or 3 million dollars in today's money. A drop in the ocean of what was on board. Much of the art, meanwhile, disappeared, while several officers requisitioned furniture, china, rugs, silverware, glassware and table and bed linen for their homes in the US.

As for the privately owned gold, what happened to that? Most of it has disappeared.

The likelihood is that much of the treasure was stolen.

The US government put an official notice of secrecy over the story, and it was kept under wraps until 1998, when President Bill Clinton created the Presidential Advisory Commission on Holocaust Assets. The report that followed detailed a catalogue of failings by the US Army in its handling of the train and its treasures. In 2001, Hungarian Holocaust survivors filed a lawsuit in Florida against the US government for the mishandling of their property, and in 2005 the US government settled the case, agreeing to pay $25.5 million to various Holocaust charities: still a fraction of the true value.

The Endgame: The Nazis Try to Get Their Gold Out

'Bury your treasure deep. You will need it to begin the Fourth Reich'

Adolf Hitler[25]

As the war turned against the Nazis, the roles reversed. Now they were the ones attempting to hide their gold. First, they scrambled to get gold back to Germany, then, as things fell apart at the end of the war, they scrambled to get it back out again. They buried their gold. They hid it in mines and tunnels. They dumped it in lakes and in the ocean. Some they even hid in a haystack.

Much of the gold splintered across Nazi organisations. Von Ribbentrop's Foreign Office had much of Italy's bullion, for example, while Himmler's SS had the concentration camp gold. US documents say Goebbels deposited the equivalent of $2 million in gold and various currencies in a Buenos Aires bank under a friend's name. Von Ribbentrop did something similar in the name of a cousin. Hitler's secretary, Martin Bormann, perhaps the most business-minded of all the Nazis, had tonnes of gold sent to Argentine banks, as well as currency, almost 3,000 troy ounces of platinum and an extraordinary 4,638 carats of diamonds, according to one version of the story.[26]

But the main hoard remained at the Reichsbank, where Hitler wanted it kept. Heavy bombing in February 1945 and the Soviet advance – they were just fifty miles away from Berlin – forced him to relent. Funk convinced him that moving the gold to Merkers was essential to keep Germany's economy going and to enable the funding of the Fourth Reich. It took almost two months to ship it all.

Germany was in chaos. Roads, bridges and railways were bombed out. The money printers weren't working so there was a shortage of currency. Nobody, including soldiers, was getting paid. Barter became widespread as farmers traded milk or eggs for anything they could get.

Gold was spilling out everywhere. Top Nazis were grabbing it in the hope it would aid their survival after the war. SS General Kaltenbrunner secretly flew nine tonnes to Salzburg. His mistress later told US interrogators that he had hidden two chests of gold, but they were never found. Von Ribbentrop hid eighty-one sacks in a castle cellar near Salzburg, more in a nearby factory, more in a monastery near Worms, more in a castle in Thuringia and two tonnes in Schleswig-Holstein, thirty miles north of Hamburg, where he planned to make a final stand. Locals and even American GIs managed to pilfer their own little stashes. At one point, GIs were seen filling their helmets with gold coins, while an officer used a kilo bar on his desk as a paperweight.

On the one hand the Nazis were fleeing, but on the other they were hanging around for the gold. That same greed for gold which, throughout history, has claimed the lives of so many almost certainly cost Heinrich Himmler his life. In May 1945, on the run not just from the Allies, but now also from his own Nazi party from which he had just been ejected, he could have easily escaped to neutral Sweden, but instead he decided to head south into territory occupied by the Allies. It's thought he was trying to get to Plauen in central east Germany, where he had 900 kg of gold coins in the vaults of the post office.[27] But he never made it. He was stopped at a checkpoint as he headed south and detained, before eventually committing suicide in captivity.

A US Army unit of seventy-five men, led by US Coast Guard Lieutenant Commander Joel Fisher, had the job of capturing Nazi gold and currency as US forces advanced through central Germany. In Plauen, after questioning, Reichsbank officials revealed that there was gold in the vaults of the post office. Fisher blew open the vaults and, sure enough, found thirty-five sacks of gold coins weighing 900 kg. Nobody knows what happened to the gold. Researcher Heintje Peter believes it made its way back to the US with those soldiers, who justified the theft on the grounds of reparations.[28]

The Mystery of the Lake Walchen Gold

Even after the shipment to Merkers, there was still gold in Berlin, ostensibly to pay for the city's defence. On 9 April, with the Russians closing in, Hitler ordered it to be transferred to the Bormann bunker in Bavaria. Reichsbank officials commandeered two freight trains to take it south to Munich: 4,000 gold bars, 365 bags of gold coins, millions of dollars' worth of foreign currency, 500 million Reichsmarks and reams of blank paper and printing plates to make more German currency. In total, at least ten tonnes of gold and another seven tonnes of other valuables.

The trains never made it. In Freising, the entire city, including the station, was on fire. The gold was loaded onto trucks and driven south instead, to be met by Funk, who had left Berlin in another convoy that included more gold. Now to find somewhere to hide it all.

Sixty-five miles south of Munich, they looked at some disused coal mines, but found them waterlogged, which would have destroyed the paper currency. In the meantime, they stored the gold in a bowling alley beneath the barracks of the Mountain Infantry School. Funk was drinking heavily by this point. Lieutenant Colonel Rauch and Colonel Pfeiffer were given the responsibility of taking the valuables into the mountains and finding somewhere to hide them.

One of Rauch's officers was the son of a forester who owned a house in the woods close to Lake Walchen. He agreed to keep the gold in a stable there until they could find somewhere better to put it. It took them three days to get it there, and from there it was carried higher into the mountains on mules and donkeys. They then buried the gold in the woods. The paper would not survive long underground, so it was stored above ground camouflaged behind logs. The printing presses were deemed useless and dumped in the lake.

A few days later, American GIs marched into the area, unaware of the treasure. But rumours quickly spread. Funk at this point had handed himself in, but he had no idea where the gold was. After a month of piecing together information, British and American forces began a serious search. Armed with metal detectors, they followed the mule droppings up into the woods, until the metal detectors went off. They looked around, saw discarded food cans and wine bottles and started digging.

All in all they recovered 9.1 tonnes of gold. Almost a tonne had gone missing. An 'unknown amount of currency' had also disappeared.[29]

A criminal investigation was eventually carried out in the 1950s. By this time, both Pfeiffer and Rauch had emigrated to Argentina, where they were enjoying successful careers working for a metallurgy company. Hmm. There were also reports of American officers seen with large rucksacks full of valuables, and one local hotel owner, linked to a plot to steal the valuables, was found murdered. Locals whisper that the Americans took most of the gold. Others say the Nazis did. Others say the locals. Two thousand ounces were later found in a hay wagon. Gold and currency sometimes resurfaced years later in people's gardens. It seems there was an almighty cover-up. This is another little tale that tells the greater story.

No one was ever charged.

After the War, Restitution of Gold

'They lied their heads off'

Jean Ziegler, Member of the Swiss Parliament

Despite following up on almost all leads, the Allies knew they were unlikely to uncover all the gold hidden in Nazi Germany. Thirteen tonnes were found at various regional banks. One tonne was found buried under a chicken coop and a pile of manure. As late as the 1960s, people were still finding gold in Bavarian forests.

So much was, simply, stolen in the chaos.

There are countless stories of hidden or lost Nazi treasure. One tells of a train loaded with gold, jewels, currency and other valuables hidden, as the Nazis retreated, in a secret tunnel near Wałbrzych,

Poland. The train has never been found. Another tells of gold stolen from concentration camp victims at Buchenwald, but, again, no large cache has been found, though small amounts have been. Thirty tonnes are rumoured to be in a well at the Polish Baroque palace of Hochberg near the Czech border.[30] Other rumours persist of gold dumped in Alpine lakes, especially Lake Toplitz in Austria. Numerous diving expeditions have been conducted with little success, however, although one notable find was a gold cauldron in Chiemsee weighing 11 kg. Initially thought to be ancient, it was later linked to the Nazis. In August 2015, a sixteen-year-old girl was paddling in Lake Königs, near Hitler's home in the Obersalzberg, when she found a half-kilo gold bar on the lakebed. She got to keep it. Such incidents only add to the speculation, of which there is no shortage. Documentaries about secret Nazi gold proliferate (I've narrated many of them). I doubt that fascination will ever go away.

Whatever monetary gold the Allies found, however, was gathered together, mostly at Frankfurt, and put into a pool to be distributed by the Tripartite Gold Commission on a proportional basis relative to losses.[31] But redistribution was no easy task. Reparations delegations could not even reach a definition of looted gold.[32]

The Soviets demanded huge gold reparation to compensate for their loss of life. Stalin initially claimed 27 per cent of the gold at Merkers, then announced he would make no claim on gold captured by Allied troops. We still do not quite know why. Ten countries submitted claims which totalled 735 tonnes, when the captured gold amounted to less than half that – 336 tonnes.[33] More gold was lost, spent or stolen than was available for restitution. The Bank of England estimated 'a maximum distribution of 58% against gold claims'.[34] Eighty per cent of claims were dealt with by 1950, but bullion was still being returned as late as the 1990s. No country would receive back all the gold it claimed to have lost.

After the war, when Poland came under Soviet control, their gold was not returned, though at some point it made its way to London, and in 2019 London dispatched it back to Poland.

There was little to no attempt to deal with stolen personal gold, perhaps because individuals are deemed less important than the state, perhaps because it would have been too complex an undertaking. This is a problem that has haunted reparations for years, particularly in the case of Jewish gold.

As for Nazi gold located outside of Germany, the Allies' legal position was 'exceedingly weak'.[35] Neutral countries said such demands conflicted both with their own legislation and their status as neutrals. The US wanted sanctions if neutral countries would not cooperate, but this idea was rejected by the British, who argued sanctions would be unenforceable in peacetime.

In 1946, the Swiss sent a delegation to Washington to negotiate an agreement on the liquidation of German assets. 'They lied their heads off,' said Swiss parliamentarian Jean Ziegler. Switzerland eventually settled for $58 million, which got negotiated down to $28 million in 1951, far below the US estimate of $200 million held in Swiss banks.[36] Spain, which received $90 million in Nazi gold, returned only a token $114,329. Neutral nations for the most part kept much of their ill-gotten gains.

Gold was silent witness to the horrors and ambitions of the Third Reich. It was a means to finance Nazi aggression, but also to escape it. The densest form of wealth there is, it was key to their pursuit of power. From their meticulous looting across Europe to the chaotic final days when gold was hidden, buried or desperately smuggled abroad, the story of Nazi gold is one of greed, skulduggery and atrocity. Gold's journey from the vaults of the conquered to secret caches in neutral countries illustrates how deeply intertwined it is with the financial machinery of war. Even as the Third Reich crumbled, the power of gold endured. Desire for it – on all sides – never abated, shaping decisions right up to the last.

12

The Mucilaginous Mystery of Japanese Gold

'Speech is silver, silence is golden'

Proverb

Japanese mass murder during the Second World War was a scale up from the Nazis', hard though that may be to believe.

The Nazis killed over 17 million. The Japanese slaughtered twice as many,[1] including 23 million ethnic Chinese. If you were a Nazi prisoner of war from the Anglosphere, you had a 4 per cent chance of dying; held by the Japanese, the death rate rose to 30 per cent.

Like the Nazis, the Japanese sent conquered people into forced labour and slavery. Twelve countries including China, Korea, Burma (Myanmar), the Dutch East Indies (Indonesia), the Philippines and Malaya fell foul. The Japanese also engaged in the looting and plunder of occupied nations, and for the same reasons: to finance their military and to exploit inferior, conquered people. As well as essential strategic commodities, such as oil, industrial metal and rubber, the Japanese stole precious metals, gems and valuables, art, artefacts and other items of historical, religious and cultural significance, for their own gain and to annihilate the cultural identities of those they conquered. They plundered sacred and ancient tombs. The Japanese government even allowed its gangsters to loot Asia's underworld and its black economy.

We know vast quantities of gold were stolen. But we do not know how much, nor where it ended up. There are all sorts of reasons for this, ranging from circumstance to policy, but when secrets are kept, and the truth is hidden, speculation and theory soon follow, especially where gold is involved. So it was with the Japanese and the treasure they amassed.

Though Emperor Hirohito announced the surrender of Japan on 15 August 1945, American forces did not land there until almost three weeks later. That left the Japanese authorities a window, even in their heavily bombed, incapacitated state, to hide or destroy evidence that might incriminate them in war crimes. Something like 70 per cent of their wartime records were destroyed. Of course, they hid wealth as well. They would need it at some stage to rebuild their nation and did not want it falling into American hands. One huge haul of bullion, as we shall discover, they even dumped into Tokyo Bay.

There was American occlusion, too. Unlike in Germany, where records of war crimes were collected and disclosed, the US kept (and still keeps) many Japanese records classified – against, many argue, its own rules. There were fewer trials for war crimes in Japan than there were in Germany. Victims of Japanese atrocities, ranging from forced labour to sexual slavery, were prevented from seeking compensation, further capping information flow. So much evidence that would otherwise have come to the surface did not. Why the different approach? Many explanations have been proffered: Japan could not afford reparations; or the Americans trod softly to stop Japan going communist. But there is also a theory based on Japan's vast hoard of gold.

In 1936–7, Emperor Hirohito put his brother Yasuhito, Prince Chichibu, in charge of Operation Golden Lily. Its purpose was to systematically plunder the nations conquered by the Japanese. Hirohito made his cousin, Prince Tsuneyoshi Takeda, second in command, to supervise looting, and he made his uncle, Prince Yasuhiko Asaka, deputy commander of the Central China Area Army. Asaka commanded the 1937 assault on the then Chinese capital Nanking, now known as the Rape of Nanking, one of the most horrific episodes in human history, which saw six unspeakable weeks of murder, rape, looting and arson.

Golden Lily's workload grew with Japanese expansion. By 1941–2 most of South-east Asia had fallen under its power. Commander of the Japanese forces General Tomoyuki Yamashita was nicknamed 'the Tiger of Malaya' for his rapid conquest of Malaya and Singapore, the 'largest capitulation' in British military history, according to Winston Churchill. The Japanese even attacked the United States, when, on 7 December 1941, they decimated the US Pacific fleet with their surprise strike on Pearl Harbor. As well as the wealth of conquered nations to plunder, there were the assets of overseas Chinese populations and the Dutch, British, French and Americans in their respective colonies. Golden Lily operatives took whatever they could find. They tore gilt from Buddhist temples and stole solid-gold Buddhas, especially from Burma. They made off with gemstones and precious metal, all the while selling copious amounts of opium: a lucrative business, and destructive to local well-being. Much of the gold was sent to a smelter in Ipoh, Malaya, where Chichibu and his staff inventoried the plunder, resmelted it and shipped it back to Japan, with their boats often disguised as hospital ships.

American submarine warfare meant that a lot of the gold bound for Japan ended up at the bottom of the ocean, so the Japanese began shipping it to the Philippines instead. Chichibu moved his headquarters from Singapore to Manila. General Yamashita was later assigned there, too. The feeling at this point was that only some kind of negotiated settlement was going to end the war, and that Japan would get the Philippines in exchange for an end to hostilities. In 1942, Chichibu ordered 175 tunnels to be constructed in secret locations across the 7,641-island archipelago to store gold and other treasure until after the war was over. This order showed some foresight, because by 1943 the only way through Allied blockades was by submarine (which is how Chichibu and Takeda eventually escaped back to Japan). Thus the Philippines became even more of a destination for looted gold. Slave labourers and prisoners of war dug the tunnels and, along with Japanese officers and soldiers, were often deliberately buried alive when the time came to seal the tunnels, so as to keep their locations secret. The tunnels were also booby-trapped: with bombs, sand traps and poison gas. In

Manila itself, Golden Lily saw treasure caves built under the cathedral, guessing rightly that the Americans would not bomb it, and in the dungeons of the old Spanish Fort Santiago, which had been US military headquarters. The gold they contained would become known as Yamashita's gold.

With the lack of disclosure and the destruction of records, we just do not know how much gold was looted. China, at this point, was more of a silver-based economy, and the British colonies tended to hold paper rather than metal, but, even so, hundreds, perhaps even thousands of tonnes.

Sitting in the Mud of the Bay

'My advice to you, my violent friend,
is to seek out gold and sit on it'

John Gardner, *Grendel*

On the morning of 4 September 1945, the advance party of the 1st Cavalry Division took to their landing crafts and landed unopposed at Yokohama docks. By nightfall, they controlled the initial staging areas throughout the harbour.

The Allied occupation was gradual and cautious at first, but it soon became apparent that the Japanese were not going to fight back. The war was over, and the occupation would not require a significant force of arms. That's not to say the Japanese were entirely cooperative. By October, as the demilitarisation of Japan began, something of a game of hide and seek had begun too. The Americans commandeered and investigated arsenals, factories, barracks, military posts, airfields and storage grounds. The search broadened to caves, mountain hideouts and other secret caches. Schools, temples and shrines were spared at first, but then it was discovered that these too were being used to stash munitions, so they too came under scrutiny. Eighteen months later, weapons of war were still being found, so widely had they been dispersed. Disease meanwhile was everywhere, especially around the ports.

One of the occupying force's most important first tasks was to take control of the financial sector. On 30 September, twenty-one teams, comprising soldiers, counterintelligence corps and interpreters, descended simultaneously on twenty-one different banks, closed them and seized all records. Then in October, the 1st Cavalry Division began the seizure of bullion, jewellery, foreign currency, and stock and bond certificates from Japanese businesses and industrial plants. At Japan's Imperial Mint in Tokyo, which had been flattened by bombing, there were millions of dollars in gold, silver, platinum and currency buried in the rubble. Teams of Japanese women were brought in to haul it out of the flooded vaults. Over $250 million worth was recovered, according to one news report,[2] which would be equivalent to around 220 tonnes. Neither the army nor the navy had accounted for its spending since 1937, it seems. Such was the state of Japanese records.

In June 1946, a tip-off meant US authorities got wind of a hoard dumped in Tokyo Bay. Recovering it would be no easy task. The harbour has a high-tide range and there is a good four feet of mucilaginous mud and silt on the seabed, into which the bullion had sunk. But so began Operation Mudsill. Visibility underwater in the harbour was bad, so the hardhat divers relied on touch alone to locate the bars, fishing about with their hands in the mud. Their very first find was a seventy-five-pound platinum bar. Another 840 silver bars were recovered, but not, it seems, much gold.

By the end of January, eighty-four tonnes of gold, eight tonnes of platinum, 9,000 tonnes of silver and large quantities of diamonds were sitting in the vaults of the Bank of Japan, confiscated by US forces. They had also seized sixty-six tonnes of narcotics.

But what about the gold in the Philippines? What happened to Yamashita's gold?

As Japan fell, the tunnels were quickly and brutally sealed. Yamashita eventually surrendered in September 1945, but there was no mention of treasure or loot during his trial for war crimes, which began in late October. The same month, US intelligence officers in Manila were beginning to learn about the hidden gold. In cahoots with the Philippine government, after torturing various members of Yamashita's staff, they began to locate some of it. What they found, it is said, amazed everyone from General Douglas Mac-Arthur to President Harry Truman in the White House.

But we just don't know how much they found, so speculation and rumour have followed. The amounts found were so huge, say some, that they could jeopardise the new monetary order for the post-war era agreed at Bretton Woods the previous year (more on this in a moment). In particular, there was the fear it could bring down the price of gold and thus, effectively, devalue the dollar. Instead, America would use the money to establish the post-war economic order in Asia and, in the fight against communism during the Cold War, to provide untraceable finance for intelligence activities and covert operations, such as manipulating elections and bribing political and military leaders. The gold almost certainly helped finance the notoriously lavish lifestyles of US-backed Philippine President Ferdinand Marcos and his wife Imelda. Indeed in 1992, Imelda Marcos actually claimed that Yamashita's gold accounted for the wealth of her husband, citing a 6,000 tonnes figure, though she was not exactly a credible witness.

Treasure hunters have been searching for Yamashita's gold ever since the war ended. They are still trying to find it now. In 1970, one of them, Rogelio Roxas, actually found gold in a cave north of Manila: a hidden chamber full of gold bars and a giant golden Buddha with gems concealed in its head. He was then arrested by President Marcos, who confiscated the gold and tortured him. After being released, Roxas died in mysterious circumstances. In 1988, his family filed a lawsuit against President Marcos in the US, and in 1996 the court ruled that the Roxas family be paid $22 billion in reparation – the largest civil settlement in history.

The missing gold has become the subject of numerous books, films and other stories. There have even been get-rich-quick schemes claiming to have discovered the treasure – but, of course, large amounts of capital are needed to 'recover it'. A Northern Irish dentist by the name of Colin Howell, who got a £400,000 insurance payout after murdering his wife and framing it as suicide, managed to lose his ill-gotten gains on one such scheme.

How much bullion was taken as a result of Operation Golden Lily? Where is it now? Does Yamashita's gold exist, or is it an urban myth? There are many more questions than answers. How much gold remains unaccounted for is impossible to say. Some of the loot is no doubt lying at the bottom of the sea. Some of it is probably hidden to this day somewhere in the land of the rising sun. Some of it is hidden in caves in the Philippines along with the bones of those who were entombed as the caves were sealed.

Even more mystery surrounds Japanese gold than the Nazis'. But that's the thing about gold: whoever has it, has it. There is nobody on the other side of the trade. It is wealth in and of itself, and its provenance is easy to hide. I'll bet most of it is long since resmelted, its origins impossible to prove.

13.

How the US Made the World
Dependent on the Dollar

'There can be no other criterion,
no other standard than gold'

Charles de Gaulle, President of France

In August 1971, President Nixon took the US off the gold standard, a 'temporary' measure that remains in place more than fifty years later. For the first time in history, gold – Switzerland aside – played no part in the global monetary system.[1]

Gold was $35 an ounce. Today, it hovers around $3,000 an ounce. Gold hasn't changed. It doesn't. We know that. It's the dollar which has been devalued – by 98.5 per cent. That's quite something.

But the US dollar has been one of the better currencies. The British pound or the Italian lira, for example, have done far worse – and they were G7 currencies. Heaven forbid you should have been a citizen subject to the currencies of Brazil, Argentina, Venezuela, Turkey or Zimbabwe.

This drastic shift had its origins in a little-known village in New Hampshire called Bretton Woods, where, towards the end of the Second World War, officials designed a new monetary order for the world.

Wishing to avoid the mistakes which followed the previous war, they had started planning as early as 1942. The US, represented by Assistant Secretary of the Treasury Harry Dexter White, wanted the dollar – backed by gold – as the world's reserve currency. Britain's John Maynard Keynes proposed a more balanced system based on a supranational currency called the 'bancor', an idea he had developed with fellow economist E. F. Schumacher.

In July 1944, with it now clear that the Axis nations were going to lose the Second World War, representatives from the forty-four Allied nations met at the Mount Washington Hotel in Bretton Woods for the United Nations Monetary and Financial Conference, where they would finalise this system of money, so that international economic relations could be rebuilt. After three weeks of deliberations, setting up rules, institutions and protocols, the delegates signed. Well, mostly. Soviet representatives declined, saying the institutions which had been created, including the International Monetary Fund (IMF) and World Bank Group, were 'branches of Wall Street'. They may have had a point.

Keynes did not get his bancor over the line. International accounts would be settled in dollars, and those dollars were convertible to gold at $35/oz. Countries had to maintain exchange rates within 1 per cent of the US dollar. In effect, the US was on a gold standard, and the rest of the world was on a dollar standard. 'Never in history had the paper money of one country been given such value and respect,' said historian Kenneth R. Ferguson.[2]

Countries contributed $8.8 billion proportionally – 15 per cent in gold – to create the IMF.[3]

The US dollar may have been exchangeable for gold, but not if you were an American citizen. Gold was still illegal. Even Keynes said the agreement was not 'a gold standard' though it 'used gold as a standard of value'. Others said this was a 'distinction without a difference'.[4] Like the failed gold standard of the inter-war years, Bretton Woods was another bogus standard, doomed to failure because it was incomplete.

The system relied on the integrity of the US dollar's gold backing to work, and that integrity was in question, even before the end of the war. The June 1945 Federal Reserve Act reduced required gold reserves for notes outstanding from 40 per cent to 25 per cent, and against deposits from 35 per cent to 25 per cent. The intentions may have been worthy: to increase the availability of dollars for the reconstruction of war-torn Europe – this was deemed more important than the inflation that might follow – but it weakened the integrity of the dollar's gold backing.

Between 1944 and 1954, because of increased supply, the dollar lost a third of its purchasing power,[5] though the $35 Bretton Woods price remained. Both sterling and the French franc devalued sharply.

The system was not even fully operational until 1958, when the major European currencies became fully convertible, but by this point the wheels were already coming off.

US government spending was soaring, and it began running balance of payments deficits – made worse by the costs of foreign aid, investment and maintaining a military presence in Europe and Asia. With many doubting the dollar's value, gold was now leaving the US. By 1960, US gold stocks had declined by 27 per cent.[6]

European central banks, meanwhile, were stockpiling. From 3,334 tonnes in 1950 (excluding Britain), stocks had tripled by 1960 and quintupled by 1965 to 16,930 tonnes. US stocks by 1965 had fallen by 9,500 tonnes, down 40 per cent from the 1949 high.[7]

France's President Charles de Gaulle wanted a return to a proper gold standard, not this quasi-system. He demanded gold for every dollar in a French bank. 'There can be no other criterion, no other standard than gold,' he said. 'Yes, gold which never changes . . . which has no nationality and which is eternally and universally accepted as the unalterable fiduciary value par excellence.' De Gaulle was challenging the entire system, knowing full well the US didn't have enough gold to back all the dollars in circulation.

Successive US administrations tried to stop the outflow. Eisenhower banned Americans from buying gold overseas, Kennedy imposed the Equalization Tax on foreign investments, and Johnson discouraged Americans from travelling altogether. 'We may need to forgo the pleasures of Europe for a while,' he said. 'I am asking the American people to defer, for the next two years, all non-essential travel outside the western hemisphere.'[8]

Private demand was also increasing. In 1960, European private buyers – both corporate and individual – took up three-quarters of new mine supply. Fears that the dollar would devalue following the election (won by JFK) sent the gold price in London to $40. The Bank of England, in collusion with the Federal Reserve, began increasing gold sales to keep the price down. Thus did the London gold pool begin, with the addition of six major European nations the following year (Belgium, France, Italy, the Netherlands, West Germany and Switzerland), which coordinated sales to suppress, or 'stabilise', to use their word, the gold price and diffuse unwanted, upward market pressure.

But the pool struggled against growing demand. As long as it kept the price below $35.20 at the London fix, they were OK, but when it exceeded that level, it became cheaper to buy from the Federal Reserve in New York, putting an unwelcome further drain on US reserves. Large sales from the Soviet Union saved them for a while, but these sales ended in 1965, just as demand rose, when speculators sold sterling for gold in anticipation of devaluation under Britain's new Labour government. Even China sold its sterling.

In 1965, an ounce of gold was still $35, but the purchasing power of the dollar had decreased by 57 per cent from 1945, while gold reserves had also fallen sharply.[9] The villain was the costs of the US government, in particular the Vietnam War and President Lyndon B. Johnson's enormous welfare spending. With inflation rising at home and international confidence in the dollar waning, these programmes were not just costly – they undermined Bretton Woods. The German and Japanese economies were growing, meanwhile. Non-American nations felt aggrieved that they had to produce $100 worth of goods and services to get a $100 bill, when the US could just print one. French Finance Minister Valéry Giscard d'Estaing called it 'America's exorbitant privilege'.

De Gaulle, meanwhile, had had enough. He ignored the pool to turn all French dollars and sterling balances into gold. The French even sent battleships to New York to collect their gold. He became the target of several assassination attempts – coincidence, I'm sure. There were rather more US dollars in the world than there was gold to back them, he felt, and he was right. By 1967, US foreign liabilities were $36 billion, but it only had $12 billion now in gold reserves – a third of what was needed to back the dollar. West Germany, Spain and Switzerland began demanding gold for their dollars. Even the British, for whom sterling was going through one of its quadrennial collapses, asked the Americans to prepare $3 billion worth of Fort Knox gold for withdrawal.

Private gold demand was overwhelming. The days of mine production going to central bank hands to become tender were over. The dollar had been debased, never mind other currencies. Yet central bankers were still set on maintaining $35 gold. Gold was worth more than that, as so many could see.

A huge industry smuggling gold emerged, especially from Dubai to India. In 1966, more gold went from London to Dubai than to any other country, except France and Switzerland: 125 tonnes. Within a few years it was double that. The average Indian peasant, said the president of the Bombay Bullion Association,

> is always faced with fear of famine, his crops depend on the whim of the monsoon, he knows nothing of banking and credit. Now what is the one thing to tide him and his village over in an emergency? When famine comes they must have something tangible to convert – gold.[10]

He was touching on a role that gold has always had – and will always have: insurance. In India, where banking systems were unreliable and natural disasters could wipe out entire communities, gold wasn't a luxury – it was a necessity.

In November 1967, the British government devalued the pound by 14 per cent from $2.80 to $2.40 in order to 'achieve a substantial surplus on the balance of payments consistent with economic growth and full employment'.[11] In that month, the London market saw greater bullion demand than it would typically see in nine: as much as 100 tonnes per day. To stem demand they banned forward buying, leverage and the purchase of gold with credit. The pool still lost 1,400 tonnes that year, more than a whole year's mine supply.

Selling pressure on the US dollar only increased when the Viet Cong and North Vietnamese People's Army of Vietnam launched the first of a series of surprise attacks on US Armed Forces in South Vietnam in January 1968. Desperate to prop up the system, US military aircraft flew tonne after tonne of gold to RAF Lakenheath from where it was trucked in military convoys to the back entrance of the Bank of England: at one point the floor of the Bank of England's weighing room collapsed under the weight of all the gold. In the four days from 11 March to 14 March, some 780 tonnes were sold to market. The effort to protect the price was deemed hopeless. On 15 March, UK Chancellor Roy Jenkins declared a bank holiday, and the gold market was closed for a fortnight, 'at the request of the United States'. Zurich also closed. Paris stayed open with gold trading at a 25 per cent premium. All in all, the final fifteen months saw over 3,000 tonnes sold to market to protect that $35 price.

Two days later, in the rushed-through Washington Agreement, governors of the central banks in the gold pool declared there would be one fixed gold market for official government transactions at $35/oz and another, free-market price for private transactions. Not for the last time, central bankers were living in a world of their own.

In the fortnight that the gold markets were closed in London, Credit Suisse, Swiss Bank Corporation and Union Bank of Switzerland pulled off a coup. They persuaded the South African Reserve Bank to market its gold futures through them. London had lost its monopoly on South Africa's gold sales, and it now had a big rival in Switzerland. This marked a major shift in the gold market. As Switzerland ascended, London's 100-year reign as the heart of global gold sales began to wane. From 1961–8, the UK sold 1,180 tonnes. It's thought the US lost eight times that figure.

The Bretton Woods era was about to end.

15 August 1971: Nixon Takes the US Off the Gold Standard

'The time has come for a new economic policy for the United States'

Richard Nixon, 37th President of the United States

Gold is one thing. Gold standards are another. They tend, as we have seen, not to last, particularly bogus ones. Keynes called them barbarous – ironic, perhaps, given he was one of the architects of this one.[12]

With inflation in the US still high, the balance of payments deficit, particularly with Japan, increasing, and the costs of war and welfare still rising, further downward pressure on the dollar was inevitable. The Washington Agreement may have lasted three years, but it was unworkable. Once gold backing for notes was removed, there was little reason to believe the United States could honour its promises. There was not enough gold in Fort Knox. More concerning was that any rogue nation could use the system as a tool of economic warfare: buy gold from the US at $35 and then sell it on the open market at a higher price. Incoming Treasury Secretary John Connally saw this danger.

An urgent meeting was called for Friday 13 August 1971. Nixon met with Connally, Federal Reserve Chairman Arthur Burns and thirteen other high-ranking White House and Treasury advisors at Camp David, the president's country home in Maryland. They made one of the most momentous decisions in the history of money. Two days later, Nixon announced that US dollars would no longer be redeemable for gold.

Of course it was the fault of the speculators. It always is. 'I have directed the Secretary of the Treasury to take the action necessary to defend the dollar against the speculators,' he said, deflecting responsibility, and 'to suspend temporarily the convertibility of the dollar into gold.'[13] They called it the closing of 'the gold window'. Really, it was a rejection of Bretton Woods and the post-war gold standard, and a devaluation of the world's leading currency. He imposed wage and price controls to counter inflation – a ninety-day freeze on prices and wages – and a 10 per cent tax on imports to protect American products. Nixon didn't have the gold to pay for all the bombs America had dropped, and was continuing to drop, on South-east Asia, nor for all its welfare.

There was also that word 'temporary' again. Here we are more than half a century on, waiting for that temporary measure to be rescinded. Like so many other temporary measures – income tax, for example – it became permanent.

'My efforts to prevent closing of the gold window . . . do not seem to have succeeded,' lamented Federal Reserve Chairman Arthur Burns, when he realised what President Nixon intended. 'The gold window may have to be closed tomorrow . . . What a tragedy for mankind!'[14]

This was a landmark in the history of money. It set the stage for an unprecedented shift in the global financial system, opening the door to the world of floating fiat currencies, untethered from any real value, and all their pernicious consequences.

Fixed exchange rates got shelved, and the dollar lost more than 12 per cent of its value in four weeks. There were attempts to restore the system. Nixon called one of them 'the greatest monetary agreement in the history of the world'.[15] They all failed.

Ever since, without the discipline of gold, western governments have bloated to unprecedented size, fat on waste, war and welfare, intervening in areas of our lives never before thought possible. The consequences of the new debt-based fiat system have taken manifold forms, from rampant inequality to successive financial crises.

'Fix money, fix the world,' is the mantra of the bitcoiners. They're right. In 1971, Nixon did the opposite.

The Bold Tricks of the Gold Smugglers' Trade

In the late 1960s, Dubai earned a reputation as the smugglers' supermarket. The year 1970, in particular, was a boom for the swinging sheikdom, as it was known, and much of the money that built it came out of this trade. Hundreds of tonnes were shipped there, quite legally, from London and Zurich and from there smuggled to India, Indonesia and elsewhere in Asia. Agents pocketed 8–10 per cent and risk was spread typically across five shipments, in case any should be caught.

One perspiring man in Jakarta's Halim Airport, queuing at immigration in 1976, suddenly had his knees buckle and he collapsed. He couldn't get back up. It took three people to get him on his feet. Concealed beneath his clothes were fifty-two kilos (115 lb) of gold on his belt and in a waistcoat.

The sheer scale of smuggling is hard to comprehend. Unlike drug trafficking today, gold smuggling was seen as having a noble purpose: helping citizens protect themselves and their families' wealth from oppressive governments and their unstable currencies. One Old Etonian who got into the game for the thrill used to advertise in *The Times*, 'Young men of initiative wanted for job with rewarding travel opportunities.'[16] These opportunities included wearing corsets loaded with thirty kilos (65 lb) of gold. They took some lifting. Smugglers had to practise standing up and sitting down with the extra weight. They were even equipped with Dextrosol tablets to give them extra strength.

He wrote a 'Smuggler's Companion' and advised that every gold runner must carry 'a belt and braces, new shoelaces, needle and cotton, safety pin and buttons'. The buttons were essential – losing one on your shirt could accidentally reveal the golden corset hidden beneath. 'Always dress English with collar and tie. Avoid casual gear. At airports nobody gets stopped unless they draw attention to themselves. Be polite and relaxed with officials, but never humble.' Sage advice, not just for smuggling, but for life, really.

Of course, with modern advances in airport security, these audacious practices are now relics of a bygone era.

14.

What to Do with All That Gold?

'Practically all governments of history have used their
exclusive power to issue money to defraud and plunder the people'

F. A. Hayek, Nobel Laureate in Economics[1]

Gold was no longer money officially, at least. Central banks and monetary institutions were sitting on 36,500 tonnes. What to do with it?

For the most part, they did nothing, at least at first. Nixon's move was only supposed to be temporary. As the gold price rose in the 1970s, the US Treasury and the IMF flirted with gold sales to curb the price, but activity was sporadic.

Who, then, would buy new mine supply, if not central banks? To the surprise of the mining industry, demand for gold from investors and from the jewellery industry actually exceeded new mine supply, particularly as restrictions on gold ownership around the world began to lighten up.

In 1974, President Gerald Ford had no idea that it was illegal – 'a federal felony' – for US citizens to own gold. He was watching TV, when he saw sound-money advocate Jim Blanchard, holding a bar of gold up and asking from his wheelchair: 'Why can I not own this?' Ford was soon signing a bill to legalise ownership, which the Treasury opposed at first, believing it would encourage speculation and affect the international monetary situation. But on 31 December 1974, the bill came into effect.

It was a classic case of 'buy the rumour; sell the news'. The price of gold, which had risen in anticipation, then fell for the next two years – perhaps because Treasury and Federal Reserve officials issued so many warnings about the dangers of buying gold, few actually did.

In 1977, the legal right to contract for payment in gold was also reinstated, meaning Roosevelt's gold laws were finally repealed in their entirety.

The British were banned from owning more than four coins – a ban which lasted until 1979 – but demand still skyrocketed during the sterling crisis of 1974–6, which ended with Chancellor Denis Healey going to the IMF to borrow a record sum of money. The influx of gold was so huge that the Labour government banned imports, though there were at this point already some five million Krugerrands in Britain.

Overall, the 1970s was an incredible time for the gold price and for gold investors. Having begun the decade at $35/oz, gold hit a historic high of $850/oz on the afternoon fix of 21 January 1980, a high that would not be seen again for more than twenty-five years. This was the day after the Iranian hostage crisis ended, and the remaining fifty-two Americans taken captive after Iranian revolutionaries seized the US Embassy in Tehran were released. It was also the day after the inauguration of a new US president, Ronald Reagan. Inflation was out of control at 13.5 per cent and unemployment rampant at 7 per cent. Elsewhere, the Soviet Union had just invaded Afghanistan.

Gold mining companies saw their share prices rocketing too. It was a classic, frenzied price spike, the kind you see during full-blown panics, especially at the end of long bull markets.

But on that historic day – 21 January 1980 – the US dollar was, effectively, fully backed by gold once again. The market value of the 260 million ounces of gold owned by the US and mostly stored in Fort Knox reached $221 billion. There were some $160 billion in paper dollars on issue, so US gold was actually worth 140 per cent of US paper. It was as if the US had been put back onto a gold standard. 'The US Treasury is once again solvent,' said one Zurich banker, 'thanks to the high price of gold.'[2]

But it was not to last. In 1980, Federal Reserve Chairman Paul Volcker tightened monetary policy, hiking interest rates as high as

17.6 per cent (the so-called Volcker Shock), and for two decades the gold price went sideways or down. The easing of geopolitical tensions with the fall of the Iron Curtain and the dissolution of the Soviet Union also meant less appetite for gold. By 1999, it had fallen to $250/oz. The world lost interest.

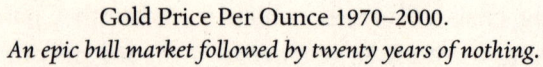

Gold Price Per Ounce 1970–2000.
An epic bull market followed by twenty years of nothing.

The 1980s and 1990s:
Central Banks Seriously Start to Sell

'Gold is the money of kings; silver is the money of gentlemen;
barter is the money of peasants; but debt is the money of slaves'

Norm Franz, *Money & Wealth in the New Millennium*[3]

Forty years of fixed $35/oz gold had left the mining industry depressed and stagnant. The abrupt shift to floating gold prices after the Nixon shock created uncertainty, and mining was hesitant to invest, unsure of how these new dynamics would play out. South Africa's production had peaked in 1970 at 1,000 tonnes per annum. Over the next decade, global supply fell by a third, hitting its lowest point in 1980 – ironically, just as gold prices soared to historic highs, indeed probably contributing to the spike.

As the gold price stabilised around $400/oz in the 1980s, mining started to expand. Advances in geochemistry and geophysics led to new discoveries, while new mining methods cut costs. Heap-leaching, for example – pile up crushed ore, spray it with cyanide, which absorbs gold, then extract the gold from the resulting solution – made low-grade ore bodies more viable.

In 1968, only sixteen countries had notable production, with South Africa and the Soviet Union between them producing 80 per cent of global supply. By 2000, there were fifty-seven countries producing significant amounts of gold, among them Peru, Brazil, China, Ghana, Mali, Guinea, Côte d'Ivoire and Spain. US output rose tenfold; Australian rose fourteenfold. Global mining output doubled from 1980 levels. South Africa and Russia's share of global production was now just 27 per cent.

In the 1980s and 1990s, bullion banks – many of which had been absorbed into larger financial institutions – began to finance mining operations. They offered gold loans, startup capital, and hedging programmes to help miners manage the volatility of the gold price.

To do so, they borrowed gold at 3 per cent from central banks and then sold the gold forward to underwrite projects. The miners would then deliver the gold from future production to settle the contracts. Some 4,650 tonnes were sold in this way.

What began as a way to support miners soon evolved into something much larger. Instead of lending gold, central banks started selling it. As sales ramped up, so did supply, and that weighed heavily on the gold market through the 1990s. Some argued that these sales were part of a deliberate effort to suppress the gold price.

This era of sales and fiat money reshaped central bank reserves. In the 1930s, gold made up over 90 per cent of central bank reserves. By 1950, that figure had dropped to 70 per cent. As central banks sold more gold, this share fell to 33 per cent by 1990 and just 12 per cent by 2000.[4] By 2015, gold's share had hit a low of 9 per cent, though it has been rising slowly ever since – a crucial trend we'll revisit in a moment.

The US dollar – and US Treasury securities – rose to take its place. In 1950, the dollar accounted for less than 10 per cent of global central bank reserves. By 2000, it accounted for 62 per cent, while the newly introduced euro held 17 per cent.

Of all those central bank sales, one stood out above all the others.

Gordon Brown's Bottom

'Governments lie; bankers lie; even auditors
sometimes lie: gold tells the truth'

William Rees-Mogg, Editor of *The Times* (1967–81)

Brown's Bottom is the name given to one of the UK's great financial blunders (and there is no shortage of those): Chancellor Gordon Brown's decision to sell more than half of Britain's gold at the bottom of the market in 1999.

Even at the time, the tabloids said the decision was 'catastrophic'.

Gold traders called it 'appalling'. Parliament was outraged – foreign central banks were, too. Brown was under no pressure to sell. What was he thinking? For many, the decision was of such incompetence, the only possible explanation is conspiracy.

It was two years into Brown's new job as Chancellor of the Exchequer. At the time, the UK held approximately 715 tonnes of gold, worth around $6.5 billion. Its gold amounted to about half of its $13 billion foreign currency reserves, and Brown and the Treasury wanted 'to achieve a balanced portfolio of our national reserves,' as he put it in Parliament.[5] There was, the Treasury said, too much exposure to a single asset, which paid no interest and whose price was volatile. The government made a surprise announcement in the House of Commons that it would be holding a series of auctions for its gold, starting in six weeks, with an eventual plan to sell 415 tonnes by 2002.

Eddie George, the Governor of the Bank of England, raised 'strong objections,' but he was 'outgunned by a coalition of the Treasury and some of his own senior officials'.[6] However, when grilled by the Treasury Select Committee, he said the Bank was consulted and that this was a 'straightforward portfolio decision' and 'a perfectly reasonable portfolio decision' to 'reduce exposure to a single asset'. He described the market reaction as 'overdone' – don't we all?[7]

London was still (just) at the epicentre of the gold market, and its many gold traders thought the decision was nuts. Gold prices move in decades-long cycles, they told Bank of England officials, and the price was likely a lot nearer the bottom than the top. 'The timing of the decision was ludicrous. We told them, "You are going to push the gold price down before you sell,"' said Peter Fava, head of precious metal dealing at HSBC. 'We thought it was a disastrous decision; we couldn't understand it.'[8]

Not only did Brown give advance notice of several weeks to the market that the UK would be selling – and how much it would be selling – thereby driving away potential buyers, but the UK lent one-fifth of its gold out, which speculators borrowed and sold in order to front run the UK's sale. Predictably, prices had fallen 10 per cent by the first auction in July, hitting lows not seen since shortly after the US left the gold standard in 1971. No wonder so many see this as among the worst decisions in British financial history.

In sterling the price achieved was £150/oz. Today we are north of £2,500 – that gives you an idea how much sterling has devalued by.

As soon as the commitment was made, a consortium of central banks – including the European Central Bank and the Bank of England – signed the Washington Agreement on Gold in September 1999, limiting gold sales to 400 tonnes per year for five years. This triggered a reversal in price, a 25 per cent rally in a week. Such gains have never been seen before or since.

In total, the UK eventually sold 395 tonnes over seventeen auctions from July 1999 to March 2002, at an average price of US$275/oz, raising approximately US$3.5 billion.[9]

Bullion traders speculate that China was on the other side of the trade, buying the gold at knock-down prices, but that is something we will never know.

The given explanation is that the decision was taken to diversify UK assets. Gold pays no interest; Brown wanted a yield. Many on the left supported the decision for that reason. How was Brown to know yield (interest rates) would fall for the next twenty years? But other theories quickly emerged: it was 'a political decision', not a financial one, said the Bank of England. Some argue, however, it was to suppress the gold price, amidst Gordon Brown and Tony Blair's plans to take Britain into the new euro currency. Others argue it was to help out certain investment banks that were heavily short (betting on the price to fall). Goldman Sachs, among others, was on the wrong side of the trade and, rumour said, facing insolvency: the depressed price enabled them to cover at a small profit. The simplest explanation is that Brown thought the price was going even lower and called the market wrong.

Macquarie's analyst Kamal Naqvi told the *Financial Times*, 'The British are looking to sell before everyone else.' Perhaps that too is true. Brown spoke about 'diversifying our portfolio and reducing the risks'.[10] The 1990s had already seen roughly 1,600 tonnes sold by

Argentina, Australia, Belgium, Canada and the Netherlands. Official sector holdings were declining. The new European Central Bank might not even bother keeping any bullion from the eleven founders of the forthcoming single euro currency. Two months earlier, in April 1999, Switzerland narrowly passed a referendum to take the franc off the gold standard (it became the last nation to do so) and the sale of another 1,300 tonnes was greenlit – though Switzerland never actually sold. The following week, the International Monetary Fund was 'practically unanimous' in its plans to follow suit.

There had been calls – led by Gordon Brown (who would repeat them in 2005) – to use the money to write off third world debt for the new millennium. '100 per cent debt relief on multi-lateral debt, IMF debt, to be written off by revaluing or dealing with IMF gold through sales,' Brown said.[11] He even claimed, 'at the time, the governor of the Bank of England Eddie George said to the Treasury Select Committee that the decision to sell gold was a perfectly reasonable portfolio decision,'[12] which rather goes against Eddie George's version of the story.

Once the decision had been taken, this famously stubborn man would not go back on it, even with all that advice from the gold markets. The result was that he nailed the bottom of the market. Of everything he did as Chancellor, this is what he'll be most remembered for.

Now gold's day was done, many thought, among them Professor Niall Ferguson, who declared the 'twilight of gold'.

Of course, they were wrong. Very wrong.

15.

Irrelevant Gold Stays Relevant

'A US dollar is an IOU from the Federal Reserve Bank.
It's a promissory note that doesn't actually promise
anything. It's not backed by gold or silver'

P. J. O'Rourke, author

The first decade of the twenty-first century was a good one for gold.
It began at below $300/oz and rose relentlessly, amidst an extraor-
dinary bull market for commodities generally, printing gains every
single year except 2008. It eventually hit a high of $1,920/oz in Sep-
tember 2011 at the peak of the Greek government-debt crisis. That
old 1980 high of $850 was long since smashed and forgotten.

The bull market in metals and commodities more generally was
driven by two things. Falling prices in the 1980s and 1990s led to
underinvestment and a shortage of supply. Supply shortages in
commodities, metals especially, cannot be fixed overnight. It takes a
long time and a lot of money to bring a new mine into production.
Never mind the prospecting and exploration; just to take a project
from discovery to production typically takes over ten years, sometimes twenty. An agricultural commodity shortage can be sorted
within a year or two, but not a metals shortage. Mining companies
and their investors really need to believe that higher metals prices
are here to stay before they risk the capital.

The supply shortage then ran into a period of extraordinary
global demand, most of which came from infrastructure spending,
especially in China. Whether it was base metals such as copper and

nickel, or more exotic metals such as platinum or rhodium, everything soared in price.

The US dollar, meanwhile, went into a prolonged period of weakness in the years that followed the dotcom crash. When the dollar is weak, gold is usually strong. Many narratives began to appear about the US dollar's imminent collapse, the evils of fiat money, and the need to return to sound money. These narratives spread quickly thanks to the new invention that was the internet: books were championed, films were viewed many times, and unlikely figures, such as the US Congressman Ron Paul – a great champion of libertarian values and sound money – became internet sensations.

Gold also benefited during this decade from the plethora of new ways that emerged to buy it. As well as the traditional means to buy gold – going to a dealer and buying coins or bars – we saw the emergence of online bullion dealers.

There was E-gold, the 1996 invention of an oncologist and economic history buff named Douglas Jackson and an attorney named Barry Downey. The idea was that you could open an account, buy some gold, and then use that gold as a means of payment to other E-gold account holders. By 1999, even though gold itself was right at the bottom of a twenty-year bear market, it had already achieved what the *Financial Times* called 'critical mass'. Jackson believed his payment system, backed by solid gold, would eventually rival government currencies. By 2008, some 4 million people had accounts with E-gold, and it was processing over $2 billion in transactions a year. The problem was many of these accounts were operated by money-launderers and drug-dealers. It fell victim to hacking, fraud and identity theft. E-gold was already under FBI investigation in 2005. In 2009, the FBI shut it down, leaving the founders in all sorts of legal trouble.

Other companies with similar models to E-gold sprang up and failed in the Noughties – eBullion, Standard Reserve, INTGold and even a multi-million-dollar Ponzi scheme that had no gold at all, OS-Gold. If nothing else, they demonstrated both appetite for gold and discontent with fiat currencies. Many online bullion companies survived and thrived, however: Goldmoney, BullionVault, Goldcore,

The Pure Gold Company and others. Here you could buy amounts as small as a gram of gold and store it in vaults in secure locations such as London, Jersey, Zurich, Singapore and Hong Kong.

The Noughties also saw the emergence of gold exchange-traded funds (ETFs), which probably did more than anything to make owning gold easy. ETFs trade on the stock exchange, and you can buy or sell them just as you would any share. In buying the ETF, you are effectively buying shares in the gold the fund holds. Their ease attracted billions of dollars of capital, especially institutional money, into the gold markets. At the peak of the market in 2020, ETFs held some 3,915 tonnes, making ETFs the second-largest owner of gold in the world after the United States, nominally at least.

This anti-fiat narrative of the Noughties only intensified with the Global Financial Crisis, the bailing out of banks, the extraordinary new practice of creating money by quantitative easing, and zero interest rate policies (ZIRP). The narrative grew so strong it led to the creation of an entirely new non-government currency: bitcoin, also known as gold 2.0 or digital gold. Its foundation, the blockchain, was hailed by computer scientists. Bitcoin roared up in value, making fortunes for its early adopters – the fortunes that goldbugs had been dreaming they would enjoy after the demise of the US dollar.

But then, for no apparent reason – market exhaustion perhaps, or a turnaround in the US dollar – the gold bull market ran out of steam. It coincided with the end of the commodities bull market more generally. The years after 2011 saw gold fall over 40 per cent from $1,920/oz to $1,040/oz. Gold mining companies were obliterated. Most saw declines of over 90 per cent. Thousands, especially those with dubious assets, went bust. Widespread malpractice and fraud were uncovered. Many investors were ruined. As someone who invests in gold mining, 2015 was probably the hardest year I have ever known.

After gold's 2015 low at $1,040/oz, the yellow metal spent the next few years trading sideways. But while the price may have been going nowhere between 2014 and 2018, trading in a range between $1,040/oz and $1,400/oz, an important and potentially very significant change was taking place. Central banks became net buyers again, especially in Asia. Their holdings in gold have been increasing ever since, while they have been reducing their holdings of euros and dollars.

Gold Price Per Ounce 2000–2025

The gold price found some strong tailwinds in 2019, which took it to new highs above $2,000/oz in 2020, before it fell back in the aftermath of Covid. Since 2022, the gold price has been climbing steadily. The main driver appears to be Asian central bank buying.

The big story of gold mining this century has been the fall of South Africa and the emergence of China. Even though South African production levels had been declining since 1970, when it mined over 1,000 tonnes – an amazing figure – it remained the world's largest producer until 2007, when it was finally overtaken by China, which has been the world's largest producer ever since.

The table on the next page, courtesy of the World Gold Council, shows the ten largest producers in the world in 2023.

Rank	Country	Annual production (tonnes)
1	China	378
2	Russian Federation	322
3	Australia	294
4	Canada	192
5	United States	167
6	Ghana	135
7	Indonesia	133
8	Peru	129
9	Mexico	127
10	Uzbekistan	120

Source: World Gold Council

1 oz Bullion Coins

The name krugerrand is an amalgamation of Paul Kruger, who was the President of the South African Republic at the time of the Witwatersrand gold rush and led the Boers in their fierce resistance against the British, and the rand, the South African currency. These coins were introduced in 1967 to help market South African gold. They were an incredible success. More than 50 million have since been minted. On one side Kruger himself is depicted, complete with magnificent beard, on the other a trotting springbok, South Africa's national animal.

Hugely popular with investors and smugglers, by 1980 krugers made up more than 90 per cent of the global coin market, the de facto bullion coin. In 1978 alone, for example, more than 6 million were minted.[1]

But krugers fell out of favour in the 1980s, partly as the gold price declined and partly with sanctions against South Africa. Krugers actually became illegal in the US in 1985, though by this point more than 22 million had been imported. Other countries began copying the model, starting with Canada in 1979 with the gold maple leaf. This one-ounce coin was also hugely popular. Like sovereigns, krugers are mixed with a bit of copper to make them harder. This gives them a reddish hue. The maple leaf was twenty-four-carat and, to my eyes at least, considerably more beautiful.

China introduced the gold panda in 1982, also twenty-four-carat. The US unveiled its American gold eagle (twenty-two-carat) in 1986, and in 1987 Australia minted its first nugget and the British their first britannia (both twenty-four-carat). Austria followed with its Vienna philharmonic in 1989, another twenty-four-carat coin and one I find particularly lovely.

As for which is the most popular and widely traded coin today, that is a close call between the kruger, the Chinese panda and the American eagle. There are more krugers than any other coin, but 'only' 600,000 were minted in 2023, compared with 921,500 eagles.[2] About a million Chinese pandas are minted annually and, because of the sheer number of Chinese, the panda will soon be the most popular bullion coin.

The most successful and widely used bullion coin of all time remains the British sovereign. First minted under Henry VII in 1489, (though more for presentation than to be circulating currency), it only found widespread use after the recoinage of 1816. Since then, more than a billion have been struck. The sovereign remains very popular today, especially in India, the US and, perhaps surprisingly, Greece.

16.

What's the Point of Gold?

'Because silver and gold have their value from the matter itself,
they have first this privilege, that the value of them cannot
be altered by the power of one, nor of a few Commonwealths . . .
But base money may easily be enhanced or abased'

Thomas Hobbes, *Leviathan*[1]

In 1970, the average house in the UK cost £4,000. Today it's £283,000.

That's an increase of seventy-one times over the last fifty years. For a basic necessity of life.

A pint of beer now costs thirty-three times more than it did in 1970.

But the average salary has gone up only twenty-two times. The result is that the ordinary worker has been left behind.

If you cast your eyes over the following two tables, you'll see the cost of various items in the UK and the US in 1970 compared to their cost today.

What can we conclude?

First, to state the obvious, the cost of everything, except phone calls, has risen. Some items have risen by more than others, but everything has gone up.

Second, things have risen by so much more in the UK than in the US. There's a simple explanation. In 1970, the exchange rate was $2.40; today, it is $1.22. The pound has become almost twice as weak.

But within these price increases, there are also some very interesting patterns.

UK Prices	1970	2025	Multiple	Fixed Supply?
Average salary (before tax)	£1,456	£31,980	22x	No
Average house	£4,057	£283,000	71x	Yes + debt
Ford Cortina	£882	£28,000 (Ford Mondeo)	32x	No + debt
Range Rover	£1,998	From £83,525	42x	No + debt
Pint of beer	15p	>£5	33x	No + tax
University tuition	Free (subsidised)	£9,250 a year (Overseas £33–48,000)	–	No + debt
Pint of milk	6p	70p	12x	No
Gallon of petrol	31p	>£7	23x	No + tax
Washing machine	£90	£400	4x	No
Phone call (1976 – 6 mins local)	10p	0	–	No

US Prices	1970	2025	Multiple	Fixed Supply?
Average salary (before tax)	$6,186	$63,795	10x	No
Average house	$23,400	£513,000	22x	Yes + debt
Ford Country Squire	$4,000	£43,620 (Ford Edge)	11x	No + debt
Cadillac Eldorado	$7,750	$94,000 (Escalade)	12x	No + debt
Pint of beer	86c	>$4	5x	No + tax
University tuition (Harvard)	$2,600	$59,000 a year	23x	No + debt
Gallon of milk	$1.32	$4	3x	No
Gallon of petrol	36c	c.$4	11x	No + tax
Washing machine (mid-range)	$280	$1,000	3.6x	No
Phone call (long-distance, 3 minutes)	$1.70	0	–	No

The price increases have been lowest in areas where there is very little debt in the market, where there is no finite supply of the product or where the product has been subject to the deflationary forces of improved productivity: milk and washing machines, for example. Whether it's through battery farming, improved technology or outsourcing to China, we have got better at producing milk and washing machines. For the most part, we don't take on debt to buy them.

Similarly, with wages, whether it is because of cheaper immigrant or outsourced labour, or more women entering the workforce, there has been no shortage of labour supply. Were there to be an actual shortage, as we saw briefly during Covid, wages would rise by more. Meanwhile, for the most part, we don't take on debt to buy labour; it is paid out of cash flow.

Where there are taxes or heavy regulation, prices have gone up by more. We see this with fuel and alcohol, both of which are taxed heavily, especially in the UK.

We do use debt, however, to buy houses, cars and university tuition. The existence of higher debt levels in these markets means more money enters these markets and so prices go up.

Remember: money is created when debt is issued. If you borrow $50,000 in student loans or $1 million to buy a house, that $50,000 or $1 million is created in the act of the bank lending it to you. Yes, *created*. That money did not previously exist. Initiating the loan creates money.

Many people struggle to get their heads round this, but money, today, is debt. The more debt there is, the more money there is.

Back to our tables. Supply of university tuition or automobiles is not finite. You can produce lots more lectures and cars. On the other hand, housing supply, especially in city centres, is more limited. We can thank onerous planning laws for that. Limited supply of the product and an increase of money entering the market to buy that product explain why houses have gone up by so much more than, say, eggs. More debt – more newly created money, in other words – in the market has pushed up house prices in a way that could not have happened if this was a cash market. This is a worldwide phenomenon. What is more, houses are prone to high costs of government, especially via planning and building regulation – your house has to meet certain building standards, even if you do not want it to.

If UK wages had gone up by as much as house prices, the average salary would be around £100,000. It is not even a third of that. If wages in London or New York had gone up by as much as house prices in those cities, well, there isn't enough space on the page to print the zeros.

That discrepancy between wages and house prices explains why housing has become so unaffordable for the young the world over.

On the other hand, if you want to see the deflationary forces of improved technology at work, look no further than the cost of phone calls. Even in a world of rampant money printing a phone call costs almost nothing. Once a local call used to cost perhaps 10p or a quarter for three minutes. A long-distance call cost a lot more. Now I can have a video conference call for hours with anyone anywhere in the world for free.

The way to benefit from this extraordinary inflation in the supply of money has been to own assets of which there is a finite supply, and which people use debt or cheap money (and that includes leverage) to buy. It is why real estate has proved such a brilliant investment. The easiest way for ordinary people to protect themselves against and even benefit from the explosion in money supply since 1971 has been via real estate. That is why houses have become savings vehicles instead of just houses. But now we have an entire generation that cannot afford anywhere to live and will put off starting a family as a result – with all sorts of long-term consequences to western civilisation. How much better for society if houses were just houses, somewhere to live, and instead money itself was the savings vehicle? A store of value as well as a medium of exchange.

Wages have of course increased, but to nothing like the extent to which the purchasing power of money has fallen. It now takes two salaries, fewer children and a lot more debt to enjoy the middle-class lifestyle that many took for granted in the 1950s.

You will have heard it said that the value of money has been eroded by the passage of time. No, no, and a thousand times no. The money's worth has been eroded not by time, but by government. Inflation is not measured properly. It is not even defined properly. Money supply growth is ignored in official inflation measures such as CPI. House prices are ignored. Only the prices of certain consumer goods and services, most of which are prone to the deflationary forces of increased productivity and for which we do not take on debt to buy, are measured. The result is that interest rates have been too low for too long, allowing for the cheap creation of yet more money, whether at the institutional level, privately or in the government bond market. The quantitative easing that followed the Global Financial Crisis and all those other forms of fiscal stimulus that came with Covid have only increased money supply. This is not erosion by the passage of time, but the incremental and compounded effects of decades of debasement.

Of course, there is one money that is not eroded by the passage of time. It is just as it was when the universe was formed.

Really, the cost of everything should have come down, because we have got better at making things. This chart from Our World in Data shows consumer prices over the course of the nineteenth century, when the world was on a gold standard. The line going down means *prices were falling* – and hence *the value of money was increasing*.

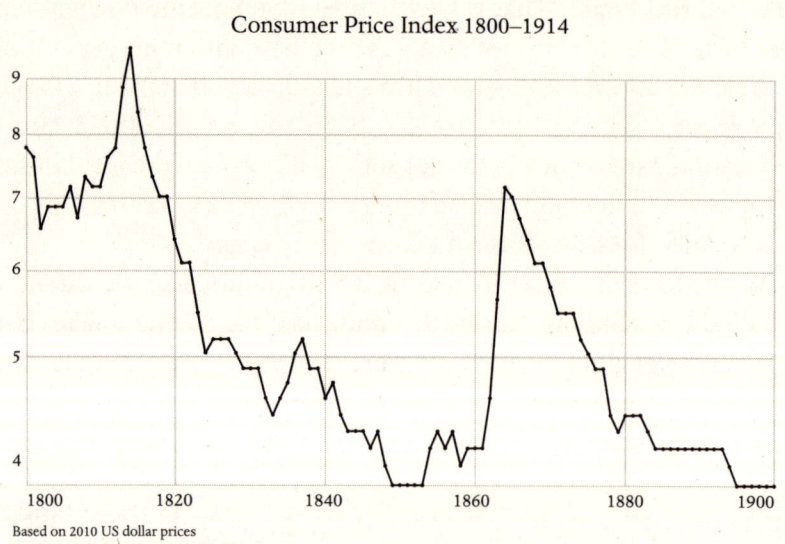

Consumer Price Index 1800–1914

Based on 2010 US dollar prices
Daniel E. Sichel (2017) & Our World in Data

In the thirty years from the end of the Napoleonic Wars in 1816, prices more than halved. That means the purchasing power of money doubled. Your salary bought you twice as much, even if it stayed the same.

Prices rose again with the US Civil War in the 1860s. But from its end to the turn of the twentieth century, prices almost halved again.

Forty years from now, do you think your dollar or your pound will buy you more or less? We all know it will be less. The only question is: how much less?

Imagine knowing your money would buy twice as much in forty years – society's entire approach to saving and planning would transform. Short-termism would evaporate.

In a way, money is stored energy. You expend energy working and in exchange you receive money, which you will then spend at some later stage for the product of somebody else's expended energy. It is essential to a healthy society that that energy keeps its power.

Now take a look at this chart, also from Our World in Data. It shows consumer prices since 1695, when central banking began. You can see how prices rose and fell a little, but traded within a range, for hundreds of years. Then, in the twentieth century, as we began to move away from gold, prices started rising, accelerating especially after 1971.

(Even though neither the inter-war systems nor Bretton Woods were proper gold standards, at least they kept something of a lid on money supply. No such restraint has existed since 1971.)

Consumer Price Index 1694–2011

Based on 2010 US dollar prices, UK CPI 1694–1784 and US CPI 1784–2011
Daniel E. Sichel (2017) & Our World in Data

Gold's Purchasing Power Endures

'There is no such thing as an inflation of prices, relative to gold.
There is such a thing as a depreciated paper currency'

Lysander Spooner, Boston anarchist

We know $100 today doesn't buy what it did ten years ago, but we still think in terms of past prices. A worker might feel great with a 5 per cent raise, but if inflation is 7 per cent, he is actually earning less than before. This is the cognitive bias of money illusion at work. It is part and parcel of fiat money. But, as Leo Tolstoy said, 'Truth, like gold, is to be obtained not by its growth, but by washing away from it all that is not gold.'

Here is a chart of crude oil prices going all the way back to 1950. You can see how in the 1950s and 1960s, oil ranged between $2 and $3 a barrel. Then after 1971, its price rapidly began to rise. Today it is around $80 a barrel.

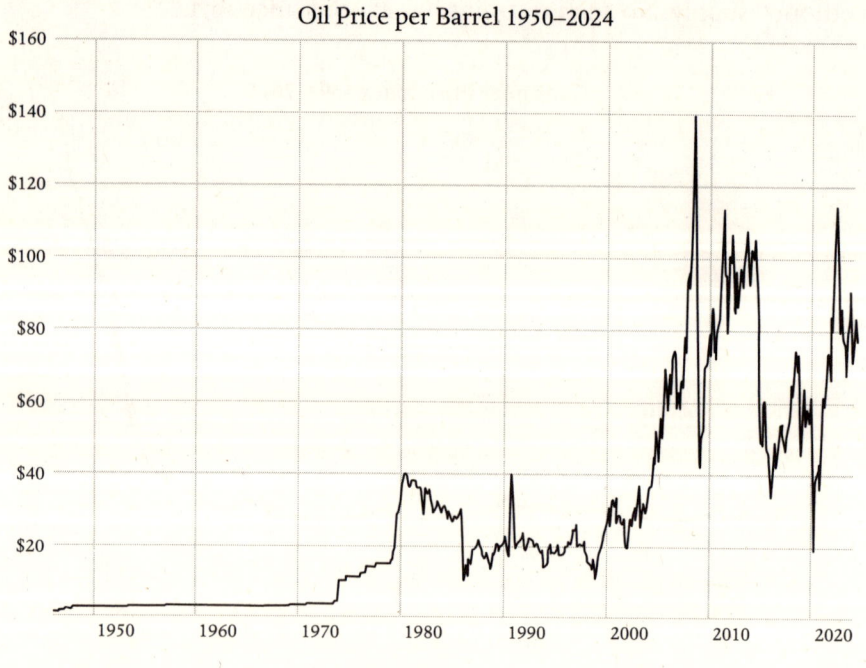

Oil Price per Barrel 1950–2024

Now we look at the same chart, but instead of pricing oil in US dollars, we price it in gold. You will notice that, while the price has risen and fallen, this has been within a range of, for the most part, 0.04 and 0.12 ounces of gold.

Oil Priced in Gold Ounces per Barrel 1950–2024

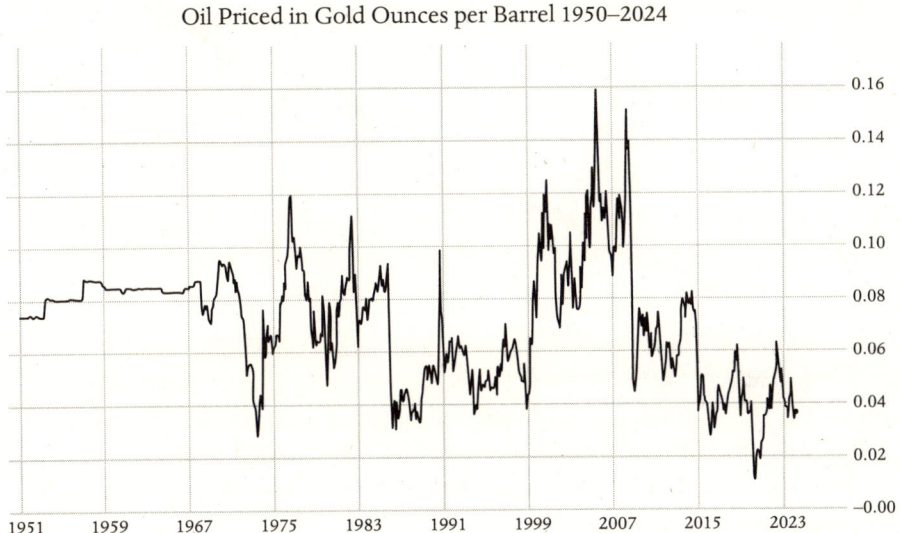

In gold terms, oil is actually cheaper today than it was in the 1950s and 1960s. Not just cheaper, half the price. It does not feel like that when you are filling up your car.

On the next page is the average price of a US house since 1964. You can see how house prices have risen relentlessly. House-price-to-earnings ratios have reached, in the past ten years, levels never before seen in history, and unaffordability has become a major issue for young Americans. It is a huge factor in shrinking family size and the rise of nihilism, fuelling feelings of hopelessness as many feel they will never be able to afford a home.

Average US House Prices 1964–2024

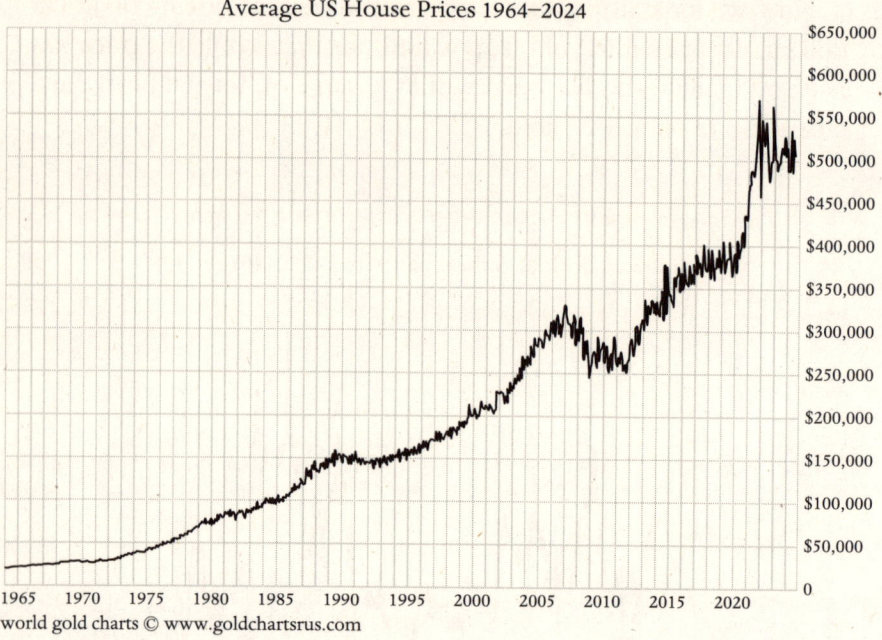

world gold charts © www.goldchartsrus.com

Now we see those same house prices but priced in gold. Amazingly, the average US home is cheaper than it was in the 1960s, and indeed the 1980s and 1990s.

How Many Ounces of Gold to Buy the Average US House 1964–2024

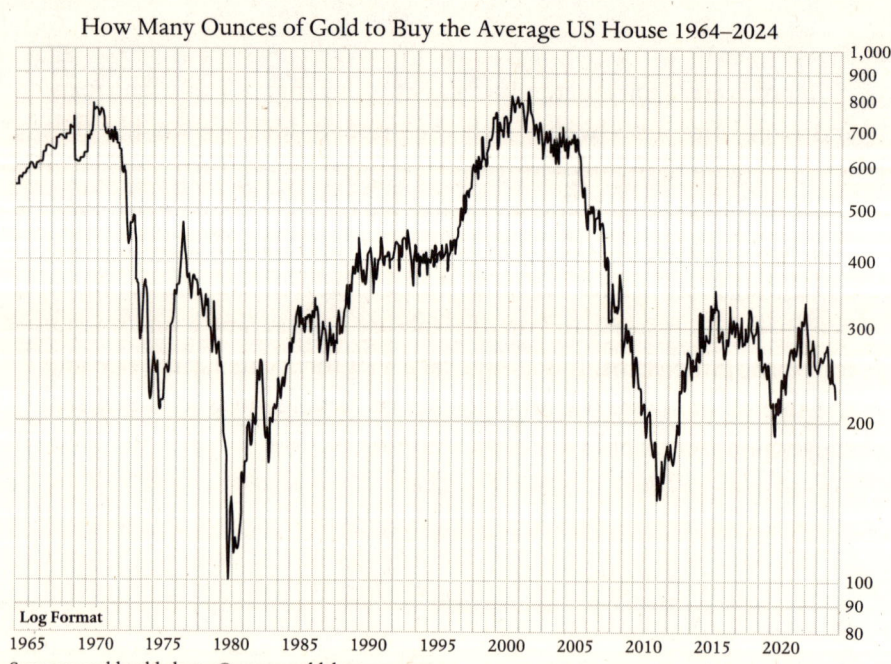

Source: world gold charts © www.goldchartsrus.com

This next chart shows the price of the average UK home since 1953, in pounds, which has risen just as it has in the US, with all the same consequences. The house-price-to-earnings ratio in the UK, at more than nine, is the highest it has been in the modern era.[2]

Average UK House Prices 1953–2024

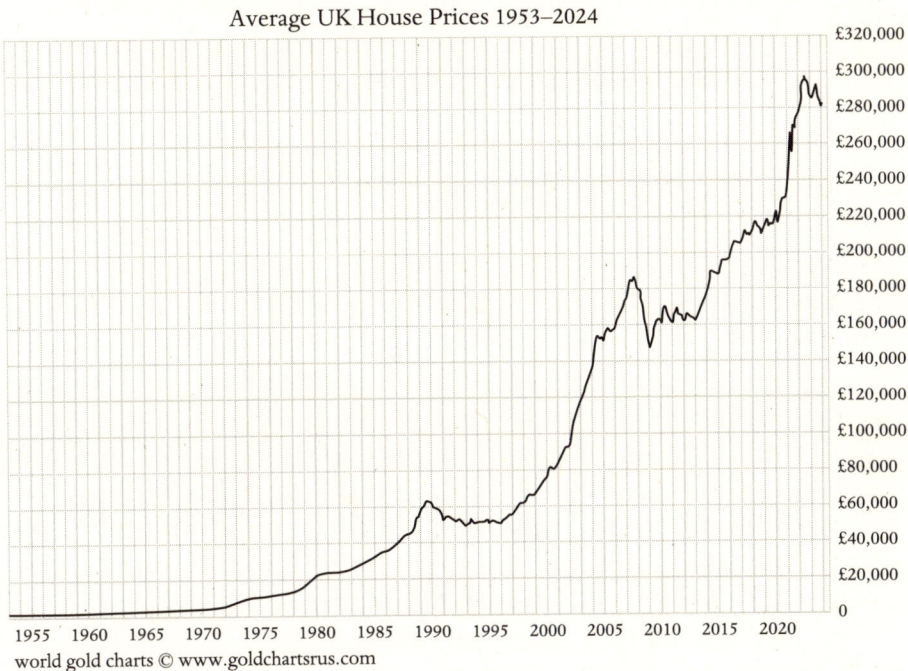

world gold charts © www.goldchartsrus.com

And then on the next page we see those same UK houses but priced in gold. The average UK house, for all the inflation that has taken place, is the same price it was in the 1950s.

When people are asked why they don't have bigger families, the most commonly given reason is the expense. The biggest expense in the westerner's life, as *Daylight Robbery* readers will know, is government. The next biggest is housing. The reaction of governments to the size and cost of government has been not to scale back, but to increase them (paid for with debt, taxes and inflation); the reaction to housing unaffordability has not been to make their money more sound, but to debase it and make it worth even less. So, life gets more expensive and people have smaller families. The reaction to the issue of slow population growth has been to increase immigration levels. In the case of Prime Ministers Tony Blair, David Cameron and others, they actively encouraged it. Thus, among the unintended consequences of fiat in the developed world have been wealth inequality, smaller families and increased immigration, which erodes local traditions, culture and livelihoods. The connections are undeniable once you understand the forces at work.

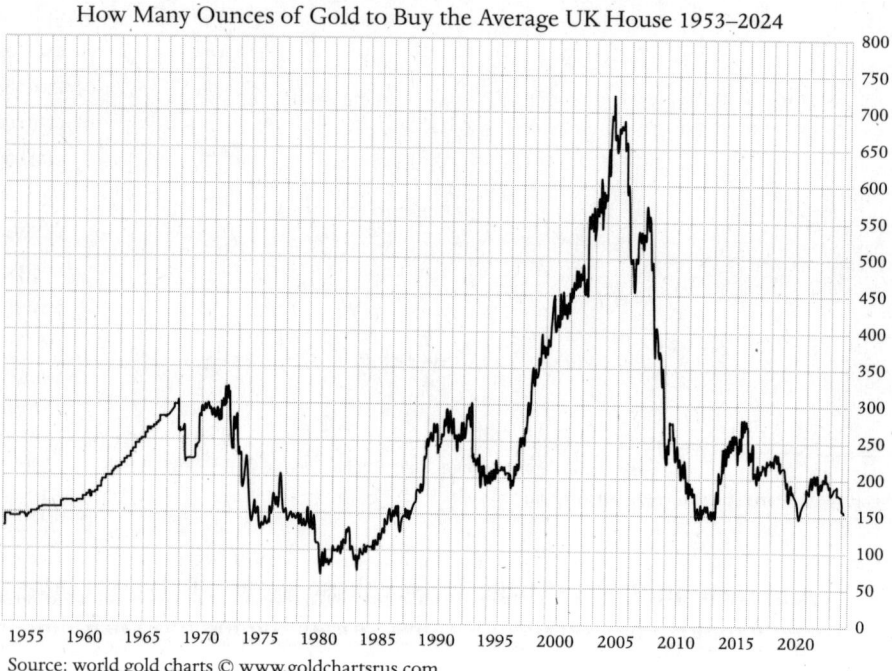

How Many Ounces of Gold to Buy the Average UK House 1953–2024

Source: world gold charts © www.goldchartsrus.com

Wages, in nominal terms, have been rising for decades. Here we see median wages in the US.

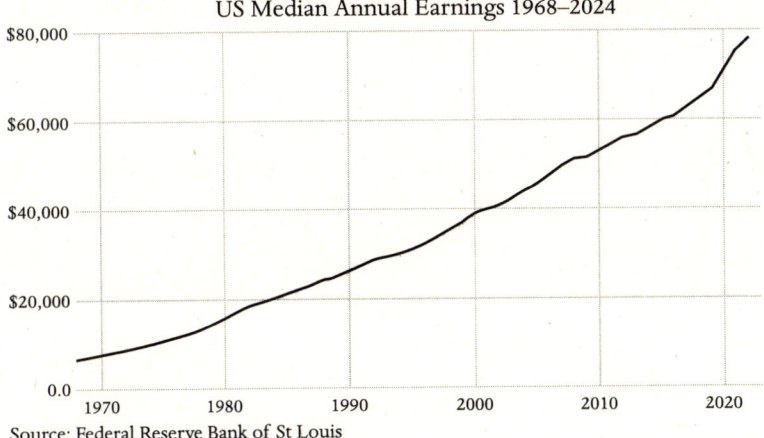

US Median Annual Earnings 1968–2024

Source: Federal Reserve Bank of St Louis

And here we see them in the UK.

UK Median Annual Earnings 1968–2024

ONS – Annual Survey for Hours and Earnings

However, if you measure wages in the constant that is gold, you see that they have only ever been this low once before, when gold hit that temporary high of $850/oz in 1980. Effectively, they are at the lowest point they have ever been since 1970 in both the US and the UK.

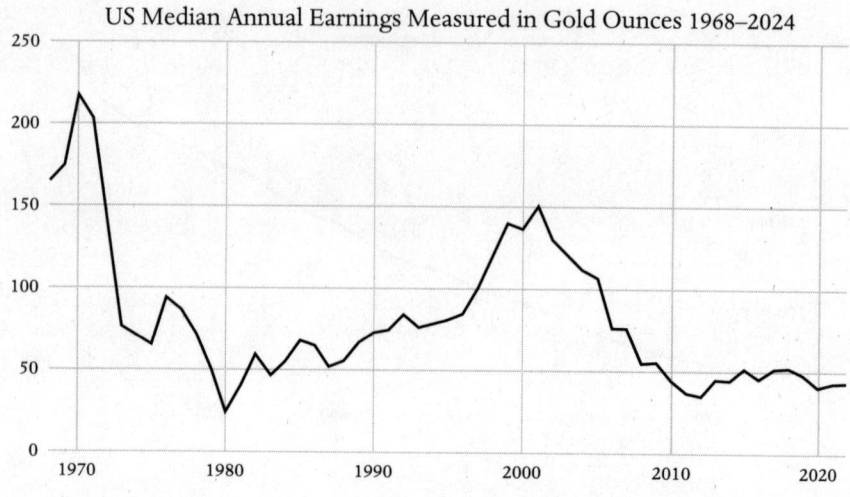

US Median Annual Earnings Measured in Gold Ounces 1968–2024

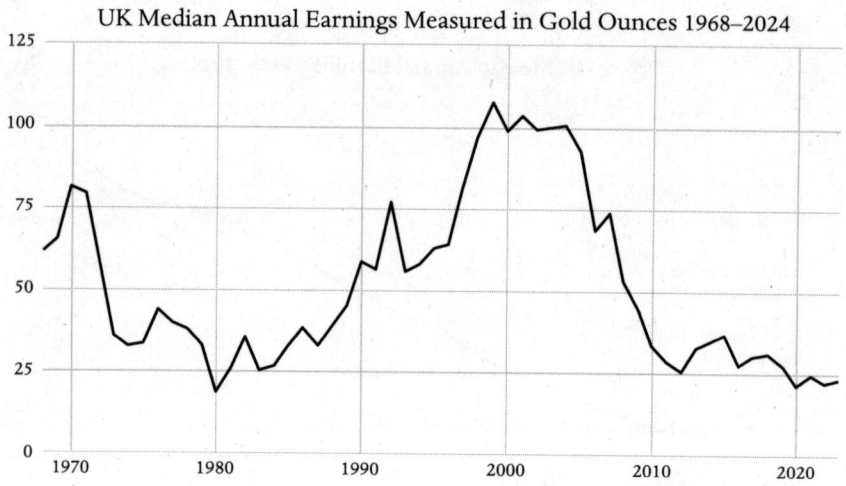

UK Median Annual Earnings Measured in Gold Ounces 1968–2024

No wonder the salaried classes feel they are being left behind. They are. Their purchasing power has plummeted.

All the injustices I have just described – from short-termism to inequality to shrinking family size – are inevitable under a fiat system. So is the expansion of government. When one body in a society has the power to create money at no cost to itself, it is inevitable that body will grow disproportionately large. Thus all the problems of excess government – waste, incompetence, corruption, crony capitalism, eroded privacy and liberty, unaccountability, bureaucratic overreach and excess regulation, manifold businesses built around wealth extraction rather than wealth creation, even war – will inevitably grow too.

Government spending is a precursor to taxation, debt, deficits and money-creation. When new money, i.e. debt, is created, those closest to its issuance benefit first – large corporations and banks. By the time it reaches ordinary people, prices have long since risen, and they find themselves priced out. This 'Cantillon Effect' ensures that the rich grow richer, while the poor are left behind. It exacerbates the wealth divide, especially between generations. Few can afford to live in the area they grew up in, for example, and so people lose touch with their roots. Fiat money does not merely damage wallets; it damages communities.

None of this would have the oxygen it needs to exist if governments had to run the same balanced books that everyone else does. The victims are ordinary people, who face rising living costs, declining real wages and financial instability. This is a systemic problem, and it is self-perpetuating. The only way to stop it is sound, independent money.

'Never trust money more than gold,' said Indonesian author Toba Beta. Indeed.

17.

The Future of Gold

'Gold will be around, gold will be money when the dollar and
the euro and the yuan and the ringgit are mere memories'

Richard Russell, writer

Consider Facebook for a moment. Two elements helped make it such
a global phenomenon.

First, it's a digital, not a physical, business. Digital things can
multiply, or 'scale', in ways that physical things simply cannot.

Second, it's a network – a huge web of millions of interconnected
nodes (in this case, people).

Over the last generation, there has been a colossal shift in our
economies from physical and tangible to digital and intangible. The
tangible economy has grown, but it has been nothing like the growth
of the intangible economy. In 1990, the three biggest companies in
Silicon Valley had a total market cap of $36 billion. Today, the three
biggest – Facebook, Google and Apple – have a combined market
cap almost 200 times higher at $7 trillion. Once, physical things like
land, mines, farms and gold were the most valuable assets. Today,
extraordinary value lies in intangible goods – software, brands, intellectual property, operating systems, networks, unique supply chains
and, perhaps above all, data.

You can send out an email and reach thousands, millions even,
in a way that is faster, simpler and cheaper than printing and distributing flyers. You can post a photo on Instagram or a song on
Spotify and reach a global audience instantly in a way that you

never could with physical photographs or LPs. Manufacturing and distributing widgets or machinery is problematic. Now you can upload an app to an app store, and it can be accessed by billions immediately. The inherent scalability of digital gives businesses unprecedented reach and efficiency compared to traditional physical methods.

With such rapid growth potential, it is no wonder the intangible economy attracts more investment. It is all facilitated by the greatest intangible of the lot: the internet. Google is an information network, YouTube a video network, Facebook a social network, Amazon a retail network and X a speech network.

So much value today is digital. The bond market is digital. The foreign exchange markets are digital. Equities are mostly digital. Even money itself is digital. Barely 1 per cent of western money exists as cash. The role of metal, be it copper, nickel, silver or gold, as a medium of exchange – which it had for thousands of years – is over. Coinage, that incredible financial technology that has roots in the legend of King Midas, is done. Even the role of paper money is close to an end. Digital payments are more convenient; and in the marketplace, convenience wins.

What is gold's role in all of this?

It is as analogue an asset as you can get – older than the earth itself and indestructible. Is it outdated, unnecessary and irrelevant?

It may be God's money. With new gold supply and the human population increasing at the same rate, it may be the money of Natural Law. But what seems 'natural' often comes to an end. The horse was 'natural' transport for almost as long as gold was money. Then the Industrial Revolution came along. By the mid-nineteenth century, railroads had become the primary mode of transportation for people and goods. Then came the automobile in the late nineteenth and early twentieth centuries. 'Horseless carriages' they were even called. Now the horse is, for the most part, an expensive luxury. Its use is often just symbolic.

Could you say the same about gold? Is it as irrelevant to modern finance as the horse now is to transport? Let's see.

The Cable That Changed History

'The President of the United States acknowledges with profound
gratification the receipt of Her Majesty's despatch'

Andrew Johnson, 17th President of the United States[1]

In the mid-nineteenth century, there were various attempts to lay cables across the Atlantic Ocean between the UK and the US. It took several failures, numerous bankruptcies and over ten years before they got it right, but eventually they did, and on 27 July 1866, Queen Victoria sent a message to US President Johnson, to which he immediately replied. To send a note by ship could take ten days or more. Now it took just a few minutes. With the dramatically reduced communication times, somebody came up with the advertising slogan 'two weeks to two minutes'.

Back then, the world was on a gold standard, of course. You could send gold by ship. You could carry gold, or paper promising gold, on your person. But you couldn't send gold down the cable, nor could you send paper. You could, however, send a promise.

Within a fortnight of Queen Victoria's first message, that's exactly what two parties who trusted each other did. They sent a promise: an exchange rate between the dollar and the pound, both gold-backed currencies, was agreed and then published in *The New York Times* on 10 August. That is why, to this day, the pound–dollar exchange rate, GBPUSD, is known as cable.

Today, millions of financial transactions take place every second. Each one is a promise between parties that trust each other: you pay with your credit card, your card talks to the card reader and its bank, which then talks to the shopkeeper's bank and so on. These promises, transferring as quickly as words, are 'promissory money'. Promissory money has evolved as communication has evolved – indeed money is often the spur for the evolution of communication technology.

But promises disappear. Gold doesn't. The two are quite different forms of money: one is based on belief; the other is real.

Gold is the only form of money that isn't a promise. That makes it not only useful, but fundamental.

Bitcoin – Gold 2.0

Actually, there is another form of money that isn't a promise: bitcoin.

I know there are some that love bitcoin – I am one of those – and some that think it is a scam, worthless or fake. Hopefully, the progress bitcoin has made in the years since it was invented is enough to now discount the latter view. If it was going to die, it would have died by now. The opposite has happened: what started as a speculative asset for a few computer coders and libertarian-minded discontents has become a core holding for investors, and now corporations and countries, with a market cap above $2 trillion.

While gold is perhaps the most analogue asset there is, bitcoin is entirely digital. You cannot see or touch it: one of the reasons so many distrust it. It was designed to be cash for the internet: a form of money you could send directly from A to B without the need for middlemen or, as its inventor Satoshi Nakamoto put it, 'trusted third parties'. In other words, money where no promise is required.

For decades, coders had wrestled with the problem of digital cash. The issue was that if I send you any form of computer code, you can copy and paste it multiple times. If you can do this with money, it quickly becomes worthless. The only way to stop this is to have a trusted third party verify transactions – at which point the money becomes promissory. Satoshi's breakthrough was to use an independent, decentralised database – the blockchain.

I hand you a gold coin; its value is immediately transferred from me to you. The gold is money in and of itself – a bearer asset. Whoever holds the gold, holds the value. The same applies to bitcoin, only the whole process is digital, not physical. I send you a bitcoin, and its value is now held by you. There is no need for promises or third parties. Every transaction is confirmed by the blockchain and is transparently visible on it. The code by which the system functions is open source and visible to all. Hence the mantra: 'Don't trust, verify.'

Obviously, gold is beautiful and compelling. Bitcoin does not have that, even with the brilliance of its design. For bitcoin to have value, other people have to feel bitcoin has value. It is possible that at a certain point few will think that way and the bitcoin price will plummet. That will never happen to gold because, even in a worst-case future scenario, gold will always have value as jewellery.

On the other hand, gold does not have bitcoin's portability. Look at the crazy wild goose chases that occurred in the Second World War as the world scrambled to either steal or safeguard its gold. Such a situation could never occur with bitcoin. It's just a matter of protecting your keys, which is easy to do. If we ever populate outer space, it will be easy to send bitcoin to one another. Gold will be harder – it's a lot heavier.

The blockchain itself is run and protected by extraordinary amounts of computer power, on a network of independent computers located around the world, and it would take quantum computing's answer to a nuclear explosion to take it down.

Like gold, bitcoin is a borderless, universal currency – designed for the borderless medium that is the internet.

Yes, bitcoin does require some trust or belief in that you have to believe that the blockchain will continue to work. Many doubt that it will, but many more simply point to the fact that it does work, that it has no central point of failure, while being backed by extraordinary amounts of computer power.

Bitcoin is the money of the future. It will be here for a long time. But gold will be around for even longer.

Promises, Promises, Promises

'All money is a matter of belief'

Adam Smith, economist (attrib.)

Look at an American or British bank note (if you still use them) and you will see a promise inscribed: 'Will pay the bearer on demand' or 'I promise to pay the bearer'. Fiat money is based on promises. Once, this meant money could be exchanged for gold or silver. Today, it is a promise of nothing. But we still use it.

In the digital world, those promises are recorded and exchanged via computers between parties that trust each other.

There is a term by which promissory money is more commonly known: credit.

'Credit is everything and everything is credit,' said financier J. P. Morgan in 1912. 'Credit' comes from the Latin 'credere', meaning 'to believe' or 'trust'. It refers to the ability to borrow money or receive goods with the promise of the creditor being paid back in the future.

Today the entire global financial system, once built on gold, is now built on credit, which perhaps explains the never-ending sense of paranoia that the whole thing is about to fall apart.

When he said that, Morgan had been called to testify before Congress in 1912, and was trying to explain the difference between money and credit. Credit, he said, is 'an evidence of banking, but it is not the money itself. Money is gold, and nothing else.'[2]

In ancient Mesopotamia, people used gold and silver, but also clay tokens – discs for sheep, cones for barley – baked inside clay balls to represent debts. When debts were settled, the balls were smashed. (Over time, man found it more efficient to inscribe the clay with pictures representing the items owed and so did the first systems of writing come about – remember what I said about money and communication technology: they evolve together.) Even though man was using gold as money, he was also using promises. There is a distinction, then, between gold and all other forms of money. Both gold and credit can be used as a store of value. Credit as a store of value is why the bond market is so enormous. Both gold and credit can be used as a medium of exchange or unit of account. Both function as money, in other words. But they are not the same.

Credit can be digital. It is therefore highly versatile. I have often said 'money is tech' and, in this sense, it is. It evolves as communication evolves, even as language evolves.

But gold never changes, and never will. It is the only form of money that exists in and of itself. It does not rely on the words of others, on promises, trust, regulation or law.

Gold will always be, if nothing else, the money of last resort, and thus will it also always lie at the top of the hierarchy of financial instruments. When all else fails, there is gold. That's why I say it is not only useful, but fundamental.

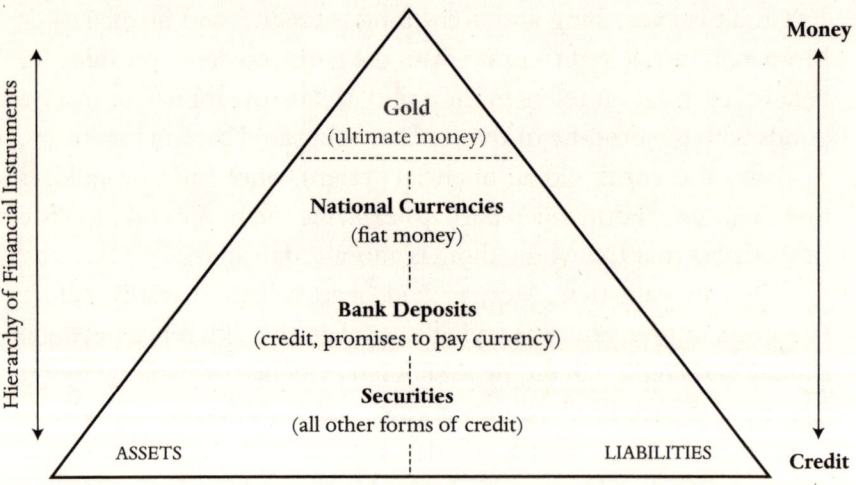

It may be that we never need gold in our lifetime. But it also means we should always have it. That is why so many see gold as insurance. You will often hear me say, 'Put 10 per cent of your net worth in gold and hope it doesn't go up.' If it is going up, it usually means there is trouble somewhere.

The Modern Financial Perspective

'Gold is still significant'

Alan Greenspan, Chairman of the Federal Reserve (1987–2006)[3]

'I ask myself, if it's a relic why is there a trillion dollars held in gold by the world's central banks plus the IMF and all of the other financial institutions,' said Alan Greenspan in 2018. 'If it's worthless and meaningless, why is everybody holding it?'[4]

One possible answer to this question came during a 2011 exchange between Congressman Ron Paul and then-Federal Reserve Chairman Ben Bernanke.

Paul: Do you think gold is money?
Bernanke: (long pause) No.
Paul: It's not money?
Bernanke: It's a precious metal.
Paul: Why do central banks hold it?
Bernanke: Well, it's a form of reserves.
Paul: Why don't they hold diamonds?
Bernanke: Well, it's tradition – long-term tradition.[5]

Perhaps that is the only reason central banks hold gold: tradition. They own it as a result of what happened in the nineteenth and twentieth centuries, and never sold it.

Paul championed gold, sound money and free markets. Bernanke was a technocrat. He not only advocated, but imposed fiat money, interest rates, quantitative easing, central planning, centrally managed economies and data-driven policy. They were on opposing sides of the culture war. But the latter, Bernanke worldview is what dominates government and policymaking today. It is not pro-gold. Those who favour central planning rarely are. Fiat money gives them more control. They are not going to cede power to gold, not voluntarily anyway.

Gold used to be the backbone of the financial system. Today, you could argue that it is just a contrarian investment, which does well in times of uncertainty. Global GDP is over $100 trillion. The total value of the world's stock markets is over $111 trillion.[6] Global bond markets (debt securities) are worth around $140 trillion.[7] The value of financial assets held by investors and central banks is $280 trillion.[8] World real estate is worth around $650 trillion.[9] The total value of physical gold demand last year was $382 billion.[10]

If you add up the value of all the gold bullion traded, all the gold mining companies, the funds, and anything related, you do not even reach $1 trillion. In the context of the global financial system – of global credit – gold, even if it has its noisy champions, is almost irrelevant.

On the other hand, the total value of all the gold in the world – some 200,000 tonnes – is a not so insignificant $23 trillion.[11] Gold futures, at $233 billion/day, are the second-most heavily traded asset in the world, more than US Treasury Bills, or euro–sterling or euro–yen futures. Only S&P 500 futures ($300 billion/day) exceed them.[12] So gold still has some significance.

In today's modern world, fiat currency is the norm. It is the basis of the global economic system. Sound money might be preferable, but to go back to gold standards would require an enormous shift. There would be such upheaval to the way that governments, the state and central banks currently operate. It would meet with huge resistance. The system would almost not allow it.

To go back to using gold-backed government currency is not practically possible without one of two things. Either, one, a dramatic increase in gold supply, as happened in the gold rushes of the second half of the nineteenth century. For this to occur, there would have to be either a plethora of new discoveries – unlikely, but never say never – or some new technology that improves the efficiency of mining. Or, two, there would need to be a dramatic upward revaluation of the gold price to offset all the fiat currency that has been created. For the US dollar to be fully gold-backed, the gold price would have to be north of $80,000/oz.[13] This is not going to happen unless there is a major regime change or the hand of government is forced, perhaps by some kind of international currency crisis. That is a possibility, though not a likelihood, I would say, though others argue that it is inevitable. (Such an upward revaluation would also trigger a huge mining boom.)

In such a scenario, I am sure governments would implement either some kind of confiscation, as happened with Roosevelt in the 1930s, or heavy taxation (for example, a windfall tax on unrealised gains of gold holdings), so that governments rather than 'undeserving' citizens would ultimately lock in the gain. The evidence of history is that governments would find a way of doing this under the pretext of an emergency. ETFs, of which both ownership and storage location is clear, would be an easy target for confiscation or taxation.

In such a scenario, digital gold – perhaps in the form of central bank digital currencies – rather than physical gold could become a medium of exchange. Gold would be held in some trusted bank or vault, and ownership of that gold would change hands by digital transfer. But then we are back to promissory money again, albeit gold-backed. Unlikely, I would have thought.

Gold's future, like its past, I suspect, will chiefly be as a store and display of value.

But this is not absolute, and there will be exceptions, especially in times of crisis. 'Russia paid Iran "in gold bullion" for drones used in attacks on Ukraine', ran a recent headline in the *Daily Telegraph*.[14] Kremlin 'paid in literal gold', said the subhead. Leaked documents posted online by a hacker group show that Russia flew more than two tonnes of gold to Iranian manufacturer Sahara Thunder. Here are two nations shut out of the SWIFT banking network, but who want to transact, and they opted to settle in gold. Great. But how impractical is flying two tonnes of gold? It's only really ever going to be a currency of last resort, as was the case here, between two nations shut out of international banking.

Will Industrial Demand Change the Future of Gold?

'Hee that labours and thrives, spins gold'

George Herbert, poet[15]

Roughly 50 per cent of annual gold demand comes from the jewellery industry: it is the single biggest buyer of gold. Another 23 per cent is investment demand, and 21 per cent – last year at least – came from central banks.[16] Jewellery is a form of saving and investment, only the gold is worn rather than stored. Just 6 per cent of demand is industrial.

Jewellery demand will increase a little as people feel wealthier, and it will decline in times of recession. It won't disappear, nor will it suddenly increase to the extent that it creates shortages. It will be overall constant.

A change in macroeconomic circumstances could easily mean, for example, that central banks become net sellers. It is not like it has not happened before. But, while de-dollarisation remains a theme (more on this in a moment), I do not see that as likely. Similarly, investment demand could easily shrink.

Industrial demand is rather more at the margin, but might we see demand growth there? Interestingly, one huge potential increase in demand will come at the final frontier in outer space.

Though both silver and copper are better conductors of electricity than gold, gold is more resistant to corrosion and oxidation, so it finds considerable use in electronics as a coating – in connectors, switches and circuit boards – especially where long-term stability is important. This makes it ideal for the aerospace and outer space industries, where it is used to coat satellite components and spacecraft. It can reflect infrared radiation and protect craft from overheating – especially important in the wild temperature fluctuations of outer space. It is also used in heat shields which protect sensitive equipment from high temperatures during re-entry into the earth's atmosphere. Astronaut umbilical cables and helmet visors are plated with gold for protection against UV radiation and extreme temperatures.

Ultimately, gold's permanence is the fundamental reason for its use. You need durable materials. When you send a spacecraft to outer space, you can't easily repair it.

This usage is not yet significant enough to radically alter gold demand, but that could change, and quite dramatically so, as space exploration increases.

Gold's reflective properties, combined with its stability, means it also finds use in optics – in lenses and mirrors, especially space telescopes, to reflect infrared light. Gold plates the mirrors of the celebrated James Webb telescope, the largest optical telescope in space, to optimise the mirrors' function, allowing it to view objects too old, distant or faint for the Hubble Space Telescope.

There is a Canadian company, Totenpass, that has been developing some interesting tech, also related to gold's longevity:

> a permanent digital storage drive constructed from solid gold that requires no energy and has no movable parts. Digital data is written onto the drive by way of a proprietary light-diffraction process. This technology allows for the permanent storage of precious digital data, thereby eliminating any future dependence on the internet and the vast amounts of energy required presently to store content.[17]

Here, it seems, is a very modern application for the extraordinary permanence of gold.

Gold is being used increasingly in nanotechnology. Gold nanoparticles are used in photonics (the science of light waves), especially in the development of light-based technologies for imaging and sensors. Gold's inertness makes it an excellent material for nanoparticles used as catalysts in various chemical reactions, improving the efficiency of many processes from air purification to solar power generation. And again, its conductivity and resistance to oxidation make it ideal for nanoscale electronic components.

Gold nanoparticles are used in medical diagnostics and treatments, including targeted drug delivery and cancer therapy, because they can be easily detected and manipulated. Additionally, gold's biocompatibility ensures it does not provoke an immune response, making it suitable for various biomedical applications. In 2013, researchers found that gold nanoparticles reduced the ability of HIV to reproduce and infect new cells.

Gold is now a weapon in the battle against malaria. Of the hundreds of millions of malaria tests sold each year, many contain gold: gold nanoparticles bind with specific malaria antigens, which allows for quick and accurate detection of the disease. The test results can be ready in fifteen minutes.

Gold nanoparticles are also sometimes used in building materials for strength and thermal regulation. Coat glass with gold and in summer it will reflect the sun, while in winter it will bounce internal heat back into rooms to retain warmth. Gold reflective glass can therefore result in substantial energy savings. It is corrosion-resistant too, which increases longevity.

But the main reason for its use in building is opulence. Gold will give your building's facade unique and striking appeal. Toronto's Royal Bank Plaza, the Grand Lisboa hotel and casino in Macau, and the Al Yaqoub Tower in Dubai are all notable examples, as is Trump International Hotel and Tower in Las Vegas: its gleaming gold-tinted glass makes it stand out even on the Las Vegas Strip. The golden-domed St Michael's Cathedral in Kyiv is also a stunning example. To use gold on a roof or facade is extravagant but perhaps not as extravagant as you might think: an ounce of gold will cover up to 1,000 square feet (ninety square metres) in gold plate, plus there are those energy savings.

All in all, lots of exciting potential, but none of this demand – in most cases we are talking about plate or nanoparticles – will be enough to significantly affect the price of gold.

The main source of gold demand will be what it has always been: investment and jewellery.

18.

How Much Gold Does China Have? And Why?

'Real gold is not afraid of the melting pot'

Chinese proverb

In China, gold is a symbol of happiness, as well as of prosperity, and the Chinese have long adored it. A wealthy child is born not with a silver spoon in his mouth, but with golden chopsticks. Indeed, China was probably the birthplace of alchemy: they even thought alchemical gold was superior to the real stuff.

If there is one thing that China is not short of, it's ambition. Nor is it short of pride. Rumours abound that it has set its eyes on the global reserve currency status currently enjoyed by the US dollar. To achieve that, it will need a banking system to match.

Over the last twenty years, China has been quietly and without sensation accumulating extraordinary amounts of gold. It has almost certainly been understating its reserves. This accumulation may mean very little beyond standard asset allocation. But it may also be linked to its ambitions for its currency. If so, the accumulation has enormous geopolitical significance.

The rise of China has been an incredible economic growth story. From a centrally planned, insular and primarily agrarian economy in the 1970s, its 'reform and opening-up' policy has seen GDP grow annually at almost 10 per cent, from $360 billion in 1990 to over $18 trillion in 2022. It has become the world's largest trading nation, its largest manufacturer and second-largest economy. Before long, it will be the largest – if it isn't already.

Trade (exports plus imports) has grown from $280 billion to above $6 trillion over the same period. Foreign direct investment is up more than thirty-five times. Almost a billion people have been lifted out of extreme poverty. Its cities have expanded, and its urban population has risen from 26 per cent to 63 per cent. Unhindered by patent law or copyright, it has made colossal strides in technological innovation. Its military has also grown, so that now it is not just by economic might that it rivals the US.

The table below, courtesy of the World Gold Council, shows reported gold holdings by nation.[1]

Gold Reserves by Country

Rank	Country	Gold Reserves (tonnes)	% F/X Holdings
1	United States	8,133	71.33
2	Germany	3,352	70.6
3	Italy	2,452	67.6
4	France	2,437	68.6
5	Russian Federation	2,333	28.1
6	China	2,262	4.6
7	Switzerland	1,040	8
8	Japan	846	4.7
9	India	822	9
10	Netherlands	612	60.5
11	Turkey	570	100
12	Taiwan	422	4.7
13	Portugal	383	73.3
14	Poland	360	12.7
15	Uzbekistan	358	74.3
16	Saudi Arabia	323	4.7
17	Kazakhstan	311	58.4
18	United Kingdom	310	12.6
19	Lebanon	287	54.5
20	Spain	282	19.3

The US is top. It has 8,133 tonnes of gold, which make up over 70 per cent of its foreign exchange holdings. But it might be worth mentioning that the US has not properly audited its gold in over sixty years. The last comprehensive audit took place under the Eisenhower administration. There have been checks and inspections, but no proper audit. The reasons given – which have ranged from the lack of urgency to the operational complexity – have been flimsy. Many argue that the gold isn't all there, and that much of it was used to defend the dollar in the 1960s. Moreover, what is there is not all of good delivery quality, meaning it would not be readily accepted in international bullion markets. Much of the gold is that which Roosevelt confiscated in the 1930s, so-called 'coinmelt', and many of the commonly confiscated coins, such as the $20 double eagle, were only 90 per cent pure and mixed with copper to make them harder. When they were melted down, they were not always properly refined to modern standards, and the new bars weighed 320–330 ounces, whereas 400 ounces is the standard today. In practice, this means Fort Knox gold would not be accepted without additional processing. But until a proper audit takes place, this is all speculation, albeit informed speculation. We don't know the full facts. Here is a joke I rather like:

Head of US Homeland Security: Mr President, there's no gold in Fort Knox.
President: What do you mean there's no gold in Fort Knox?
Head of US Homeland Security: The vaults are empty. There's no gold in Fort Knox.
President: Double the guard!

However, shortly after his inauguration in 2025, President Donald Trump said there will be a full audit of Fort Knox, a sentiment echoed by his 'chief fixer' Elon Musk. So, we should not be long waiting. Given that they have both made light of it – there have been plenty of jokes – one can assume that there are no terrible secrets being kept. In an interview with Bloomberg's *Surveillance* on

20 February 2025, newly appointed Treasury Secretary Scott Bessent said, 'I can tell the American people on camera right now, there was a report, September 30th, 2024, all the gold is there.'[2] It must have been an internal report! A full audit is a different matter. Even so, this appears to be an area where we will soon have clarity.

Returning to the above list of gold holdings, we see the UK sits proudly in eighteenth position (thank you, Gordon Brown), behind Kazakhstan, Turkey and Uzbekistan – all, notably, members of the Shanghai Cooperation Association, which we will come to in a moment.

China currently lies in sixth place. It says it has 2,262 tonnes of gold.

At $2,500/oz, those gold holdings are worth $182 billion. Yet it has $3.2 trillion in US dollars[3] – more than UK annual GDP. Its US dollar holdings eclipse those of every other nation: three times as many as Japan, the second-largest owner.

China's gold holdings amount to 4.6 per cent of its foreign exchange reserves (this number was just 3 per cent in 2022 – it is increasing all the time); the US's gold holdings equate to over 70 per cent of its reserves. If China were to approach a similar level to the US, it would need more than thirteen times as much gold: somewhere in the region of 29,000 tonnes.

It is possible China is close to that level already.

The World's Biggest Producer and the World's Biggest Importer

'We must not shine too brightly'

Deng Xiaoping, leader of the People's Republic of China (1978–89)

There are two parts to my argument: some simple maths and some guesswork.

In 2007, China overtook South Africa to become the world's largest gold producer. It has remained so ever since. Last year it produced 377 tonnes, roughly 10 per cent of global supply. This past decade it has produced about 15 per cent of all the gold mined in the world. Since 2000, China has mined roughly 7,580 tonnes.[4] Over half of Chinese gold production is state-owned.[5] The China National Gold Group Corporation (CNGGC) alone accounts for 20 per cent.

The export of domestic mine production is not allowed. The export of goods manufactured from imported gold – i.e. jewellery – is, though China is actually a net importer. This is, it says, to ensure the stability of its domestic gold market and to promote the development of its domestic gold industry.

If over 50 per cent of Chinese gold production is state-owned, and few of those 7,580 tonnes of production have been exported (China is, actually, a net importer of gold jewellery), then already that official figure of 2,262 tonnes is exceeded.

There is more.

With reserves in decline at home, Chinese mining companies have also been acquiring properties abroad, especially across Africa, South America and Asia. It is impossible to get a precise number, but estimates are that annual Chinese international production is in the 50–100-tonne range and growing. What percentage of that internationally produced gold, more than half of which is state-owned, is making its way to the Chinese government? A considerable amount, I would say.

The second side to this argument is that, as well as being the world's biggest producer of gold, China is the world's biggest importer. Imports largely come via Switzerland, London, Dubai or Hong Kong. Gold imports via London, Switzerland and Dubai go undeclared, but we know that via Hong Kong alone 8,000 tonnes have entered the country since 2000.[6] However, some of that gold exits and re-enters the country as part of one of China's largest industries – money-laundering – so there is a probability of some double-counting here.

Whether imported, mined or recycled, a large part of the gold entering China goes through the Shanghai Gold Exchange

(SGE), including the gold imported from Hong Kong. So SGE withdrawals – for which we do have numbers – can act as something of an approximation for demand (although again not entirely accurate, as some of the deposits are via recycled jewellery). It is possible to get numbers for SGE withdrawals: since 2008, over 26,300 tonnes have been withdrawn from the SGE.[7]

Then we have to add in gold held in China, whether as bullion or jewellery, prior to 2000. The World Gold Council estimates a figure of 2,500 tonnes in privately owned jewellery. If you add this to domestic mining and official reserves, you get a figure of around 4,000 tonnes.

Cobble it all together – cumulative production, imports and existing stock – and you arrive at a figure of around 38,000 tonnes. This figure is agreed upon by many of the world's top analysts.

But there is more. As one of those analysts, Ross Norman, points out to me:

'Not all gold entering China is accounted for by SGE withdrawals. The People's Bank of China (PBOC), the central bank, likes internationally recognised 400-ounce bars, which do not trade on the SGE. The SGE sells its gold in yuan, while the PBOC often uses dollars on exchanges in London, Dubai and Switzerland. Many trades are kept from the public eye. The army, too, owns gold and does not have to declare its purchases. There are other state agencies that hold gold as well, such as the sovereign wealth fund: the State Administration of Foreign Exchange and China Investment Corporation.'

According to this logic, it is easy to estimate there is comfortably in excess of 40,000 tonnes of gold in China. In the US, however, if you cobble together domestic production, imports and existing holdings, both private and public, there are closer to 27,000 tonnes in total.[8] Hence why I say there is more gold in China. In India, which is the largest retail consumer, the total is thought to be 21,000 tonnes.

If we ignore domestic mining in China, on the grounds that it is sold through the SGE, we can discount 7,580 tonnes. And if we say that 75 per cent of imports via Hong Kong are circular, money-laundering gold, we can discount a further 6,000 tonnes. Then we have a lower total figure of 26,420 tonnes, to which we can add the roughly 2,500 tonnes (a low estimate) of gold secretly imported via London, Dubai and Switzerland, which has not passed through the SGE. This gives us a figure of 28,920 tonnes, a number comparable to the US.

But how much of that gold is state-owned? Given state control of its mining, as well as state power generally, an estimate of 50 per cent or more is not unreasonable. The implication is that China owns anything from 13,000 to 20,000 tonnes, considerably more than the US's 8,133 tonnes. (In the US, nationally owned gold stands at about 30 per cent of total holdings.)

'Chinese official gold holdings are 2,262 tonnes,' says Ross Norman. 'But few of us believe that. Put an additional zero on the end (22,620 tonnes) and I should not be surprised if that is not much closer to their actual holdings.'

Alasdair Macleod of Goldmoney thinks it is higher still. 'The PRC probably has over 30,000 tonnes hidden in various accounts, but not declared as official reserves,' he tells me.

Gold analyst Rhona O'Connell says that a

cumulative excess of gold since the start of 2015 has not all gone onto the Shanghai Gold Exchange or the Shanghai Futures Exchange by any stretch of the imagination; neither has it gone into ETFs . . . If, and it is 'IF', this excess has gone into one form or other of reserves then government bodies' holdings could be four times as much as is reported to the IMF, at more than 8,900t. In which case gold at $2,400 would comprise 18% of China's gold and Forex combined.[9]

Analyst Jan Nieuwenhuijs has a rather more sober estimate – still in excess of official declared holdings – of over 5,000 tonnes held by the PBOC, with about 30,000 tonnes in total held in China.[10]

In stark contrast to the US under Roosevelt, China has been encouraging its citizens to buy gold since the mid-2000s. In 2010, the government ran adverts across mainstream television and on huge billboards urging citizens to buy gold and silver as an investment. It introduced savings programmes advising citizens to make regular monthly purchases. Interestingly, the gold price has never traded below the level it was when these adverts began, leading many to infer that China defended that price to ensure it did not lose face with its citizens.

Why would China be reluctant to declare such large holdings? Perhaps because the effect would be destabilising. It could panic financial markets. It would cause an unwanted surge in both the yuan and the gold price, while China is still accumulating, and a fall in the value of the dollar, which would negatively impact its $3.2 trillion US dollar foreign exchange reserves. Perhaps most significantly, to declare so much gold would be a direct challenge to America's financial supremacy, which China, even with all its ambition, is probably not yet ready for. Parity first, then supremacy.

For now, the Chinese government has followed Deng Xiaoping's doctrine: 'Hide your strength, bide your time.' Its declared 2,262 tonnes are, perhaps, the bare minimum it could currently declare and look credible.

We will probably never know the exact number. But we do know that China, even with its extraordinary production and imports, has ramped up its accumulation over the past three years. Since 2022, the PBOC has been reporting increased gold holdings every month. Previously, it would only update its holdings every few years. By April 2024, there were seventeen successive months of increases – each month a few per cent higher. Perhaps this is China's means of disclosing its holdings by gentle information.

'I calculate the PBoC bought 1,600 tonnes since the war in Ukraine,' says analyst Jan Nieuwenhuijs.[11] 'It keeps roughly 65 per cent of its purchases hidden.'[12] How many more imports prior to 2022 do we not know about?

What might China's purpose be in accumulating so much gold, and encouraging its citizens to do the same? One likely explanation is diversification. It makes sense to own some gold in a balanced, diversified portfolio. It makes sense to diversify away from the US dollar and national currencies generally. Gold, as the only currency that is nobody else's liability, should be the core holding for any central bank.

But another possibility is that this accumulation is part of China's ambitions for its money: for the yuan to be the global reserve currency. As we have seen, there has never been a global reserve currency that did not start out backed by gold and/or silver. Whether it was the pound, the dollar, the florin or the currencies of the ancient world, they were all at least as good as gold, if not gold itself. They may have ended up debased into oblivion, but they started off with gold backing and sometimes some silver, too. It was only because the money was sound that it won global trust in the first place. If China has similar designs, and it wants the world to recognise the integrity of its money, all it has to do is make it exchangeable with gold. In this regard, in 2023, the PBOC created the facility for citizens to convert their personal cash savings into physical gold at the simple click of a mouse. Perhaps China's aim is not necessarily some modern gold standard but, simply, to be in a position where it could adopt one, if it wanted.

If China decides to go one stage further and weaponise money, as the US has done (more below), all it has to do is declare its actual gold holdings, perhaps even partially back the yuan with them. Unbacked western currency risks losing a great deal of its purchasing power in such an event. To back western fiat even partially with gold would mean a dramatic upward revaluation of gold – into the tens of thousands. But that is the card China now has with its twenty years of relentless accumulation.

As was demonstrated by Alexander the Great, he who owns the gold makes the rules. Even in today's computerised world in which so much value is now digital, surely that maxim still applies.

De-dollarisation and Bitcoin

'An international reserve currency based on a basket of
currencies of our countries is being worked out'

Vladimir Putin, President of Russia

The United States likes to weaponise the dollar, to exploit its status
as global reserve currency and use it as both carrot and stick. Cuba,
Iran, North Korea and Venezuela have all fallen foul at some point.
There are many historical examples in Latin America of regimes
suffering for not playing by US rules.

While the US has showered billions in foreign aid to 'friends'
(until the recent re-election of Donald Trump at least), its enemies
can find themselves frozen out of the global financial system, which
the US effectively controls using the international payment system,
SWIFT.

In 2022, after its invasion of Ukraine, Russia's US dollar reserves
($300 billion) were confiscated, and it was removed from SWIFT.
Modern digital technology meant this happened with speed.
Imagine that: simply confiscating another country's money. China,
and other countries besides, were watching. Since that confiscation there has been a rapid uptick in gold buying – not by retail
investors, but by central banks. What's more, many of those banks
are not reporting their gold purchases, but keeping them quiet,
China being the most obvious example. What we are witnessing is
de-dollarisation.

Whether to protect its national interests or its citizens' wealth, or
simply as a matter of national pride, China cannot be reliant on or
subordinate to a banking system that is controlled by the US, and
which the US is prepared to use as a weapon of war. It makes it too
vulnerable. Others clearly feel the same way.

Both Vladimir Putin and Xi Jinping of China have called for a
reshaping of the international financial system. Every time there is

a summit that involves BRICS nations – such as 'Russian Davos' or, as it's properly known, the St Petersburg International Economic Forum, or the BRICS summit itself – the same theme recurs: the need for a new, non-western international currency. (BRICS+ is currently Brazil, Russia, India, China, South Africa, Iran, Egypt, Ethiopia and the United Arab Emirates.)

In terms of geographical scope and population, the Shanghai Cooperation Organisation (SCO) is the world's largest regional organisation, covering 40 per cent of the world's population and over 30 per cent of global GDP. Its members are China, Russia, India, Pakistan, Iran (which has just joined), Kyrgyzstan, Tajikistan, Kazakhstan and Uzbekistan. Turkish President Recep Tayyip Erdoğan says he is considering membership. These are not exactly pro-western nations. Numerous infrastructure projects are being developed, notably a trans-Afghan railway to link Uzbekistan to Pakistan, a China–Central Asia natural gas pipeline and a China–Kazakhstan–Uzbekistan railway. China, which, as we know, is beholden to both Europe and the US for its exports, wants to open up new markets. Are these nations going to want to trade in dollars, if they don't have to?

In the first few months of 2023, China agreed deals with Russia, Brazil and Saudi Arabia to bypass the dollar and trade using the Chinese yuan. On a trip to China in March 2023, even French President Emmanuel Macron said to President Xi: 'I want to take the opportunity to insist on one point: we should not depend on the extraterritoriality of the US dollar.'[13]

Many of Eurasia's brightest minds are plotting an alternative system. One such system is being spearheaded by Sergey Glazyev, a former Kremlin advisor, now Commissioner for Integration and Macroeconomics at the Eurasia Economic Union (EAEU). He is working on a digital payment currency backed by a basket of BRICS+ currencies and natural resources. 'The basket could contain an index of prices of main exchange-traded commodities: gold and other precious metals, key industrial metals, hydrocarbons, grains, sugar, as well as water and other natural resources,' he says.[14]

But to back a currency with commodities generally raises all sorts of problems relating to storing raw materials. Most degrade over time, especially grains and fibres. Many, such as copper and oil, can be expensive or impractical to store for long periods. Futures are another possibility, but you need to trust your trading partner to honour the contract, and all sorts of date-related complexities open up.

One simple solution is a shiny yellow metal. The issue is where to store it. The likes of Singapore, Dubai and Hong Kong are all possibilities for carrying out the roles of Switzerland, London or New York. Would such a system be practical today for the SCO nations? Possibly.

Russia's State Duma Deputy Chairman Alexander Babakov has also stated that a BRICS alliance was working on a new currency secured by gold and other commodities, including rare-earth metals. Fifty-nine countries have said they would join.[15]

Then there is mBridge (Multiple Central Bank Digital Currency Bridge), a new international payments system based on blockchain technology, being developed by China, Hong Kong, Thailand, Saudi Arabia, the UAE and the BIS in Hong Kong. mBridge is designed to 'facilitate faster, cheaper, and more transparent cross-border payments using CBDCs [central bank digital currencies] bypassing some of the friction associated with the traditional international banking infrastructure'. Settlements take minutes rather than days. Its designers say it is quicker, cheaper, safer, more accessible and more transparent than existing systems, and that it is especially useful 'between regions that do not share a direct payment corridor'. I'm thinking that's code for the likes of Russia and Iran. It's peer-to-peer – so no US or any other third parties getting in their way with their weaponisation of finance. Indeed, mBridge is not compatible with US dollars.

Instead, mBridge will provide settlement for the UNIT, a new currency for BRICS+ nations. The UNIT is 60 per cent made up of a basket of local currencies of BRICS+ nations. The other 40 per cent is gold. The gold will be put into an escrow account inside the country that owns the gold, and independently audited with significant penalties for any deviation from the UNIT proto-col. This would eliminate the need for trusted banks to carry out the role that the Federal Reserve or the Bank of England currently plays. Gold would also be deliverable on demand.

Of note is that the countries involved in mBridge have all been buying gold hand over fist in recent years: even Thailand, which in the last five years has become the seventh-largest buyer of gold in the world. In one heck of a scoop, analyst Jan Nieuwenhuijs found in September 2024 that Saudi Arabia secretly bought 160 tonnes. 'One thing is for certain,' he said. 'Saudi Arabia owns much more gold than it wants the world to believe.'[16] This is significant because Saudi Arabia was such a key player in establishing the petrodollar in the early 1970s after the US came off the gold standard, enabling the dollar to retain its status as global reserve currency. Is Saudi Arabia quietly repositioning itself as an ally of the next global superpower?

mBridge has another thirty 'observing members'. They, and almost every country in the SCO, have been increasing their gold holdings. Between 2006 and 2020, Russia's central bank more than quintupled the country's gold holdings, from around 400 tonnes to today's 2,333 tonnes. It's now the world's fifth-largest gold owner. Since 2022, cen-tral banks have been buying at the fastest rate since the 1960s. Most of those central banks come from nations within the SCO. Even the non-aligned middle-ranking nations are now starting to increase pur-chases. What has confounded commentators about this recent bull market in gold (2022–5) is that the traditional driver – western retail buying – has been absent. Central banks' buying has been the driver, and they have been buying aggressively and on the quiet, barely wait-ing for the price to pull back before making their purchases.

What has also enabled all this buying is that the international banking regulations known as Basel III, which introduced stricter capital requirements for banks, upgraded gold from a Tier 3 to a Tier 1 asset – giving it a status similar to cash or government bonds. This effectively de-risked gold. The result is that many countries have been reducing their holdings of US treasuries and increasing their holdings of gold. Gold is increasing as a percentage of international reserves the world over, while US treasuries are decreasing. China, which has reduced its treasury holdings by more than 40 per cent since 2013, is the most telling example.

In summary, new international payments systems that bypass the US dollar are being developed, and the countries that are developing these systems have been buying lots of gold.

The problem with gold is settlement. You can't send gold over the internet. You have to use banks or gold dealers. Numerous solutions to this have been proposed, and they may work, but they all rely on trusted third parties of some kind, whether auditor or independent bank. If only there was a form of money that you could transfer over the internet from A to B that eliminated the need for trusted third parties . . . Indeed, Russia's President Vladimir Putin did his best bitcoin maximalist impression in November 2022, when he called for an international, independent, blockchain-based settlement network:

> The technology of digital currencies and blockchains can be used to create a new system of international settlements that will be much more convenient, absolutely safe for its users and, most importantly, will not depend on banks or interference by third countries . . . I am confident that something like this will certainly be created and will develop because nobody likes the dictate of monopolists, which is harming all parties, including the monopolists themselves.[17]

I would say the probability of a national or supranational currency that is *fully* exchangeable for gold actually materialising is low, even with all that plotting and Asian buying. A more prosaic explanation is that they are buying gold to store wealth, de-dollarise and diversify.

Whether the future of money involves gold, bitcoin or something new, the desire to de-dollarise is most certainly there. Gold, an alternative store of money, is part of that. De-dollarisation is a gradual process. Russia may want to accelerate it – its needs are more pressing. But other nations – China, in particular – are biding their time. Gradually then suddenly.

Conclusion: Beauty, Freedom and Truth

'Gold is forever'

Proverb

Gold is wealth in its simplest, most elemental form. It is also wealth in its most universal form: everyone, everywhere has always understood that gold has significant worth.

Broadly speaking, I see three potential futures for gold. First, and most likely, is that gold's role continues much as it is today, as jewellery, a store of wealth and insurance. Second – not probable in my view, though some see it as inevitable – is that governments start to back their currencies with gold once again and its official monetary role resumes. Third, and least likely, is that central banks and investors dishoard, and gold demand comes from jewellery and industry alone.

Unlike money in the bank or a bond, there are no strings attached to gold: it carries no promise from a third party, no liability. Hand it to someone else and its value is transferred. It is a 'bearer' asset, owned by whoever has possession of it. This strength also shows its weakness. It's all very well having a pot of gold, but if somebody comes along and takes it from you, then you're left with nothing at all. As wealth in such distilled, transferrable form, it will always be the target of thieves and conquerors. Keeping it safe will always be a problem.

Here is a couplet common to older economic texts:

Money is a matter of functions four,
A medium, a measure, a standard, a store.

Let's look at each of these in turn.

We'll start with medium. Gold's primary role was never so much as a day-to-day medium of exchange. There is too much wealth in a single gold coin – even a coin the size of a quarter or 2p is worth over $700. Silver, nickel and copper – then paper and digital messages – have been preferred, for lower-value transactions at least. Today, with modern communication, promises are more instantly transferrable than metal, so we use those.

It is possible that promises representing gold in vaults, or central bank digital currencies backed by gold, become a medium of exchange. But this would be some form of gold standard. The gold itself would stay in some vault somewhere and ownership of the gold would change. For the system to be trustworthy, users have to know they can exchange their digits for gold, even if they don't actually do it. But this is really gold functioning as a store of wealth, as backing, with an exchange system built on top. Gold coins are unlikely to be physical currency, as they were under Newton's gold standard, if only for the simple reason that physical cash is disappearing from use.

Central bank gold could find use as 'last resort money', as final guarantee, as with Russia's purchase of drones from Iran. But for everyday transactions? Unlikely, I would have thought.

As a unit of account – 'measure' in the above couplet – for the most part we will use whatever currency the government demands we use. If we're in the US and we must pay taxes in the US, we will use the US dollar as our unit of account. Fiat might be a rubbish unit because it gets debased by 5–15 per cent each year, and a dollar today is not the same as a dollar ten years ago, but the law is the law. In such circumstances, gold will only find use as a unit of account by those few seeking something more truthful, such as yours truly when measuring house prices.

Gold is a better unit of account because its value is recognised wherever and whenever, totally fungible and truly universal. There will be places and times where it buys you more or less than in other places or times, but that is the whole point of a unit of account – it is used to measure relative value. Gold is the constant. However, until gold reclaims some official role, it will not find common use as a unit of account even if superior: the currency in which we must pay tax will have that role.

So to standard. In the couplet, 'standard' means 'standard of deferred payment': an accepted unit for settling debts over time. Here, too, gold's constancy makes it better than fiat – at least for larger payments – because it preserves its value. It's why many successful currencies and economies were built on gold standards. However, gold will not find common use in this regard either, unless, somehow, it becomes official money once again.

Finally, we have store: to store value is gold's primary monetary function. We have always used gold for this, and we always will. At the national level, central banks will continue to hold gold. They have been net buyers since 2015. They are growing their holdings. At the private level, people will continue to wear gold and keep gold, particularly as trust in governments falls. People will do this more when they are worried, and less when times are unthreatening.

A gold-backed system of money would force everyone in an economy, including governments, to operate by the same rules. It is equitable. The citizen can hold his government to account. Government becomes limited. Gold would restore not only financial stability but also societal trust; people could work and prosper without being exploited by inflation or manipulated by lies. Gold is inherently honest. It brings a natural order to things. Nobody has the power to create it from nothing, and its value cannot be distorted by the whims of politicians or bankers. The world would be a better place with a monetary system underpinned by gold, with the pernicious consequences of fiat eradicated. If money is sound, a sounder society will follow. One leads to the other.

I am not holding my breath for this. Never mind the practicalities, politicians would have to cede too much fiat power.

But whether officially embraced or not, gold will remain a cornerstone of human civilisation. People will always want it. Economically, it has always underpinned money. It is a form of power. Culturally, it has adorned our bodies and our sacred spaces. It is embedded in our myth and legend, a consistent thread through the tapestry of human history. Psychologically, our desire for it has driven human progress. It has motivated us to attempt the bravest and most ambitious things, to venture out into the unknown and explore, to innovate and invest, to take incredible risks. It has also driven us to commit abhorrent, crude and terrible crimes. Our instinct for gold is almost as timeless as the metal itself. Such is its fundamental allure, humans will desire it, fight for it, steal it, work for it and treasure it for as long as we are human.

And, when we are long gone, gold will still be there – inert and unchanged, exactly as it always was.

Gold may be older than the planets, but perhaps its story has only just begun.

Author's Note

Needless to say, I urge everyone to own some gold in their portfolio. If you are interested in buying gold, there is a how-to guide at my Substack, The Flying Frisby – www.theflyingfrisby.com.

It tells you everything you need to know.

And if you've enjoyed my writing, please go to The Flying Frisby, www.theflyingfrisby.com, and subscribe. I blog there twice a week.

Thank you so much for reading this book. Tell a friend.

Acknowledgements

I thank my agent, Sally Holloway, for the enormous effort she put into getting this book commissioned, and for all the support and level-headedness she has shown. The proposal was almost as much work as the book itself.

I thank the editorial team at Penguin: Celia Buzuk for the original commission, then Shanika Hyslop, Alice Johnstone, Elisabeth Merriman, Robert Drew and Sam Wells for their incredible diligence and eye for detail.

I thank Toby Bray for reading an early draft and for the hundreds of suggestions he made. What would I do without you? This book wouldn't have a title for a start.

There are several authors and experts whose work has helped me enormously with this book: Ross Norman, James Turk, Timothy Green, George M. Taber, Jan Nieuwenhuijs, Nick Laird and Kenneth R. Ferguson. Thank you all.

Finally, I thank my daughter Eliza for telling me about the Anunnaki from the planet Nibiru.

Select Bibliography

Ahamed, L., *Lords of Finance: The Bankers Who Broke the World* (London: Penguin, 2009).

Bradsher, G., 'Nazi Gold: The Merkers Mine Treasure', Prologue: *Quarterly of the National Archives and Records Administration*, 31(1) (1999).

Baum, L. F., *The Wonderful Wizard of Oz* (New York: George M. Hill Co., 1900).

Bernstein, P. L., *The Power of Gold: The History of an Obsession* (Hoboken: John Wiley & Sons, 2000).

Bernstein, P. L., *A Primer on Money, Banking, and Gold* (3rd ed.) (Hoboken: John Wiley & Sons, 2008).

Boyle, R. W., *Gold: History and Genesis of Deposits* (Berlin: Springer, 1987).

Brands, H. W., *The Age of Gold* (London: Arrow Books, 2006).

Buffett, H., 'Human Freedom Rests on Gold Redeemable Money', *Commercial and Financial Chronicle* (6 May 1948) https://www.fgmr.com/wp-content/uploads/2017/02/Howard-Buffett-explains-sound-money-4-May-1948.pdf [Accessed 18 April 2025].

Cobbett, W., *Paper Against Gold and Glory Against Prosperity* (London: J. McCreery, 1815) https://archive.org/details/cobbettspaperaga00cobbrich [Accessed 5 September 2024].

Dunstan, S. and Williams, G., *Grey Wolf: The Escape of Adolf Hitler* (New York: Sterling Publishing, 2011).

Eichengreen, B., *Golden Fetters: The Gold Standard and the Great Depression, 1919-1939* (New York: Oxford University Press, 1996).

Ferguson, K. R., *Confiscation: Gold as Contraband 1933–1975* (self-published, 2018).

Ferguson, N., *The Cash Nexus: Money and Power in the Modern World, 1700–2000* (New York: Basic Books, 2001).

Frisby, D., *Life After the State* (London: Unbound, 2013).

Frisby, D., *Bitcoin: The Future of Money?* (London: Unbound, 2014).

Frisby, D., *Daylight Robbery: How Tax Shaped Our Past and Will Change Our Future* (London: Penguin, 2019).

Green, T., *The Ages of Gold* (London: GFMS, 2007).

Green, T., *The New World of Gold* (London: Weidenfeld and Nicolson, 1981).

Greenspan, A., 'Gold and Economic Freedom', *Objectivist* (July 1966) constitution.org/1-Activism/mon/greenspan_gold.htm [Accessed 11 July 2024].

Gregorietti, G., *Jewelry Through the Ages* (New York: Crescent Books, 1969).

Hart, M., *Gold: The Race for the World's Most Seductive Metal* (New York: Simon & Schuster, 2013).

Jastram, R. W. and Leyland, J., *The Golden Constant: The English and American Experience 1560–2007* (Cheltenham: Edward Elgar, 2009).

Keynes, J. M., *A Tract on Monetary Reform* (London: Macmillan, 1923).

King, R., *The Shortest History of Italy* (London: Old Street Publishing, 2024).

Kwarteng, K., *War and Gold: A Five-Hundred Year History of Empires, Adventures and Debt* (London: Bloomsbury Paperbacks, 2015).

Levenson, T., *Newton and the Counterfeiter* (Boston, MA: Houghton Mifflin Harcourt, 2009).

Lourie, P., *Sweat of the Sun, Tears of the Moon: A Chronicle of an Incan Treasure* (New York: Atheneum, 1991).

Marx, K., *Capital: A Critique of Political Economy* (1867) Vol. 1 (New York: International Publishers, 1967).

Rickards, J., *The New Case for Gold* (New York: Portfolio, 2016).

Ridley, M., *The Rational Optimist: How Prosperity Evolves* (London: Fourth Estate, 2010).

Ruskin, J., 'Unto This Last' (1860), in Rosenberg, J. D. (ed.), *The Genius of John Ruskin* (London: George Allen & Unwin Ltd, 1985).

Shaw, G. B., *The Intelligent Woman's Guide to Socialism and Capitalism* (New York: Brentano's, 1928).

Taber, G. M., *Chasing Gold: The Incredible Story of How the Nazis Stole Europe's Bullion* (New York: Pegasus Books, 2014).

Select Bibliography

Turk, J., *Money and Liberty: In the Pursuit of Happiness & The Theory of Natural Money* (self-published, 2021).

Turk, J. and Rubino, J., *The Coming Collapse of the Dollar and How to Profit from It: Make a Fortune by Investing in Gold and Other Hard Assets* (New York: Doubleday, 2004).

Notes

1. The Eternal Metal

1 Atkinson, V., 'World's thinnest gold leaf, dubbed "goldene," is just 1 atom thick', Live Science (25 April 2024) https://www.livescience.com/chemistry/worlds-thinnest-gold-leaf-dubbed-goldene-is-just-1-atom-thick [Accessed 10 January 2025].

2 Dissolving gold in aqua regia does change its atomic structure. The strong oxidising properties of aqua regia break down the metallic bonds in gold, resulting in the formation of gold ions in solution and a change in the arrangement of its atoms.

3 Mortished, C., 'Demand for global listing helps to put new gloss on gold', *The Times* (21 July 2003), p. 21.

4 Lewis, N., '3 facts of a gold standard', BullionVault (2015) https://www.bullionvault.com/gold-news/history/3-facts-gold-standard-09022015 [Accessed 2 March 2025].

5 World Gold Council, 'Gold reserves by country' (n.d.) https://www.gold.org/goldhub/data/gold-reserves-by-country [Accessed 24 January 2025].

6 Wilson, A. and Bowman, A. K. (eds.), *Trade, Commerce, and the State in the Roman World* (Oxford: Oxford University Press, 2018), p. 413.

7 Laird, N., 'World population and gold production', GoldChartsRUs (n.d.) http://www.goldchartsrus.com/gold/WorldPopGoldProduction.php [Accessed 9 July 2024].

8 Bernstein, P. L., *The Power of Gold: The History of an Obsession* (Hoboken: John Wiley & Sons, 2000).

9 Ibid., p. 321.

10 Shaw, G. B., *The Intelligent Woman's Guide to Socialism and Capitalism* (New York: Brentano's, 1923), p. 263.

11 Keynes, J. M., *A Tract on Monetary Reform* (London: Macmillan, 1924), p. 172.

12 Paul, R. and Lehrman, L., *The Case for Gold: A Minority Report of the U.S. Gold Commission* (Washington, DC: Cato Institute, 1982), p. 183.

13 Ferguson, N., *The Cash Nexus: Money and Power in the Modern World, 1700–2000* (New York: Basic Books, 2001), p. 325.

14 Pindar, Fragment 222, in *The Odes of Pindar*, trans. J. E. Sandys (London: William Heinemann, 1915), p. 611.

15 Taber, G. M., *Chasing Gold: The Incredible Story of How the Nazis Stole Europe's Bullion* (New York: Pegasus Books, 2014), p. 2.

16 Diodorus Siculus, *Bibliotheca historica* (first century BC), cited in Hyndman, H., *The Evolution of Revolution*, Chapter 12 (1921) https://www.marxists.org/archive/hyndman/1921/evrev/chapter12.htm [Accessed 24 January 2025].

17 Ruskin, J., 'Unto This Last' (1860), in Rosenberg, J. D. (ed.), *The Genius of John Ruskin* (London: George Allen & Unwin Ltd, 1985), p. 260.

2. The Ancient Genesis of Gold

1 Moskvitch, K., 'Neutron-Star Collision Shakes Space-Time and Lights Up the Sky', Quanta Magazine (16 October 2017) https://www.quantamagazine.org/neutron-star-collision-shakes-space-time-and-lights-up-the-sky-20171016/ [Accessed 25 February 2023].

2 Letzter, R., 'Gravitational Waves from Neutron Star Collisions Show How the Universe Creates Gold', Live Science (16 October 2017) https://www.livescience.com/60701-ligo-neutron-stars-heavy-metals-gold.html [Accessed 25 February 2023].

3 Marlowe, H., 'Neutron star smashup seen for first time, "transforms" understanding of Universe', Phys.org (16 October 2017) https://phys.org/news/2017-10-neutron-star-smash-up-discovery-lifetime.html [Accessed 13 May 2025].

4 Loeb, G. M., *The Battle for Investment Survival* (Hoboken: John Wiley & Sons, 2007), p. 102.

5 Boyle, R. W., *Gold: History and Genesis of Deposits* (Berlin: Springer, 1987), p. 23.

6 Yannopoulos, J. C., *The Extractive Metallurgy of Gold* (Boston, MA: Springer US, 1991), p. ix.

7 Plato, *Hippias Major* (n.d.) 289e.

8 Keats, J., 'Ode on a Grecian Urn', in *Lamia, Isabella, The Eve of St Agnes and Other Poems* (London: Taylor and Hessey, 1820).

9 Gregorietti, G., *Jewelry Through the Ages* (New York: Crescent Books, 1969), p. 40.

10 Green, T., *The Ages of Gold* (London: GFMS, 2007), p. 22.

11 Boyle, *Gold: History and Genesis of Deposits*, p. 27.

12 Bernstein, P. L., *The Power of Gold: The History of an Obsession* (London: Wiley, 2000), back cover.

13 Pester, P., 'What did the ancient Egyptian pyramids look like when they were built?', Live Science (5 February 2023) https://www.livescience.com/how-egyptian-pyramids-originally-looked [Accessed 21 January 2025].

14 Teach, E., 'Remembering Peter Bernstein', CFO (10 June 2009) https://www.cfo.com/news/remembering-peter-bernstein/669948 [Accessed 13 April 2023].

15 Haggai 2:8 (King James Version).

3. Myths and Dragons, Coins and Kings

1 Jackson, P. (dir.), *The Lord of the Rings: The Fellowship of the Ring* (New Line Cinema, 2001), based on the novel by J. R. R. Tolkien. Note: this quote appears to be Jackson's line, not Tolkien's.

2 'Ford would replace gold with energy currency and stop wars', *New-York Tribune*, 4 December 1921, p. 1, ed. 1 https://chroniclingamerica.loc.gov/lccn/sn83030214/1921-12-04/ed-1/seq-1/ [Accessed 27 August 2024].

3 Marx, K., op. cit., p. 135. 'The metals ... are by their nature money (Galiani, *Della Moneta*, in Custodians collection, Parte moderna, Vol. 3, p. 137).

4 Britannica on Money, 'Origins of coins' (n.d.) https://www.britannica.com/money/coin/Origins-of-coins [Accessed 13 December 2024].

5 Green, *The Ages of Gold*, p. 111.

6 Early humans might have made little distinction between gold and electrum, but by around 3500 BC firing techniques for separating gold from silver using ordinary salt had been discovered.

7 Yule, H. and Burnell, A. C., *Hobson-Jobson: A Glossary of Anglo-Indian Colloquial Words and Phrases* (London: John Murray, 1903), p. 161 https://archive.org/details/hobsonjobsonglosooyulerich/page/161/mode/1up?view=theater [Accessed 24 January 2025].

4. Gold in the Classical World

1 Parker, B. and Hart, J., *Remember the Golden Rule* (New York: Fawcett, 1985), front cover.
2 Green, *The Ages of Gold*, p. 128.
3 Ibid., p. 130.
4 Ibid., p. 133.
5 Ibid., p. 187.
6 Ibid., p. 188.
7 Pliny the Elder, *Natural History: A Selection*, trans. by Healey, J. (London: Penguin, 1991), XXXIII:70.
8 Green, *The Ages of Gold*, p. 191.
9 Ibid., p. 194.
10 'Rome: A Thousand Years of Monetary History', American Numismatic Society (2014) https://numismatics.org/rome-a-thousand-years-of-monetary-history/ [Accessed 19 September 2023].
11 Ibid.
12 Green, *The Ages of Gold*, p. 207.

5. The Middle Ages, International Trade and the Changing Nature of Money

1 Mohamud, N., 'Is Mansa Musa the richest man who ever lived?' (10 March 2019) https://www.bbc.co.uk/news/world-africa-47379458 [Accessed 24 January 2025].

2 *The Book of Ser Marco Polo the Venetian, Concerning the Kingdoms and Marvels of the East*, 2 vols, trans. by H. Yule (London: John Murray, 1871), vol. 1, p. 379.

3 Kemble, S., *Odes, Lyrical Ballads, and Poems on Various Occasions* (Edinburgh, 1809), p. 287 https://www.google.co.uk/books/edition/Odes_Lyrical_Ballads_and_Poems_on_Variou/1cwjAAAAMAAJ?hl=en&gbpv=0 [Accessed 24 January 2025].

6. Lust for Gold Brings Violence to South America

1 Aldenferder, M., et al., 'Four-thousand-year-old gold artifacts from the Lake Titicaca basin, southern Peru', *Proceedings of the National Academy of Sciences*, 105(13) (2008), pp. 5002–5 https://www.pnas.org/doi/10.1073/pnas.0710937105 [Accessed 22 June 2024].

2 Green, *The Ages of Gold*, p. 261.

3 Columbus, C., 'Letter to Ferdinand and Isabella' (July 1503), Columbus, C., *Writings of Christopher Columbus: Descriptive of the Discovery and Occupation of the New World*, ed. by Ford, P. L.. (New York: C. L. Webster, 1892), p. 230.

4 Jones, J., 'Gold of the Indies', The Metropolitan Museum of Art: Heilbrunn Timeline of Art History (1 October 2022) https://www.metmuseum.org/toah/hd/ingd/hd_ingd.htm [Accessed 29 December 2023].

5 Minster, C., 'Treasure of the ancient Aztecs', ThoughtCo (25 February 2019) https://www.thoughtco.com/the-treasure-of-the-aztecs-2136532 [Accessed 17 December 2024].

6 Ibid.

7 Al-Bukhari, M. I., *Sahih al-Bukhari* (9th century), hadith 6436–9.

8 Dobyns, H. F., *Their Number Become Thinned: Native American Population Dynamics in Eastern North America* (Knoxville: University of Tennessee Press, 1983).

9 Green, *The Ages of Gold*, p. 284.

10 Minster, C., 'Where is the lost treasure of the Inca?', ThoughtCo (19 July 2019) https://thoughtco.com/lost-treasure-of-the-inca-2136548 [Accessed 24 January 2025].

11 Minster, C., 'About the ransom of Atahualpa', ThoughtCo (6 March 2017) https://thoughtco.com/the-ransom-of-atahualpa-2136547 [Accessed 24 January 2025].

12 Taylor, L., ' "Holy grail of shipwrecks": recovery of 18th-century Spanish ship could begin in April', *Guardian* (18 March 2024) https://www.theguardian.com/environment/2024/mar/18/san-jose-shipwreck-recovery [Accessed 24 January 2025].

13 Olympic Museum, 'Olympic Games – Winner Medals 1908', Olympic-Museum.de (n.d.) https://www.olympic-museum.de/w_medals/olympic-games-winner-medal-1908.php [Accessed 25 March 2023].

14 Tan, S., 'Are Olympic gold medals actually made of gold?', Evidentscientific.com (11 October 2022) https://ims.evidentscientific.com/en/insights/are-olympic-gold-medals-actually-made-of-gold [Accessed 25 March 2025].

7. The Birth of Central Banking and the Accidental Gold Standard

1 Bank of England, 'Why Was the Bank of England Founded?', Bank of England Museum Online Collections (19 February 2021) https://www.bankofengland.co.uk/museum/online-collections/blog/why-was-the-bank-of-england-founded [Accessed 30 September 2023].

2 Old Currency Exchange, 'Banking collapse in London as Charles II defaults on royal loans' (2015, August 20) https://oldcurrencyexchange.com/2015/08/20/financial-crisis-1676-as-charles-ii-defaults-on-royal-loans/ [Accessed 16 May 2025].

3 Bank of England, 'Why Was the Bank of England Founded?'.

4 Paterson, I. *The God of the Machine* (United Kingdom: Taylor & Francis, 2017), p. 204.

5 Levenson, T., *Newton and the Counterfeiter* (Boston, MA: Houghton Mifflin Harcourt, 2009), p. 63.

6 Ibid., p. 112.

7 Ibid.

8 Ibid., p. 243.

9 Green, *The Ages of Gold*, p. 296.

10 Ibid.

11 Ibid., p. 299.

12 Ibid.

13 A pound was twenty shillings, or 113 grains of gold. A guinea, at twenty-one shillings, was just over.

14 Green *The Ages of Gold*, p. 301.

15 Ibid., p. 304.

16 Ibid., p. 294.

8. The Mysterious World of Alchemy

1 Levenson, *Newton and the Counterfeiter*, p. 242.

2 Haven, K. F., *Marvels of Science: 50 Fascinating 5-Minute Reads* (Littleton, CO: Libraries Unlimited, 1994), p. 182.

3 Hauck, D. W., *The Complete Idiot's Guide to Alchemy* (Indianapolis: Alpha Books, 1999).

4 Encyclopædia Britannica, 'Paracelsus' (n.d.) https://www.britannica.com/biography/Paracelsus [Accessed 7 March 2023].

5 Act 5, Scene 1.

6 Levenson, *Newton and the Counterfeiter*, p. 89.

7 Ibid., p. 91.

8 Ibid., p. 94.

9 Ibid., p. 245.

10 Franke, M., 'Der Alchemist der Nazis', *Der Spiegel* (18 June 2010) https://www.spiegel.de/geschichte/der-alchemist-der-nazis-a-946449.html [Accessed 18 December 2024].

11 Ibid.

9. Gold Fever Everywhere

1 Weingarten, T., 'Travel: Gold in Those Hills', *Newsweek* (18 May 2003) https://www.newsweek.com/travel-gold-those-hills-137253 [Accessed 18 December 2024]

2 Smithsonian Institution, 'The Gold Rush and Westward Expansion', Smithsonian American Art Museum (n.d.) https://americanexperience.si.edu/wp-content/uploads/2015/02/The-Gold-Rush-and-Westward-Expansion.pdf [Accessed 16 May 2024].

3 PBS, 'Samuel Brannan: Gold Rush Entrepreneur' (n.d.) https://www.pbs.org/wgbh/americanexperience/features/goldrush-samuel-brannan/ [Accessed 18 December 2024].

4 Smithsonian Institution, 'The Gold Rush and Westward Expansion'.

5 Mason, R. B., 'Mason Report', San Francisco Museum (n.d.) https://www.sfmuseum.org/hist6/masonrpt.html [Accessed 18 December 2024].

6 Smithsonian Institution, 'The Gold Rush and Westward Expansion'.

7 Ibid.

8 Green, *The Ages of Gold*, p. 328.

9 Ibid.

10 Ibid.

11 Ibid., p. 330.

12 Smithsonian Institution, 'The Gold Rush and Westward Expansion'.

13 Green, *The Ages of Gold*, p. 330.

14 Smithsonian Institution, 'The Gold Rush and Westward Expansion'.

15 Encyclopædia Britannica, 'California Gold Rush' (n.d.) https://www.britannica.com/topic/California-Gold-Rush [Accessed 16 May 2024].

16 Norwich University, 'Historical Impact of the California Gold Rush' (n.d.) https://online.norwich.edu/online/about/resource-library/historical-impact-california-gold-rush [Accessed 18 December 2024].

17 Australian Government, 'The Australian Gold Rush' (archived 20 January 2013) https://web.archive.org/web/20130120025546/http://australia.gov.au/about-australia/australian-story/austn-gold-rush [Accessed 16 May 2024].

18 Ibid.

19 '"KEEP IT QUIET!"', *Examiner* (15 February 1934), p. 6 https://trove.nla.gov.au/newspaper/article/51857157 [Accessed 16 May 2024].

20 Green, *The Ages of Gold*, p. 333.

21 Ibid., p. 334.

22 Australian Government, 'Australian Gold Rush'.

23 Ibid.

24 Ibid.

25 ' "Council Paper" ', *Sydney Morning Herald* (28 March 1854), p. 2 (archived from the original on 2 July 2021) [Accessed 16 May 2024].

26 Green, *The Ages of Gold*, p. 335.

27 Ibid., p. 336.

28 Baum, L. F., *The Wonderful Wizard of Oz* (Chicago: George M. Hill, 1900), p. 27.

29 Green, *The Ages of Gold*, p. 336.

30 Ibid., p. 337.

31 'Bryan's "Cross of Gold" Speech: Mesmerizing the Masses', History Matters (n.d.) https://historymatters.gmu.edu/d/5354/ [Accessed 13 May 2025].

32 Baum, *The Wonderful Wizard of Oz*, p. 183.

33 Littlefield, H. M., 'The Wizard of Oz: Parable on Populism', Ethan Lewis (n.d.) https://www.ethanlewis.org/history/downloads/wizoz.htm [Accessed 24 January 2025].

34 Library of Congress, 'The Wizard of Oz: An American Fairy Tale', Library of Congress Exhibition (n.d.) https://www.loc.gov/exhibits/oz [Accessed 1 October 2023].

35 Littlefield, 'The Wizard of Oz: Parable on Populism'.

36 Paton, A., *Cry, the Beloved Country* (London: Jonathan Cape, 1948), p. 3.

37 There is no definitive figure, but see Riemer, K. L. and Durrheim, R. J., 'Mining seismicity in the Witwatersrand Basin: monitoring, mechanisms and mitigation strategies in perspective', *Journal of Rock Mechanics and Geotechnical Engineering*, 4(3) (2012), pp. 228–49 https://doi.org/10.3724/SP.J.1235.2012.00228 [Accessed 16 May 2024]. Others have it closer to 40,000 tonnes, e.g. Norman, N. and Whitfield, G., *Geological Journeys* (Cape Town: Struik Publishers, 2006), pp. 38–49, 60–1.

38 Hartnady, C. J. H., 'South Africa's gold production and reserves', *South African Journal of Science*, 105 (9–10) (2009), pp. 328–9 https://www.scielo.org.za/scielo.php?script=sci_arttext&pid=S0038-23532009000500004 [Accessed 16 May 2024].

39 Green, *The Ages of Gold*, p. 347.

10. *The First World War and the End of Sound Money*

1 Hemingway, E., 'Notes on the Next War: A Serious Topical Letter', *Esquire*, September 1935, available at *Harper's Magazine* https://harpers.org/2007/09/hemingway-on-the-politics-of-war/ [Accessed 11 July 2024].

2 Green, *The Ages of Gold*, p. 351.

3 Ibid.

4 Ibid., p. 352.

5 Damant, G. C. C., 'Notes on the "Laurentic" salvage operations and the prevention of compressed air illness', *Journal of Hygiene*, 25(1) (1926), pp. 26–49 https://www.ncbi.nlm.nih.gov/pmc/articles/PMC2167577/ [Accessed 23 May 2024], p. 48.

6 National Library of Australia, 'Salvage of Laurentic Gold', *Sydney Morning Herald*, 22 December 1926, p. 7 https://trove.nla.gov.au/newspaper/article/1209746 [Accessed 23 May 2024].

7 Officer, L. H., 'Dollar-pound exchange rate from 1791', MeasuringWorth (n.d.) https://www.measuringworth.com/datasets/exchangepound/result.php?year_source=1900&year_result=2012 [Accessed 26 May 2024].

8 The fourteen participants are: Bank of China, the Bank of Communications, Coins 'N Things, the Industrial and Commercial Bank of China, INTL FCStone, Jane Street Global Trading, HSBC Bank USA, JPMorgan Chase, Koch Supply and Trading, Marex Financial, Morgan Stanley, Standard Chartered, the Bank of Nova Scotia, and the Toronto-Dominion Bank.

9 DeMatos, D., 'The Gold Standard Between the Wars: Part I', LinkedIn, 5 June 2023 https://www.linkedin.com/pulse/tch-gold-standard-between-wars-part-i-daniel-dematos-cfa/ [Accessed 26 May 2024].

10 Green, *The Ages of Gold*, p. 357.

11 Ahamed, L., *Lords of Finance* (London: Penguin, 2009), p. 169.

12 Green, *The Ages of Gold*, p. 358.

13 Ibid.

14 Ibid., p. 350.

15 Summary of data from Crabbe, L., 'The International Gold Standard and U.S. Monetary Policy from World War I to the New Deal', *Federal*

Reserve Bulletin (June 1989) https://fraser.stlouisfed.org/files/docs/meltzer/craint89.pdf [Accessed 24 January 2025], itself consisting of data from Ragnar Nurkse, Barry Eichengreen and William Adams Brown, Jr.

16 Bell, E. V., 'Panic and Crash: 1929', Original Sources (n.d.) https://www.originalsources.com/Document.aspx?DocID=US3JCSGUWU4ZP3X [Accessed 15 May 2025].

17 Green, *The Ages of Gold*, p. 362.

18 Funnell, B., Draaisma, T. and Neville, H. 'How to Beat a Depression: Lessons from Franklin Delano Roosevelt', Man Institute (27 January 2021) https://www.man.com/documents/download/vtvcg-dASAx-XmyhR-oryl1/Man_Solutions_Insights_How_to_Beat_a_Depression_English_%28United_States%29_27-01-2021.pdf [Accessed 17 May 2025].

19 Federal Reserve Bank of St. Louis, 'Documents and Statements Pertaining to the Banking Emergency, Part I: Presidential Proclamations, Federal Legislation, Executive Orders, Regulations, Documents, and Official Statements' (1933) https://fraser.stlouisfed.org/title/documents-statements-pertaining-banking-emergency-709/part-i-presidential-proclamations-federal-legislation-executive-orders-regulations-documents-official-statements-23564/fulltext [Accessed 28 May 2024].

20 Ferguson, K. R. *Confiscation: Gold as Contraband 1933–1975* (self-published, 2018), p. 15.

21 Roosevelt, F. D., 'Executive Order 6102 – Forbidding the Hoarding of Gold Coin, Gold Bullion, and Gold Certificates', The American Presidency Project (1933) https://www.presidency.ucsb.edu/documents/executive-order-6102-forbidding-the-hoarding-gold-coin-gold-bullion-and-gold-certificates [Accessed 28 May 2024].

22 Ferguson, *Confiscation*, p. 41.

23 Green, *The Ages of Gold*, p. 365.

24 Taber, *Chasing Gold*, p. 52.

25 Green, *The Ages of Gold*, p. 369.

26 Ibid., p. 367.

11. *The Nazis and the Greatest Hoard of Treasure Ever Discovered*

1 Trevor-Roper, H. R., *Hitler's Table Talk 1941–1944: Secret Conversations* (New York: Enigma Books, 2007), p. 98.

2 Bradsher, G., 'Nazi Gold: The Merkers Mine Treasure', *Prologue: Quarterly of the National Archives and Records Administration*, 31(1) (1999) https://www.archives.gov/publications/prologue/1999/spring/nazi-gold-merkers-mine-treasure.html [Accessed 5 July 2024].

3 Taber, *Chasing Gold*, p. 400.

4 Foreign & Commonwealth Office, 'History Notes: Nazi Gold: Information from the British Archives' (1997) https://issuu.com/fco-historians/docs/history_notes_cover_hphn_11 [Accessed 5 July 2024].

5 Dunstan, S. and Williams, G., *Grey Wolf: The Escape of Adolf Hitler* (New York: Sterling Publishing, 2011), p. 136.

6 Taber, *Chasing Gold*, p. 5.

7 Ibid., p. 45.

8 Ibid., p. 6.

9 Dunstan and Williams, *Grey Wolf*, p. 44.

10 Ibid.

11 There are 2,790 gold marks to a kilo.

12 Taber, *Chasing Gold*, p. 30.

13 Ibid., p. 439.

14 'Es reicht nicht, Geld zu haben. Man muss es auch in der Schweiz haben.'

15 Taber, *Chasing Gold*, p. 376.

16 Dunstan and Williams, *Grey Wolf*, p. 50.

17 Ibid., p. 51.

18 Ibid.

19 Foreign & Commonwealth Office, 'History Notes: Nazi Gold: Information from the British Archives' (1997) https://issuu.com/fcohistorians/docs/history_notes_cover_hphn_11 [Accessed 5 July 2024].

20 Taber, *Chasing Gold*, p. 171.

21 Ibid., p. 359.

22 Ibid., p. 360.

23 'Historikerkommission – Reichsfinanzministerium von 1933 – 1945', Reichsfinanzministerium-geschichte.de, 2018 https://www.reichsfinanz ministerium-geschichte.de [Accessed 30 June 2018].

24 Zweig, R. W., *The Gold Train* (New York: William Morrow, 2002).

25 Manning, P., *Martin Bormann: Nazi in Exile* (New York: Lyle Stuart, 1981), pp. 29–30.

26 Dunstan and Williams, *Grey Wolf*, p. 264.

27 Mark Felton Productions, 'The Death of Himmler – Episode 6: Himmler's Gold' [Video] (15 July 2022) https://www.youtube.com/watch?v=05JI4BSIM1E [accessed 1 July 2024].

28 Allan, H., 'Americans "looted £25m of Nazi gold": coins hidden in a post office by Himmler were taken by troops days after the war', *Daily Mail* (8 June 2015) https://www.dailymail.co.uk/news/article-3114663/Americans-looted-25m-Nazi-gold-Coins-hidden-post-office-Himmler-taken-troops-days-War.html [accessed 1 July 2024].

29 Taber, *Chasing Gold*, p. 414.

30 'Nazi gold is in the well, says the Daily', Lovec Pokladu https://www.lovecpokladu.cz/en/home/nazi-gold-is-in-the-well-says-the-daily-8051 [Accessed 7 July 2024].

31 Foreign & Commonwealth Office, 'History Notes: Nazi Gold: Information from the British Archives' (1997) https://issuu.com/fcohistorians/docs/history_notes_cover_hphn_11 [accessed 5 July 2024].

32 Ibid.

33 Taber, *Chasing Gold*, p. 430.

34 Ibid.

35 Ibid.

36 Ibid.

12. *The Mucilaginous Mystery of Japanese Gold*

1 New Visions, 'The Asian Holocaust killed twice as many people as the Nazis did', Medium (16 January 2017) https://medium.com/dose/the-asian-holocaust-killed-twice-as-many-people-as-the-nazis-did-877f0a7c664 [Accessed 18 November 2023].

2 King Rose Archives, 'Japan's Bombed Out Imperial Mint Yields Gold' [Video] (30 December 2014) https://www.youtube.com/watch?v=S5UHDp_75g0 [Accessed 24 January 2025].

13. *How the US Made the World Dependent on the Dollar*

1 Switzerland did not abandon the gold standard until 1999 in favour of floating exchange rates, much later than other countries. Caution and Switzerland's long history with gold were probably what held the Swiss back.

2 Ferguson, *Confiscation*, p. 84.

3 Ibid., p. 63.

4 Ibid., p. 64.

5 Ibid., p. 69.

6 Ibid., p. 73.

7 Green, *The Ages of Gold*, p. 372.

8 Congressional Record – Extensions of Remarks, US Government Printing Office (GPO) (5 February 1968), p. 2176 https://www.govinfo.gov/content/pkg/GPO-CRECB-1968-pt2/pdf/GPO-CRECB-1968-pt2-5-3.pdf [Accessed 24 January 2025].

9 Ferguson, *Confiscation*, p. 84.

10 Green, *The Ages of Gold,* p. 374.

11 National Archives, 'Pound Devalued – The National Archives' (n.d.) https://www.nationalarchives.gov.uk/education/resources/sixties-britain/pound-devalued/ [Accessed 23 April 2024].

12 Keynes, *A Tract on Monetary Reform*, p. 210.

13 Nixon, R., in *Public Papers of the Presidents of the United States: Richard Nixon, Containing the Public Messages, Speeches, and Statements of the President – 1971*, ed. by Office of the Federal Register (Washington: US Government Printing Office, 1972), pp. 886–90.

14 Burns, A. F., 'Transcript of Arthur F. Burns' Handwritten Journals, January 20, 1969 – July 25, 1974', Accession: 2006-NLF-057, Journal I (Green Notebook) (Ford Library & Museum, 2008) https://www.

fordlibrarymuseum.gov/library/document/0428/Burnstranscript1. pdf [Accessed 24 January 2025].

15 Ferguson, *Confiscation*, p. 87.

16 Green, T., *The New World of Gold* (London: Weidenfeld and Nicolson, 1981), p. 1.69.

14. What to Do with All That Gold?

1   Hayek, F. A., 'Choice in Currency', Mises Institute (1976) https://mises. org/online-book/choice-currency/author [Accessed 16 May 2025].

2   'Business: Stampede for Precious Metal', *Time* (28 January 1980) https://content.time.com/time/subscriber/article/0,33009,923918-2,00.html [Accessed 4 October 2023].

3   Franz, N., *Money & Wealth in the New Millennium: A Prophetic Guide to the New World Economic Order* (Newark: Ascension, 2002), p. 128.

4   World Gold Council, 'Central bank gold reserves – an historical perspective since 1845' (1999) https://www.gold.org/goldhub/research/central-bank-gold-reserves-historical-perspective-1845 [Accessed 28 September 2024]; SWCS, 'Gold Reserves by Country 1845–1998' (1998) https://www.swcs.com.au/goldreserves.htm [Accessed 28 September 2024]; World Gold Council, 'Gold reserves by country' https://www.gold.org/goldhub/data/gold-reserves-by-country

5   'House of Commons Debate', Hansard, 22 July 1999, vol. 335, col. 5010a5a1-78ef-42b2-81d4-84b911924fc8, https://hansard.parliament.uk/Commons/1999-07-22/debates/5010a5a1-78ef-42b2-81d4-84b911924fc8/Treasury [Accessed 28 February 2025].

6   Brummer, A. and Atkinson, M., 'Bank governor in clash over gold sale', *Guardian* (6 August 1999) https://www.theguardian.com/politics/1999/aug/06/uk.politicalnews1 [Accessed 27 February 2023].

7   Commons Treasury Select Committee (25 May 1999) https://publications.parliament.uk/pa/cm199899/cmselect/cmtreasy/480/9051813. htm [Accessed 12 May 2025].

8   Knowles, T., 'Why Britain is still paying the price for Gordon Brown's gold bullion blunder', *Telegraph* (4 March 2024) https://www.

telegraph.co.uk/money/investing/gold-hits-all-time-high-gordon-brown-blunder-cost/ [Accessed 1 May 2024].

9 Farrow, P., 'Gold: Does Gordon Brown regret selling half of Britain's gold reserves 10 years ago?', *Telegraph* (8 May 2009) https://www.telegraph.co.uk/finance/personalfinance/investing/gold/5296526/Gold-Does-Gordon-Browns-regret-selling-half-of-Britains-gold-reserves-10-years-ago.html [Accessed 28 May 2024].

10 'Brown says 1999 gold sale was right', Reuters (9 August 2007) https://www.reuters.com/article/uk-imf-brown-gold-idUKROB48540820070415 [Accessed 15 May 2025].

11 Blakely, R., 'Brown calls IMF to sell gold to cut debt', *The Times* (28 January 2005) https://www.thetimes.co.uk/article/brown-calls-imf-to-sell-gold-to-cut-debt-t2f888lswxd [Accessed 28 May 2024].

12 Reuters, 'Brown says 1999 gold sale was right'.

15. Irrelevant Gold Stays Relevant

1 LBMA, 'The Krugerrand' (n.d.) https://www.lbma.org.uk/wonders-of-gold/items/the-krugerrand [Accessed 24 January 2025].

2 APMEX, 'American gold eagle mintage charts (1986-present)' (31 March 2023) https://learn.apmex.com/learning-guide/bullion/american-gold-eagle-mintage-charts-1986-present/ [Accessed 24 June 2024].

16. What's the Point of Gold?

1 Hobbes, T., *Leviathan*, Part II, Chapter 24 (1651) https://historyofeconomicthought.mcmaster.ca/hobbes/Leviathan.pdf [Accessed 15 May 2025].

2 Lamont, D., 'Your house, your wealth: what happens in an era of rising rates?', Schroders (21 February 2023) https://www.schroders.com/en-gb/uk/intermediary/insights/your-house-your-wealth-what-happens-in-an-era-of-rising-rates/ [Accessed 30 June 2024].

17. The Future of Gold

1 Deane, J. (1866) 'Diary of the Atlantic Telegraph Expedition' https://atlantic-cable.com/Article/1866Deane/index.htm [Accessed 10 May 2025].

2 Turk, J., 'What did J.P. Morgan mean?', Goldmoney (17 August 2016) https://www.goldmoney.com/research/what-did-jp-morgan-mean [Accessed 15 May 2025].

3 World Gold Council, 'Comments made at World Gold Summit, April 2018' [Video] (14 May 2018) https://x.com/GOLDCOUNCIL/status/996012857228742658?s=20y [Accessed 24 January 2025].

4 Ibid.

5 CNN, 'Bernanke and Paul Spar over Gold' [Video] (13 July 2011) https://www.youtube.com/watch?v=iKYKLgzyF9o [Accessed 18 April 2025].

6 Statista, 'Value of global domestic equity mutual fund assets 2000–2023' (2023) https://www.statista.com/statistics/274490/global-value-of-share-holdings-since-2000/ [Accessed 5 July 2024].

7 Neufeld, D., 'Ranked: the largest bond markets in the world', Visual Capitalist (12 April 2023) https://www.visualcapitalist.com/ranked-the-largest-bond-markets-in-the-world/ [Accessed 5 July 2024].

8 World Gold Council, 'Gold market primer: market size and structure' (2023) https://www.gold.org/goldhub/research/market-primer/gold-market-primer-market-size-and-structure [Accessed 5 July 2024].

9 Statista, 'Real estate – worldwide' (2024) https://www.statista.com/outlook/fmo/real-estate/worldwide [Accessed 5 July 2024].

10 World Gold Council, 'Gold demand trends: full year 2024' (5 February 2025) https://www.gold.org/goldhub/research/gold-demand-trends/gold-demand-trends-full-year-2024 [Accessed 10 May 2025].

11 There are 216,000 tonnes at $108,000/tonne.

12 World Gold Council, 'Trading Volumes' (2024) https://www.gold.org/goldhub/data/gold-trading-volumes [Accessed 24 April 2025].

13 $21 trillion (US M2) ÷ 261 million ounces of gold = $80,460.

14 Buncombe, A., 'Russia paid Iran "in gold bullion" for drones used in attacks on Ukraine', *Telegraph* (7 February 2024) https://www.telegraph.

co.uk/world-news/2024/02/07/russia-paid-billions-gold-bullion-shahed-drones-ukraine-war/ [Accessed 24 June 2024].

15 Herbert, G., *The Complete Works of George Herbert: Prose* (1874), p. 332.

16 Statista, 'Distribution of gold demand worldwide in 2024, by sector' (2025) https://www.statista.com/statistics/299609/gold-demand-by-industry-sector-share/ [Accessed 15 May 2025].

17 World Gold Council, 'Gold demand trends: full year 2024' (2025) https://www.gold.org/goldhub/research/gold-demand-trends/gold-demand-trends-full-year-2024 [Accessed 10 May 2025].

18. *How Much Gold Does China Have? And Why?*

1 World Gold Council, 'Gold reserves by country'.

2 Bloomberg Television, 'Bessent Says the Gold Is in Fort Knox' [Video] (20 February 2025), https://www.youtube.com/watch?v=lZBGsMmyf30 [Accessed 18 April 2025].

3 Trading Economics, 'China Foreign Exchange Reserves' (2025) https://tradingeconomics.com/china/foreign-exchange-reserves [Accessed 15 May 2025].

4 Jia, R., 'China's gold market in 2023: demand improved and premiums rose', World Gold Council (2024) https://www.gold.org/goldhub/research/chinas-gold-market-2023-demand-improved-and-premiums-rose [Accessed 8 July 2024].

5 Ibid.

6 Laird, N., 'China gold imports and exports: monthly statistics', GoldChartsRUs (n.d.) http://www.goldchartsrus.com/gold/CNimpex-port02.php [Accessed 20 January 2025].

7 Laird, N., 'China SGE withdrawals', GoldChartsRUs (n.d.) http://www.goldchartsrus.com/gold/ChinaSGEWithdrawals.php [Accessed 20 January 2025].

8 Laird, N., 'US gold production and imports', GoldChartsRUs (n.d.) http://www.goldchartsrus.com/gold/USprodimport01.php [Accessed 8 July 2024].

9 O'Connell, R., 'China's gold fundamentals – what the trade numbers tell us in particular', StoneX (2024) https://tinyurl.com/2haz629e [Accessed 16 May 2025].

10 Nieuwenhuijs, J., 'Estimated Chinese official gold reserves cross 5,000 tonnes', Gainesville Coins (5 September 2023) https://www.gainesvillecoins.com/blog/estimated-chinese-gold-reserves-cross-5000-tons [Accessed 8 July 2024].

11 Nieuwenhuijs, J., 'Saudi Central Bank caught secretly buying gold: Saudi Arabia owns way more gold than it wants known', The Gold Observer (25 September 2024) https://www.thegoldobserver.com/p/saudi-central-bank-caught-secretly [Accessed 24 January 2025].

12 Nieuwenhuijs, J., 'China secretly snaps up more gold' (27 December 2024) https://www.thegoldobserver.com/p/china-secretly-snaps-up-more-gold [Accessed 20 January 2025].

13 Worldcrunch, 'Full Macron interview: on China, U.S., Ukraine, and more' (2023) https://worldcrunch.com/world-affairs/full-macron-interview-china-us/ [Accessed 15 May 2025].

14 Escobar, P., 'Exclusive: Russia's Sergey Glazyev introduces the new global financial system', The Cradle (14 April 2022) https://thecradle.co/articles/exclusive-russias-sergey-glazyev-introduces-the-new-global-financial-system [Accessed 15 May 2025].

15 Al Mayadeen, 'SPIEF sees 1,000 $72bln worth of deals, contracts signed' (9 June 2024) https://english.almayadeen.net/news/Economy/spief-sees-1-000--72bln-worth-of-deals--contracts-signed [Accessed 1 October 2024].

16 Ibid.

17 NASDAQ, 'Russia calls for payment system based on blockchain technology' (30 November 2022) https://www.nasdaq.com/articles/russia-calls-for-payment-system-based-on-blockchain-technology [Accessed 9 February 2023].

Index

Page references in *italics* indicate images.

Index